Country, Class or Craft?

Country, Class or Craft?
The Politicisation of the Skilled Artisan
in Nineteenth-Century Cork

Maura Cronin

CORK UNIVERSITY PRESS

First published in 1994 by
Cork University Press
University College
Cork
Ireland

British Library Cataloguing in Publication Data
A CIP catalogue record for this book is available from
the British Library.

ISBN 1 85918 027 2

Typeset by Tower Books of Ballincollig, Co. Cork.
Printed by ColourBooks, Baldoyle, Co. Dublin.

CONTENTS

TABLES

ACKNOWLEDGEMENTS

Of the many who helped me through this work, I will mention just a few; Professor John A. Murphy who first set me on the road of historical research; the late Seán Daly who so generously shared his understanding of Cork working-class history and Professor Donnchadh Ó Corráin who encouraged me to publish.

To my parents I owe much – Mary, my mother, for her endless encouragement, and Tom, my late father, for his combination of traditional nationalism and healthy cynicism. Thanks to my own children for treating me as 'Mam' rather than as a historian, and for all his support, the biggest thank-you to the best Cork artisan of all, my husband, Dónal.

INTRODUCTION

The main function of local historical studies has been aptly described as posing 'big questions about small places'.[1] Though few Corkonians would react with equanimity to the designation of their city as a 'small place', and others might doubt that the experience of the artisan could give rise to 'big questions', this study attempts to examine the 'big' through the 'small', the general through the specific, by using the development of artisan identity in nineteenth-century Cork as a possible microcosm of skilled-working-class politicisation in the country as a whole.[2]

My interest in this subject first began with a study of Cork politics in the O'Connellite period of the 1830s and 1840s. Finding that the trade societies of the city, like those of other Irish towns, were deeply involved in the popular campaign for Repeal of the Act of Union of 1800, I wondered whether this political involvement of the artisan stretched into the later reaches of the century. The result was a tortuous journey through the elusive history of nineteenth-century Cork economic developments, trade unionism and popular nationalism.

The English visitor who, in 1844, dismissed the city of Cork as 'a pork and butter salting provincial' may have been unduly contemptuous of an urban centre where many a large fortune was made on beer, butter and provisions, but he also captured the essence of a city where the high hopes of the recent past had given way to the disillusionment of the present.[3] Nineteenth-century Cork exuded a sense of disgruntlement at two levels. Firstly, among the merchant classes, there was a massive deflation of late eighteenth-century expectations that the Act of Union would bring both political prestige and unbounded prosperity. One disillusioned local merchant's reminiscences of pre-Union hopes clearly reflected the sad realism of the early 1830s:

> Cork was to be especially and peculiarly favoured: warehouses were to be erected and stocked with all descriptions of goods to be made up in the country. The fleets destined for the east and the west were to take in their assorted cargoes here. It was destined, in the illusive anticipation of the period, to rival Liverpool. We were to have a naval depot and an arsenal – wet and dry docks were to be constructed – ships of war were to be built and launched from our shores, and our fine harbour was to be the constant *rendez-vous* of the British fleet.[4]

At the second level – that of the working classes – the effects of industrial stagnation and collapse produced levels of distress which combined with nostalgic (and largely distorted) memories of eighteenth-century prosperity to produce a ferment of social and political disaffection.

In some ways, nineteenth-century Cork was a classic Victorian city, with a sizeable population, a charter and long-established civic government, and a population with a strong sense of civic pride. As in many contemporary cities, too, acute poverty and squalor prevailed among the lower classes, local government was introspective and limited, labour was emerging but slowly from violence and subversion to respectability, and towards the end of the century the geographical structure of the city was slowly altering as sprawling expansion of the suburbs was accompanied by depopulation of the central parts.[5] But unlike contemporary English cities, Cork's population was declining, so that by 1901 it was some six per cent less than it had been in 1841 (Table 1).

As the population of the city declined in the course of the century, so too its occupational structure changed. Within the male workforce the numbers employed in the building trade rose slightly, the shopkeeping sector remained fairly stable, and there was a steady decline in the manufacturing workforce with a

TABLE 1: POPULATION OF CORK CITY, 1831–1901[6]

	1831	1841	1851	1861	1871	1881	1891	1901
Males	36,254	35,489	39,040	37,509	36,847	37,663	35,427	35,789
Females	43,860	45,231	46,692	42,612	41,795	42,461	39,918	40,333
Total	80,114	80,720	85,732	80,121	78,642	80,124	75,345	76,122

corresponding rise in the transport sector.[7] Within the female workforce, there was less obvious fluctuation, for right through the century the main area of female employment continued to be domestic service, closely followed by the dressmaking and tailoring sectors. Though from the 1870s onwards more women entered the sphere of clerical and office work, one out of every two women in paid labour was still a domestic servant, one in every five was a dressmaker or tailoress, and between one in five and one in seven worked in the dealing sector as shopkeepers, huxters or shop assistants.[8]

The main area of flux in the local employment market was the manufacturing sector. Firstly, many areas of production were falling prey to mechanisation, foreign competition and lack of investment capital.[9] Secondly, although in absolute terms the numerical strength of the female workforce in this area remained far lower than that of the male, it was clear that in many cases the skilled male worker was being progressively displaced by lower-paid boy and female labour. What remained more or less constant, however, was the craftsman's traditional employment milieu of the small workshop. While the trades employed in the local breweries and distilleries formed part of a workforce ranging in size from three to five hundred, and those in the ship-building sector were likely to work in yards employing between three hundred and eight hundred workers, the small employment unit was much more common. Both the building industry and craft-based manufacture tended to operate on the basis of the small workshop, with an average of perhaps five to eight workers, including both journeymen and apprentices. Variations were, of course, endless: the city's newspaper offices each employed between twenty and forty printers; small builders might give work to a total of seven carpenters and painters, while the larger contractors employed twenty of each with as many more labourers; a tailoring business could be carried on with anything from seven to fifty workmen; and coopering shops might employ from ten to forty journeymen.[10] Workforce size generally reflected the personal fortune of the employer, the two together enabling us to draw up a rough classification between 'big' and 'small' employers which, as will be discussed later, is particularly relevant in tracing politicisation patterns.[11] In terms of personal wealth, merchants scored highest, as suggested by surviving abstracts of wills and administrations. While some merchants left as little as £800 on their deaths, others' personal fortunes amounted to as much as £60,000. In between these two extremes was a multiplicity of variations, many between £2,000 and £3,000, with a large proportion in the range between £20,000 and £40,000.[12] At the lower end of the scale, master craftsmens' wills varied between £100 and £4,000 in the course of the century. In 1851 a baker's will amounted to £170, while in 1872 that of a tailor totalled £100; sums of between £300 and £450 were left by a merchant tailor (1858), master bakers (1860 and 1879), a master cooper and a printer (1880). The wills of others were as large as those of the lesser merchants, a cabinetmaker in 1861 and a master cooper in 1870, each leaving £3,000.[13] Reliance on the abstracts of wills is of little help in attempting to distinguish between personal wealth and business capital, but one can state that the further one descends the social ladder within the employer community, the less easy it is to make this distinction. Indeed, among smaller businessmen there may well have been no such distinction in reality. That relatively few small craft employers either made wills or opened bank accounts in itself suggests a lack of both personal wealth and business capital.[14] Recurring complaints by contemporary trade unions against the cost-cutting exercises of 'men of small or equivocal capital' also suggest the ubiquitous nature of the minor employer who ran his business on a shoestring.[15]

Just as these patterns of employer and establishment size remained largely unchanged in the course of the century, equally constant was the geographical location of different industries within the city. Not until the mid twentieth century was Cork really affected by industry's move from city centre to periphery, and the traditional street location of the various trades continued unbroken through the nineteenth century – tanning on the Watercourse Road, textiles in Blackpool, coopering on the northern slopes around the Butter Market, higher-class shoemaking in Old George's Street and Great George's street, and coachmaking and cabinetmaking in Grattan Street, Duncan Street, Coach Street and Devonshire Street. Residential patterns within the city showed a similar continuity. The working classes, skilled and unskilled alike, were concentrated in the lanes and alleys of the city centre and on the northern and southern slopes around Shandon Street and Barrack Street. Since the late eighteenth century there had been a tendency on the part of the more prosperous business and professional classes to move out to new and elegant detached villas on the periphery of the city, and from the mid nineteenth century this move towards the suburbs was followed by the lower ranks of the monied classes – prosperous master tradesmen, bank officials and minor manufacturers, who took up residence in solid and impressive terraced housing being built from the late 1860s onwards.[16]

The religious structure of Cork city remained predominantly Roman Catholic during the nineteenth century.[17] It was not, of course, a simple matter of strict social division of the population along denominational lines. As Ian D'Alton expressed it in his study of Cork Unionism,

> at every level of city society, the Unionist/Protestant had his Nationalist/Catholic counterpart. All along the economic and social line, from the railway director to the labourer, from the university professor to the refuse collector, there were Protestants and Catholics, Unionists and Nationalists to be found. On either side, there was not any unique stratum of society.[18]

Yet, because the Protestant working class had been contracting since the late eighteenth century, the Protestant population of the city a century later was very much an upper class, represented most strongly within the medical profession, banking service, magistracy, army and large-scale business sector. At the lower end of the social scale, among the trades and unskilled occupations, the dominance of Catholics was apparent, and since as a general rule the less skilled the occupation, the greater the proportion of Catholics, the 'most Catholic' occupations were those of the tanners, dockers, carters and general labourers, whereas printers and engineering workers had a sizeable proportion of Protestants in their ranks. While the connection of the latter occupations with English-based unions may partly explain this phenomenon, there are indications among other trades like the coopers, shoemakers and weavers, who for most of the century had no union links outside the city, that the sizeable Protestant presence in their ranks was a throw-back to the more vibrant local Protestant working class population of the eighteenth century.[19]

Nineteenth-century Cork, though its population hovered between seventy-five and eighty thousand, was, like many equivalent centres throughout the British Isles, a relatively small and intimate society where, in public matters, personalities were frequently more important than policies. Public men found it advisable to court the goodwill of the city populace which, though it had no voice in politics, could render most unpleasant the career of an unpopular local public man. Election time was the lower classes' opportunity to voice their support or dislike for a local politician, and as the degree of excitement at elections showed, the opportunity was not wasted.[20] Thus, the dominant note of politics was essentially local. In the mid-1840s, for example, while the imminent break between Daniel O'Connell and Young Ireland appeared to dominate the national scene, Cork was rocked by a conflict between the merchant-dominated Chamber of Commerce and the lower-middle-class People's Hall concerning the political composition of the local harbour board. Similarly, in the elections of the 1870s Home Rule was overshadowed by a conflict between the local vintners' interest and that of the Farmers' Club. Even in the 1880 election, in which Parnell was returned as MP for the city, it was significant that he had been invited to stand for Cork as the result of yet another local squabble and that he was not returned at the head of the poll but second to the local moderate nationalist, John Daly.[21] Moreover, the 'Irish Manufacture' movements which unfailingly made their appearance each decade after 1832, though reflecting successive country-wide campaigns, were geared to advancing the local industry of Cork rather than that of Ireland as a whole, and might more correctly have been termed 'Cork Manufacture' movements.[22]

On the other hand, whatever the preoccupation with local issues, rising literacy rates and the increasing accessibility of a cheap daily press in the course of the century ensured a growing awareness of outside events. This meant that even remote happenings like the Indian Mutiny of 1858 and the Franco-Prussian war of 1870 were viewed as being of direct interest to the local populace.[23] Still more did the national issues of Repeal, Home Rule, and parliamentary and agrarian reform prove increasingly effective in rousing interest on a wide scale, so that in Cork, as elsewhere, they formed the main foundation upon which popular politics were built. Indeed, one of the most obvious developments of the nineteenth century was the way in which skilled artisans and the trade unions to which they belonged became increasingly involved in the popular movements connected with these wider issues, so that by 1900 the common perception in Cork was that trade unionism and nationalism went hand in hand. Another trend equally reflective of developments outside the immediate local scene was the way in which trade unionism, regarded in the earlier decades as socially subversive, became increasingly acceptable, not only before the law, but equally in the eyes of clergy, press and middle-class society.

As this picture of nineteenth-century Cork emerged, certain questions presented themselves. If trade unionism among skilled craftsmen was becoming more socially acceptable, how effective was it in reality as an economic and political pressure group? How conscious were local trade unionists of belonging to a wider working-class society? Why did artisans individually and trade unions collectively support nationalist politics? By what means were organised artisans politicised? Finally, and most fundamentally, what was the artisan's ultimate source of identity? Each question seemed quite easy to answer at the outset, but having rummaged through incomplete runs of trade-union records, the cryptic and often contradictory evidence of the Dublin Castle files, and the episodic and heavily biased material of rival local newspapers, the answers grew more elusive as clear-cut ideas disappeared over an ever-receding horizon.

This study has been greatly facilitated by a number of parallel and related studies both of the Cork scene and of other urban centres. Cork social, economic and political developments in the nineteenth century have been particularly well-served by historians and historical geographers since the 1970s. Ian D'Alton's *Protestant Society and Politics in Cork 1812–1844* (1980) provides an insightful analysis of Protestant politics in the city in the first half of the century, while his 'Southern Irish Unionism: a study of Cork City and County Unionists 1885–1914' (1972) performs a similar function for the later decades. The late Seán Daly's *Cork: A City in Crisis* (1978) and his *Ireland and the Second International* (1984) provide an invaluable source for anyone wishing to understand working-class society in Cork in the period after 1870, while John B. O'Brien's studies of Cork merchant society in the pre-famine period and Angela Fahy's work on residential patterns in the city throw considerable light on the social and political spectra of middle class life.[24] More recently, Andy Bielenberg's *Cork's Industrial Revolution 1780–1880: Development or Decline?* (1991) fills in a hitherto gaping void in our knowledge of economic development and recession in nineteenth-century Cork.

The organised labour scene outside Cork, in both its economic and political aspects, has been the subject of a number of excellent studies. J. D. Clarkson's *Labour and Nationalism in Ireland* (1925) was the pioneering work which paved the way for later studies like Fergus D'Arcy's 'Dublin artisan activity, opinion and organisation 1820–50' (1968), Patrick Holohan's 'Daniel O'Connell and trade unions' (1968), Andrew Boyd's *The Rise of the Irish Trade Unions 1729–1970* (1972), Arthur Mitchell's *Labour in Irish Politics 1890–1930* (1974), Charles McCarthy's *Trade Unions in Ireland 1894–1960* (1977), and Brendan McDonnell's 'The Dublin Labour Movement 1894–1907' (1979). Since 1980 other valuable contributions which have appeared include John Boyle's *The Irish labour movement in the Nineteenth Century* (1988), which deals comprehensively with the organised labour scene in Dublin and Belfast, Henry Patterson's *Class Conflict and Sectarianism: The Protestant Working Class and the Belfast Labour Movement 1868–1920* (1980), Dermot Keogh's *The Rise of the Irish Working Class: The Dublin Trade Union Movement and Labour Leadership 1890–1914* (1983), Emmet O'Connor's two most recent works, *A Labour History of Waterford* (1989) and *A Labour History of Ireland 1824–1960* (1992), and the Trojan work published annually both in *Irish Economic and Social History* and in *Saothar*, the journal of the Irish Labour History Society.

Obviously, as the stock phrase puts it, much still remains to be done. Although local publications like the *Old Limerick Journal, The Other Clare* and *Decies* do publish valuable related material, nineteenth-century organised labour in centres outside Dublin, Belfast and Cork has received relatively little attention. The overall state of labour studies in the nineteenth-century Irish urban context, moreover, indicates a certain narrowness of approach. Because scholarship in this area is still, in fact, in its infancy, we have not yet (this study included) made that vital step 'from labour history to social history'.[25] While many studies of British urban centres have made that move, we in Ireland are generally hedged into the more confined institutional history of trade unionism rather than branching out into wider investigations of working-class identity, the interplay between sub-sections of the lower classes, the controversial issue of bourgeoisification of the artisanate, and the whole area of popular politicisation.[26] K. T. Hoppen's fascinating *Elections, Politics and Society in Ireland 1832–1885* (1984) is a model which might well be adapted if we wish to move to a more comprehensive and sophisticated analysis of urban working-class culture in the nineteenth century.

This venture into artisan political and economic activity in Cork attempts to insert one more rung – no matter how rickety – into that very incomplete ladder which leads towards an understanding of nineteenth-century Irish working-class life. Limitations which will be obvious to the reader include a very cursory treatment of semi-skilled and unskilled working men, as well as an almost deafening silence on women in both politics and workplace. The reasons for such omissions are simple enough. Unskilled workers were not unionised until late in the century, and then only sporadically. Hence, the trade-union records which provide such a large proportion of our knowledge of the skilled artisan are missing in the case of the non-craft working man. Moreover, as a corollary of this circumstance, the sense of cohesiveness and solidarity which derived from the skilled craftsman's membership of a tight-knit and relatively élitist occupational community is to a great extent absent from the experience of the unskilled worker.

The virtual omission of women from this study is quite deliberate. It is not that their role in political, economic and social life is being dismissed. At every level, the presence of women was obvious. In simple numerical terms females outnumbered males, accounting for over fifty-three per cent of the city's population right through the century.[27] Women did not vote, it is true, but this does not necessarily imply absence from the public sphere. At the level of organised politics, particularly in nationalist circles, middle and lower-middle-class women were becoming more actively involved. Though the precise rate of integration has yet to be delved into by historians, there is a world of difference between the active, if secondary, role of women in Fenianism and the post-1879 land agitation, and the genteel spectator role accorded to ladies in O'Connellite times, when their function appears to have been simply to grace the gallery at public meetings and dinners. In the sphere of more spontaneous but no less significant activity, working-class women were prominent in food riots, election disturbances and inter-locality mêlées. In the world of paid (or, more correctly, badly paid) employment, the admittedly unreliable census figures suggest that women accounted for between thirty-four and forty-two per cent of the workforce, and though their numerically strong presence (eighty-nine to ninety-four per cent) in domestic service may skew the figures slightly, they also accounted for thirty-four to forty-eight per cent of the manufacturing sector and between forty-one and forty-eight per cent of dealers.[28]

However, at the present juncture, the indications for omission of women from this study outweigh those for their inclusion. Firstly, any attempt to integrate our presently limited knowledge of women's politicisation would smell suspiciously of tokenism, and the subject must await a study in its own right. Secondly, from the vantage point of the workplace, the difficulties of investigation already mentioned in relation to unskilled male workers apply to them with added force. If, in his study of European labour protest, Dick Geary overstated the case in describing women as 'the archetype of the unskilled worker . . . Oppressed at home and at work, regarded as social inferiors by all but the most enlightened males, [and] educated into limited expectations', he was not that far off the mark.[29] Just as in English textile towns women showed little interest in trade unionism until the 1890s, so in Cork they were totally unorganised until the beginning of the new century. This means that while the community of work and workplace may well have been just as strong among them as that operating among women earners of later times,[30] they lacked the nucleus and mouthpiece provided by the trade unions of their male counterparts. Thirdly, and most importantly, this study is about artisans – skilled male workers who had served an apprenticeship to a recognised craft. Like it or not, in nineteenth-century terms women were not artisans and, as far as the average skilled craftsman was concerned, they were not even regarded as being part of the legitimate workforce. Women were viewed solely in terms of 'de-skilling' – i.e. their perceived capacity to undercut the earning power and skill-based status of the time-served artisan by their ready availability as cheap labour in areas of manufacture where mechanisation and rudimentary mass production were displacing the craft trades.[31] Individual artisans may well have had a less negative attitude towards women in the workplace, but collectively the artisanate (and the unskilled male workforce, too) was unapologetically chauvinist. All the verbal imagery used by trade unions and sympathetic observers to describe the organised craftsman exuded popular concepts of masculinity – 'stalwart', 'sturdy', 'independent', 'upstanding'. The paid woman worker did not, then, fit easily into their scheme of things, and neither, therefore, does she fit into this study. Whatever her conditions of work, her earning capacity, her feelings of independence or enslavement, or her ultimate sense of identity, to the skilled artisan she was – just as were non-union workers and illegal apprentices – the feared and despised 'other'.

So if no women and very few labourers have made it into the pages of this study of the Cork trades, is not this in itself the ultimate reflection of artisan identity? As the combined forces of modernisation and recession threatened their livelihood, and post-Union disappointments injured their civic pride and whetted their political appetites, organised craftsmen put their hopes for the future in an amalgam of traditional social élitism and emerging romantic nationalism. Just how this process took shape is the subject of the following chapters.

NOTES

1   Lecture delivered by Prof. Lawrence J. Taylor, Lafayette College, Easton, Pennsylvania, at University College Cork, 3 July 1992.
2   One must also recognise the limitations of local studies. As pointed out by John Foster, *Class Struggle and the Industrial Revolution: Early Industrial Capitalism in Three English Towns* (London, 1974), pp. 2–3, the locality is simply 'an arbitrary geographical bite out of a larger political system', while Eugen Weber's *Peasants into Frenchmen: The Modernisation of Rural France 1870–1914* (London, 1977), p. xiii, also stresses the problems of both local and general studies: 'La Rochefoucauld remarked that one can know things well only when one knows them in detail, yet detail is infinite, hence our knowledge is fated to remain superficial and imperfect.'
3   James Johnson, *A Tour in Ireland with Meditations and Reflections* (London, 1844), p. 140.
4   *Pilot*, 10 Dec. 1830.
5   Asa Briggs, *Victorian Cities* (Harmondsworth, 1968), *passim*.
6   The increase in population in 1851 is to some extent due to the influx of rural immigrants during the famine and immediate post-famine period.
7   For detailed tables on the changing occupational structure of the city, see Maura Murphy, 'The working classes of nineteenth century Cork', *Journal of the Cork Historical and Archaeological Society* (cited hereafter as *JCHAS*), vol. lxxxv, nos 241–42, 1980, p. 31. The change in the proportion of males employed in each major employment sector in Cork between 1841 and 1901, as a percentage of the total occupied male population was as follows:
    Agriculture – changed from 9·99 to 2.86 per cent; building – from 7·95 to 9·17 per cent; manufacture – from 40·88 to 19·15 per cent; transport – from 1·60 to 15·29 per cent; dealing – from 10·29 to 11·47 per cent; industrial service – from 18·50 to 23·22 per cent; public service and professions – from 3·63 to 15·69 per cent. *Census of Ireland, Province of Munster, City of Cork* (cited hereafter as *Census of Ireland*), 1841–1901.

8   In 1841 30·89 per cent of women in paid labour worked in manufacture, the proportion dropping to 28·09 per cent in 1901. The rate of change in other female employment sectors (as a percentage of the total number of women in paid employment) over the same time-span was: dealing – from 13·68 to 19·01 per cent; industrial service – from 0·99 to 0·25 per cent; domestic service – from 49·19 to 41·87 per cent; public service and professions – from 2·39 to 7·76 per cent.

9   Andy Bielenberg, *Cork's Industrial Revolution 1780–1880: Development or Decline?* (Cork, 1991), *passim.*

10 *Cork Examiner* (cited herafter as *CE*) 4 Sept. 1888, 23 Aug. 1892, 3, 4, 8 Apr., 31 May, 25 Aug. 1893; *Cork Daily Herald* (cited hereafter as *CDH*), 31 Dec. 1867; Cork Coopers' Society Minute Books, 4 May 1886, 12 June 1895, 6, 10 May 1896.

11 See below, pp. 144–45.

12 Albert E. Casey, *O'Kief, Coshe Mang, Slieve Lougher and Upper Blackwater in Ireland* (Birmingham, Ala., 1966–68), vol. xi, pp. 1399, 1405, 1415, 1434, 1447, 1452, 1534; vol. xiv, pp. 1027, 1036, 1058, 1078.

13 Albert Casey, *O'Kief, Coshe Mang*, vol. xi, pp. 1391, 1451, 1460, 1469, 1660; vol. xiv, pp. 1019, 1022, 1024, 1040.

14 While further work needs to be done on the pattern of wills in nineteenth-century Cork, some sampling shows that most recorded wills were left by merchants, gentlemen, farmers and shopkeepers rather than by small workshop masters. Albert Casey, *O'Kief, Coshe Mang*, vols. xi, xiv. Similarly, bankruptcy records for the later years of the century suggest that many small employers had no bank account. Maura Murphy, 'The economic and social structure of nineteenth century Cork', David Harkness and Mary O'Dowd (eds.), *The Town in Ireland* (Belfast, 1981), p. 137; Cork Bankruptcy Records, 1892/31A, 1893/41, 1894/102.

15 *CE*, 19 Jan. 1855.

16 Henry Inglis, *A Journey Throughout Ireland during the Spring, Summer and Autumn of 1834* (London, 1836), vol. 2, p. 185, speaks of the Cork upper classes' 'passion for country houses'. See also *Report of the Royal Commission Appointed to Enquire into the Boundaries and Municipal Areas of Certain Cities and Towns in Ireland*, HC 1881 [c–3089–II], l. 65, pp. 231, 237, 251; Angela Fahy, 'Residence, workplace and patterns of change 1778–1863', in L. M. Cullen and P. Butel (eds.), *Cities and Merchants: French and Irish Perspectives on Urban Development 1500–1900* (Dublin, 1986), pp. 46–8.

17 Census of Ireland 1871–1901: the religious structure of the city in the years between 1871 and 1901, when the statistics are most reliable, appears as follows:

	1871	1881	1891	1901
Catholics	83·52	84·24	83·83	84·21
Church of Ireland	12·37	12·64	13·03	12·32
Other denominations	2·47	2·41	2·31	2·21

18 Ian D'Alton, 'Southern Irish Unionism: a study of Cork City and County

Unionists 1885–1914' (Unpublished MA dissertation, National University of Ireland, 1972), p. 61.

19 Ian D'Alton, 'Southern Irish Unionism', pp. 28–9; Maura Murphy, 'The economic and social structure of nineteenth century Cork', pp. 133–4.

20 *Minutes of Evidence before the Select Committee on the Cork Election 1852*, HC 1852–53 (521) xi, (528) xi; Question (hereafter Qs.) 511794; Patrick Joyce, *Work, Society and Politics: The Culture of the Factory in Later Victorian England* (London, 1980), pp. 274–6; Seán Daly, *Cork: A City in Crisis* (Cork, 1978), pp. 42–3.

21 Daniel Owen Maddyn, *Ireland and Its Rulers* (London, 1844), vol. iii, pp. 197–8; *CE*, 2, 4 Feb. 1874; 15, 20 May 1876; 2, 7 Apr. 1880; *CDH*, 1, 2 Apr. 1880. In the election of 1880 when the local vintners' interest backed Nicholas Daniel Murphy, some supporters of the Irish Republican Brotherhood, in conjunction with the local Farmers' Club, invited Parnell to stand for the city.

22 *Cork Mercantile Chronicle* (hereafter cited as *CMC*), 11 June 1832; *CE*, 3 Jan. 1842, 23, 30 Oct., 11 Dec. 1850, 19 Feb. 1851, 22 Dec. 1882, 19 Jan., 29 Mar., 4 July 1883.

23 *Cork Constitution* (hereafter cited as *CC*), *15 Jan 1858; CE*, 25 July 1870. The narrower matter of Irish nationalism was, however, at the core of this apparently wider range of interests. The Indian Mutiny became a matter of interest because the embryonic Fenian movement portrayed the matter in an anti-English light, while the French side in the Franco-Prussian war was backed precisely because Prussia was seen as an ally of Britain.

24 John B. O'Brien, *The Catholic Middle Classes in Pre-Famine Cork*, O'Donnell Lecture (Dublin, 1979); 'The Hacketts: glimpses of entrepreneurial life in Cork 1800–1870', *JCHAS*, vol. xc, no. 249, 1985, pp. 150–7; Angela Fahy, 'Residence, workplace and patterns of change, Cork 1778–1863', L. M. Cullen and P. Butel (eds.), *Cities and Merchants: French and Irish Perspectives on Urban Development 1500–1900* (Dublin, 1986); Seán Daly, *Cork: A City in Crisis* (Cork, 1978).

25 Royden Harrison, 'From labour history to social history', *History*, vol. 60, 1975, pp. 236–9.

26 See, for example, Clive Behagg, *Politics and Production in the Early Nineteenth Century* (London, 1990); Richard Price, *Labour in British Society: An Interpretative History* (London, 1986); Dennis Smith, *Conflict and Compromise: Class Formation in English Society 1830–1914. A Comparative Study of Birmingham and Sheffield* (London, 1982).

27 Women accounted for fifty-five per cent of Cork's population in 1841, fifty-six per cent in 1841, fifty-five per cent in 1851, and fifty-three per cent from 1861 to 1901. *Census of Ireland*, 1841–1901.

28 *Population of Counties in Ireland*, 1831; *Census of Ireland*, 1841–1901; Mary E. Daly, *Dublin, the Deposed Capital: A Social and Economic History 1860–1914* (Cork, 1985), p. 78.

29 Dick Geary, *European Labour Protest 1848–1939* (London, 1981), p. 78.

30 Mary E. Daly, 'Women in the Irish workforce from pre-industrial to modern times', *Saothar,* 7, 1981, pp. 150–63; Mary Jones, *These Obstreperous Lassies: A History of the Irish Women Workers' Union* (Dublin, 1988).

31 In the early 1830s, for instance, the Cork hatters flatly refused to allow women into the trade. *Royal Commission on the State of the Poorer Classes in Ireland,* HC 1836, (35), xxx (cited hereafter as *Poor Enquiry* 1836), App. C, First Report, p. 27.

1

THE CRAFT UNDER SIEGE

It's easy seen how far two-and-sixpence or three shillings a week would go in them days when a man could get a full meal of floury potatoes and butter-milk for a penny, so that if he got a place in a chimney corner when he got old, in his son's house, or his son-in-law's, or maybe even a friend would not deny him the shelter of his roof, he'd be able to get along first-rate, and have a penny or so to buy tobacco at the end of the week. As to clothes, old men don't wear out their boots much, and a frieze coat went down from father, or grandfather for the matter of that, to son, wanting only occasional repairs and darning as it went along. In the present day a man must keep up appearance more in Dublin. He must be better dressed if he wants to appear dacent [sic] and not be laughed at. A cardriver was taken before the magistrate the other day, and tould [sic] that his license would be took [sic] away unless he dressed himself better. Everything, then, being so much dearer and worse than it used to be, a pension of three-and-six or three shillings a week won't go half so far as it used.[1]

Thus did one working-class Dubliner giving evidence to a parliamentary commission in 1872 describe what he saw as the deteriorating fortunes of the poor, contrasting contemporary living standards with those of his youth in the 1830s. As the century neared its close, such a perception that life was getting tougher was not uncommon among working people with limited incomes, unskilled and artisanate alike. Whether such assessments were skewed by the distorting lenses of nostalgia or accurately reflected existing conditions is difficult to decide. It is certainly true that even for skilled artisans, many of them far better off than their unskilled contemporaries, living and working conditions were disimproving or at least changing drastically with the gradual disintegration of the pre-industrial society, which had originally shaped their crafts, customs and status. In British centres from London to Edinburgh, the craftsman's traditional independence was assailed by employers' attempts to cut costs through the subdivision of labour, technical change, hiring labour on a casual basis, and employing women and boys in place of skilled craftsmen. In Dublin, too, the craft unions attempted to shore up their slipping fortunes by campaigning against wage reductions and the employment of unskilled and apprentice labour in what had traditionally been the preserve of the trades.[2] The experience of the Cork artisan followed the same pattern, for as manufacture declined and traditional skills were pushed aside by mechanisation, many craftsmen found their wages and employment opportunities progressively eroded.

However, the resulting 'monotonous reiteration of woe', as one historian has expressed it,[3] cannot be accepted without some qualification, since there is no doubt that in attempting to make the greatest possible public impact, craft spokesmen specialised in 'worst-case scenarios', particularly in years of depression. There was little political capital to be made out of tales of good fortune, so that, for instance, while the healthy state of the city's engineering and coachmaking trade seldom found mention at trades council meetings in the 1880s, the abysmal plight of dying trades like ropemaking, nailmaking and corkcutting made more dramatic headlines.[4] On the other hand, no-one understood as well as the artisans themselves the degree of distress suffered by their respective crafts – something tacitly admitted by contemporaries who, for example, during the famine years of the 1840s, went straight to the trade societies when seeking information on poverty and unemployment.[5] Moreover, trade society accounts of distress in such periods were amply backed up by witnesses from other backgrounds. Yet, for all this, it proves surprisingly difficult to pinpoint the precise impact of the famine years on the fortunes of the trades. That artisan distress appears subsumed into the general misery of the time is, of course, partly due to the nature of the sources on which the historian relies. Trade-union records are well-nigh non-existent for the period, while the contemporary newspapers and official documents dealt with that wide social category described as 'the poor' rather than with any specific substratum thereof. Where contemporaries did pick out a particular occupational group for special attention, they understandably concentrated on the unskilled labourers, many of them rural immigrants, whose high numbers and consequent lack of employment prospects rendered them particularly vulnerable to the horrible sufferings of a famine period. That the artisan population shared in the general misery is not at all to be doubted. Episodic newspaper reports of living conditions in the city's tenements included, hardly surprisingly, accounts of starving tailors, shoemakers and carpenters as well as of the ubiquitous unemployed labourer.[6] A meeting in the city in January 1847 to discuss relief measures gave some indication of the seriousness of craftsman distress when one speaker's asser-tion that unemployment was not serious among the city's artisans drew forth a storm of protest. One man in the body of the hall shouted up that 'all the trades in the city [were] idle', a journey-man cooper in the gallery stood up to declare that 200 of his 350-strong trade society were idle, while another man claimed that only three members of the forty-strong painters' society were employed. All in all, it was stated, over one thousand city tradesmen were idle, without counting any of the paupers and country labourers who had lately come into the city.[7]

Artisan distress in these years, like that of the labourers, was due to the conjunction of high food prices and underemploy-ment. In mid 1847 potato prices rose from fourpence-halfpenny to one shilling per twenty-one pound weight, and by December of the same year they had risen further to one-and-threepence per twenty-one pound weight, while by January 1847 the cheapest quartern loaf cost tenpence – four to five pence dearer than prices in 1845.[8] Even in an economy in which food price fluctuations were the norm, these increases were extreme, throwing the en-tire subsistence mechanism of poorer families out of kilter. Even the Indian Meal sold at the relief depots of the city for one-and-twopence per seven-pound weight was well beyond the means of impoverished families whose daily incomes frequently ranged downwards from eightpence to nothing.[9] As one woman, questioned as to how she kept her family alive in such circumstances, expressed it,

> I could not tell you how I lived, only 'twas God himself that supported me – 'tis a hard question for me to answer.[10]

Artisans in full employment, while feeling the pinch of price rises, could survive the worst periods of scarcity because their wage levels were between two and three times those of labourers. However, as will be discussed later, since theoretical wage levels and real income were frequently quite different, unemployed or underemployed artisans were often as penurious as the labourers. Where an artisan belonged to a trade society with a healthy unemployment fund or whose working members were able to contribute to a special levy for idle members, then there was some buffer against destitution. The unionised stonemasons, for example, prided themselves in later years on having supported unemployed members through the bad days of 1847.[11] Other trades like the carpenters attempted to meet the economic crisis of the early 1840s by opening an emigration fund to send some of their members to Sidney and Port Philip, and to which both society members and the public could subscribe. The sources, however, do not indicate whether or not this safety valve survived into the famine years later in the decade.[12] For a trade like the coopers, however, no such cushions against pauperism appear to have existed. Described in 1846 as facing 'beggary and the workhouse' and a year later as 'gone – extinct – dead', the coopering trade had no resources of its own to rely on, and resorted unsuccessfully to seeking government aid to emigrate its redundant members to Canada.[13]

The greater part of artisan distress in the late 1840s, however, seems to have owed less to the immediate food price crisis than to the deep-set and ongoing problems of changing patterns of demand and production which faced many trades in the course of the nineteenth century. The coopers, for example, had been complaining of the decline of their trade since the early 1830s, and the distress of the mid-1840s merely aggravated their already desperate situation. For other craftsmen like the carpenters and masons, distress was due to the inbuilt seasonality of their trades and their reliance on contracts, rather than any conditions specific to the famine years. Still others, like the casually employed tailors and shoemakers, whose livelihood depended on supplying to the poor, had always walked the subsistence tightrope, but found themselves totally ruined when the scanty funds of those lower classes on whom they relied for custom were eaten away by the provision crisis of the famine years.[14] It is to this multiplicity of ongoing problems that we must now turn in more detail.

In examining the various manifestations of craft decline in nineteenth-century Cork, one must take into account not only the difficulties of interpreting contemporary craftsmen's complaints, but also the limitations of apparently less partisan sources like the census and parliamentary enquiries. This is particularly apparent when one investigates such vital factors as fluctuation in craft numbers, variations in income levels and the seriousness of unemployment. On what initially seems the clearcut issue of numbers, both contemporary artisan statements and census columns seem to coincide in testifying to the decline of craft fortunes. As table 2 indicates, a great number of trades contracted dramatically in the course of the century, reflecting the local manufacturing sector's decline.[15] Thus, the weavers, who in the 1840s had numbered over three hundred, were completely absent from the 1901 census, while the coopers, who had been seven hundred strong in the 1830s, were reduced to less than three hundred by the early twentieth century. On the other hand – and this is something craft spokesmen neglected to mention – numerical decline was far from universal. Printers, bakers and craftsmen in the building industry showed little loss of numbers in the course of the century, while the number of engineers and coachmakers, whose skills were in increasing demand with the expansion and modernisation of the transport system, proved similarly buoyant.[16]

But just as artisan statements must be interpreted with some caution, so one must also recognise the limitations of the census

TABLE 2: NUMBERS IN THE PRINCIPAL SKILLED TRADES IN CORK CITY, 1841–1901

	1841	1851	1861	1871	1881	1891	1901
Farriers	3	24	34	27	28	32	43
Printers	116	143	181	191	189	227	184
Engineers	183	142	116	333	242	232	298
Coachmakers	76	68	147	158	161	139	179
Saddlers	140	99	117	97	97	81	76
Shipwrights	91	153	166	111	74	44	43
Builders	51	47	47	48	59	156	212
Carpenters	603	500	645	603	522	612	586
Masons	241	324	300	256	250	284	214
Stonecutters	98	114	117	116	154	93	98
Slaters	150	125	123	90	50	60	35
Plasterers	101	49	55	88	121	111	135
Plumbers	259	226	282	301	102	146	201
Painters	—	—	—	—	247	276	341
Cabinet makers	218	175	227	142	124	129	120
Weavers	325	160	113	25	7	7	0
Hatters	98	63	56	37	26	18	0
Tailors	748	551	638	564	442	397	275
Shoemakers	1398	1216	1078	702	590	510	425
Bakers	253	367	353	348	322	290	274
Ropemakers	109	90	—	64	34	23	14
Tobacco workers	20	63	77	140	106	254	216
Tanners	288	258	89	137	96	101	36
Brushmakers	45	59	55	39	25	25	11
Coopers	725	551	638	564	442	397	275
Blacksmiths	316	231	322	273	213	172	147
Nailors	131	105	98	78	49	23	7
Sawyers	163	173	172	95	65	55	93

as a gauge of craft fortunes. The census can, in particular, hide the depth of depression in a given occupation since its unqualified listing of figures is unaccompanied by any differentiation between the vibrant and the moribund craft. In the first place, because artisans unable to find alternative employment lived on for many years in their home area, there is a time-lag of about forty years between the collapse of a local trade and the point at which that collapse is reflected in the census. The death-knell of the Cork domestic textile trade, for example, had already been sounded in the 1820s but it was not until the 1860s that the last handloom weavers disappeared from the census columns. Similarly, the nailors', corkcutters' and ropemakers' crafts had fallen into decline in the 1860s but their numbers in the census did not plummet until the early twentieth century. Secondly, the prosperity suggested by high census numbers was largely illusory, for while a plentiful labour supply might indicate buoyancy in the trade as a whole, it also betokened deteriorating conditions for individual artisans. It was, in fact, the numerically weak trades like the farriers who were generally the most secure, their very lack of numbers ensuring them a fairly strong bargaining position and reasonably steady wages. In contrast, the numerically strong trades like the shoemakers and coopers were most difficult to organise and were constantly dogged by low wages, high unemployment, and vulnerability to undercutting and displacement by those willing to work under price. Thus, even though contemporary crafts spokesmen frequently cited declining numbers as evidence of their trade's decay,[17] rising numbers actually were less indicative of prosperity than of a brief boom period followed almost immediately by a disastrous oversupply of workers. Such periodic swings between employment boom and glut occurred because whenever news spread of an expansion of employment prospects in the city there soon followed an influx of non-local artisans many of whom, when the boom ended, stayed to add to the oversupply of labour and to the progressive erosion of the artisan's livelihood and status. As one witness before a select committee on vagrancy calculated in 1828, Cork had one of the highest levels of urban unemployment in the island and was 'the great place where the mass of the misery will come from, for they come from Limerick to Cork.'[18]

Being most numerous, the unskilled workers were the most vulnerable, their capacity to maintain wage levels being eroded not only by their own high numbers but also by the precarious and temporary nature of their employment and the 'relentless and inexhaustible movement of labour from the countryside'.[19] The Cork labourers, as grossly underorganised as their peers elsewhere, and easily replaced if they did prove recalcitrant, lacked both cohesion and militancy until the last three decades of the nineteenth century. In 1870, however, a major strike by the city's tailors led to such widespread popular disturbance that the contagion of unrest spread to the unskilled workers. Beginning among the Cork Steam Ship Company's labourers and soon taking in the factory operatives and the waterside men in the city, and extending even to the labourers of a number of county towns, this unrest, which centred on wage rise demands, was still simmering a year later.[20] Similarly, in 1881, following the example of militant rural labourers egged on by the more radical Land Leaguers, the unskilled city workers again turned out for a general wage rise, marching from one business concern to the next in an ever-increasing body, until the greater part of the unskilled workforce was on strike.[21]

Such strikes were largely futile. Subject, as one historian has expressed it, to 'waves of organisational enthusiasm followed by defeat and disintegration'[22] and lacking even the limited leverage which the skilled trades could employ, the largely unorganised labourers were backing a loser. The heart was taken out of their agitation in 1870 by the severe prison sentences passed on the ringleaders, and though some employers panicked and conceded the strikers' demands, employers in general had regained their composure within a matter of weeks. By 1872 they had drawn up a blacklist of all those who had struck work, while over the succeeding decade they had succeeded in eroding even the limited wage gains of 1870.[23] In 1881, too, lack of direction, organisation and funds combined with the ready availability of strike breakers to defeat the agitation. Even when in 1890 a wave of sympathetic strikes broke out among several categories of unskilled workers following the organising drives of the 'new unions', these proved no more successful, the activists being either permanently replaced by strike breakers or eventually returning to work on the employers' terms.[24]

Similar weaknesses were obvious even in the case of the builders' labourers who, though forming a relatively well-organised élite within the ranks of the labourers, were unable to extract lasting concessions from employers. Between 1890 and 1895 their society entered at least six separate disputes in futile attempts to secure and maintain a fifteen-shilling weekly wage plus overtime pay.[25] These explosions of militancy were easily offset by the easy availability of blackleg labour (a feature of the building trade all over the British Isles) which allowed individual builders to deal with the Builders' Labourers' Society just as they chose; for instance, one prominent city builder, Daniel Hill, consistently refused to pay the fifteen shilling rate and from 1891 ran his concern exclusively on the labour of non-unionists. When the local Master Builders' Association followed Hill's example in refusing to recognise the labourers' union, the latter's rule against working with non-union men became totally inoperative and the fifteen-shilling rate became ever more remote, the average wage by 1893 being a mere thirteen shillings.[26]

Craft workers were almost as vulnerable as labourers, many being susceptible not only to undercutting by members of their own craft but also to displacement by unskilled workers. Since the artisan's bargaining power depended to a great extent on 'the scarcity of his skill',[27] the most vulnerable craftsmen were those whose trade or aspects of it were easily learned, enabling masters determined to break unionisation among their journeymen to train labourers as strike breakers within a matter of weeks. Thus, a local bakers' strike in 1834 was quickly turned into a lockout by the ready availability of strike breakers while in the same year a city-wide strike by the journeymen tanners was crushed with ease when some five hundred country labourers were found to fill the strikers' places.[28] Even better organised and more specialised craftworkers – described in 1857 as the 'higher trades' – were also vulnerable, though less in the face of unskilled competition than of skilled non-union tradesmen and apprentices. In 1834 a turnout by journeymen shoemakers, crushed by this use of non-union workers, resulted in the strikers tramping through the county in search of work so that the town of Fermoy, some twenty miles north-east of the city, was reputedly flooded by Cork shoemakers vainly looking for employment, their very presence posing a threat to the bargaining strength of the local shoemakers.[29]

The tailors' experience was no different. In 1859, in response to an attempted wage cut, a call to strike was answered by almost two hundred journeymen tailors – the entire union strength in the city – but in spite of its wide extent and initial militancy the strike collapsed after only four days, for when the masters threatened to use strike breakers, the journeymen returned to work on the employers' terms.[30] Much the same problems were faced even by trades whose bargaining position, unlike that of the shoemakers and tailors, was enhanced by low membership numbers, a strike by boilermakers in a local shipyard in 1853 being quickly crushed by the employment of non-union strike breakers.[31]

From the mid century, the same problems faced the printers who were especially affected by the incursions of non-union men as 'rats' or strike breakers. The term 'rat' referred specifically to society men who had left the ranks in times of dispute, and in spite of union attempts to deter such desertion by fining heavily any renegades who wished to rejoin, the problem remained. It was apparently most serious in the 1850s when there were five 'unfair' houses in the city out of a total of between twelve and eighteen. The situation in the local *Southern Reporter* office provided a classic example. In 1851 a wage strike in that office was effectively met by the ready availability of blacklegs, including both non-union men and society deserters, so that within four years the office was run entirely on non-union labour and by 1860 was described by local society men as 'the worst rat-house in the city'.[32] The plumbers and coopers, too, constantly faced the problem of undercutting by non-union and apprentice labour. As late as the 1870s, the bar by the coopers' society on non-union labour was largely unenforceable, some employers running their establishments completely on the work of non-union men, while the plumbers' union bye-law forbidding members to work with non-union men had to be waived in 1892 because it had proved impossible to enforce.[33]

Such easy availability of non-union labour over a wide spectrum of occupations – and the consequent ease with which strikers could be replaced – was in the nineteenth century a Europe-wide phenomenon which encouraged economising employers to cut wages well below the 'official' rates – i.e. those approved by trade unions.[34] Undercutting of this type was not, of course, always easily enforced, as evidenced during a major strike by Cork masons and carpenters in 1830. Though idle for two months, the two societies refused to accept the builders' proposed daily rate of three shillings, one individual reflecting the common determination in his claim that he would work for no less than three-and-tenpence, 'and if there was a man-of-war at Cove [he'd] rather go aboard her than work for three shillings a day'. Fighting words seldom won strikes, however, and although this particular dispute ended in a compromise, most were settled to the satisfaction of the employers who could, in the last resort, employ blackleg labour to break the union and unilaterally enforce lower rates of pay, or at least prevent any pay rises.[35]

On the matter of wage rates and income levels, further balancing of official records and contemporary artisan complaints is necessary. As is evident from table 3, wage rates in almost all sectors increased in the course of the century, especially from the 1850s onwards. Though the most complete figures are available for the building trades, where the overall wage increase between 1850 and 1900 was in the region of forty-four per cent, other sectors show, despite the scrappy nature of the evidence, increases of between twenty-five and fifty per cent over the same period.[36] Therefore, though the wide variations evident – from the modest increase of twenty-five per cent among the cabinet makers to the builders' labourers' dramatic advance of between sixty-six and 166 per cent – preclude any generalisations, one can suggest that the rates for skilled men almost doubled, and those for labourers trebled in the course of the century. Another indication of this improvement, though the erratic survival rate of documentation makes any comparison difficult, is that the gap between wage rates in Cork and those in Dublin and Belfast closed slightly towards the end of the century. Though generally higher than those paid in the smaller provincial towns, most Cork rates, with the exception of those in engineering and plumbing, lagged behind those of Dublin and Belfast.[37] Among some trades, the gap between Cork rates on the one hand and those of Dublin and Belfast on the other remained constant: the cabinet makers' rates, for instance, remained at between eighty-two and eighty-seven per cent of Dublin levels in the course of the century, while the coopers worked for ninety-five per cent of the Belfast rate and only sixty-six per cent of the Dublin rate.[38] Among others, the gap between wage rates in Cork and those in Dublin and Belfast closed perceptibly. In the building trade, Cork rates for most of the century varied between sixty-four and seventy-five per cent of those paid in Dublin and Belfast, though by the 1890s they had risen to some ninety-seven per cent of the Belfast and Dublin levels. A similar narrowing of the gap was evident in the case of the Cork printers, whose rates in the 1830s were seventy per cent of Dublin levels, but had risen to ninety per cent by the 1890s.[39]

Such rising wage rates suggest that by 1900 artisans and labourers were considerably better off than their counterparts of seventy years before.[40] This is further borne out by the fact that in the course of the century living costs, though subject to considerable seasonal variations, had increased more slowly than wages. The cost of fuel in Cork, for example, rose only slightly, a ton of coal at seventeen shillings in 1870 costing little more than it had done forty years previously. Food prices also rose slowly: in 1890 the four-pound loaf of bread priced at sevenpence-halfpenny cost no more than it had done in 1835 and threepence less than in 1830; potatoes at eightpence per twenty-one pound weight sold at the same rate in 1870 as in 1835; while the price of lowest quality meat – fourpence per pound – was still the same as it had been in 1845.[41] However – and this is where the problem of interpreting source material lies – both rising wages and the apparent fall in costs of basic necessities were frequently offset by other factors. Seasonal fluctuations in food prices, the decreasing availability of cheap meat as more sophisticated processing methods removed it from the counters to the salting barrels,[42] the purchase of clothing and footwear,[43] and sudden and unexpected expenses like funerals,[44] all cut into the income of working people. Moreover, in the course of the century the budget of the poor was detrimentally affected by apparent steep increases in rent, which doubled and even quadrupled between the 1830s and the early twentieth century. A slum tenement room

TABLE 3: DAILY WAGE RATES IN CORK CITY 1800–1900[45]

	1820	1830	1840	1850	1860	1870	1880	1890	1900
Masons	3s.–3s.6d.		4s.		4s.2d.		5s.	5s.6d.	5s.9d.
Bricklayers				4s.					
Plasterers		3s.	4s.	4s.			5s.	5s.6d.	5s.9d.
Carpenters	3s.–3s.6d.			4s.	4s.	5s.	5s.	5s.5d.	5s.9d.
Plumbers				4s.	5s.4d.	5s.8d.	5s.8d.	6s.6d.	
Painters				4s.		5s.	5s.	5s.6d.	5s.9d.
Paperhangers						4s.8d.–5s.10d.			
Stonecutters			3s.6d.	4s.					
Builders' labourers							2s.2d.–2s.4d.	2s.6d.–2s.8d.	
Boilermakers				5s.					
Engineers				4s.–10s.	4s.6d.–4s.8½d.			5s.8d.	
Millwrights				4s.–10s.				5s.8d.	
Gunsmiths				4s.5d.					
Ironfounders				4s.5d.			4s.5d.	4s.8d.	5s.
Nailors				4s.					
Cabinet-makers	3s.–3s.4d.			4s.	4s.	4s.4d.		4s.6d.	4s.10d.
Coopers				3s.	5s.				
Sawyers						3s.4d.–5s.			
Corkcutters							3s.4d.		
Paperstainers				4s.					
Chandlers				3s.–4s.					

TABLE 3 (Cont.)

	1820	1830	1840	1850	1860	1870	1880	1890	1900
Shipwrights (iron)				4s.–10s.					
Shipwrights (wood)				4s.–6s.					
Sail & rope makers				3s.–4s.					
Printers		3s.6d.		3s.–5s.	4s.–5s.4d.	7s.		5s.5d.–7s.1d.	
Litho printers							5s.6d	5s.6d.	
Millers								2s.5d.–2s.10d.	
Bakers		2s.–3s.		3s.–4s.	3s.4d.		4s.8d.–6s.	5s.–6s.	
Butchers				3s.–5s.					
Tanners		10d.–1s.		2s.6d.–3s.					
Weavers				1s.–3s.					
Tailors				4s.		4s.			
Shoemakers				3s.–4s.		6s.			
Bootrivetters							2s.10d.–4s.4d.	2s.10d.–4s.4d.	
General labourers		10d.–1s.	1s.4d.–2s.	1s.4d.–2s.		2s.2d.–2s.6d.	2s.6d.	2s.6d.	2s.6d.–2s.8d.
Firemen						4s.6d.			
Lamp-lighters						2s.6d.			
Brewery workmen				2s.					

which cost between a shilling and one-and-sixpence per week
in 1835 cost around two shillings by 1909, while the weekly rents
of small houses rose from ninepence to between two and three
shillings over the same period.[46]

Similar problems emerge when assessing artisans' and
labourers' earnings. Wage rates such as those cited in table 3
are calculated for individuals in full-time work, and since they
fail to take account of complicating factors like the prevalence
of piecework and the undercutting capacity of non-union labour,
they must be regarded as a faulty barometer of working men's
fortunes. In 1843, for example, though the general rate of payment for masons was four shillings a day (showing that somewhere in the preceding decade the building trades' rates had
improved), the average mason's earnings were about half that
figure. In the same year, the coopers' daily rate was three-
and-fourpence, but many men earned as little as four to five
shillings per week, while as late as the mid-1880s, when the best
paid men earned between twenty and twenty-four shillings, many
earned as little as seven shillings weekly.[47] Moreover, in the
case of several trades, the complications of undercutting were
further compounded by the prevalence of piecework, some trades
like the sawyers, shoemakers, bakers and printers working
almost exclusively on piece rates, while in the shipbuilding and
coopering sectors, time and piece rates applied to different processes.[48] Tailors' earnings were the least clear-cut of all,
operating on the piece-cum-time system of the 'log'. This system
was defined as

> the printed statement of times allowed for making garments . . .
> agreed upon between employers and employed. The number of
> hours allowed to a garment multiplied by an agreed price per
> hour fixes the remuneration to be given to the workman.[49]

In Cork, where rates were slightly lower than in Dublin and
Belfast, the log rose from between threepence and threepence-
halfpenny (at which it had stood since the 1840s) to fourpence
in 1874 and fourpence-halfpenny four years later. But actual daily
earnings, determined by the amount of work available, averaged
from two to four shillings in the 1850s, and around four shillings

from the 1870s onwards, though in a busy season men could earn over ten shillings per day.[50]

A further complicating factor in calculating real income in the nineteenth-century context is the erosive effect of periodic unemployment. It is difficult to pinpoint the worst slump periods, for different sectors felt the pinch at different times. Clothing, textile and building workers recorded high levels of unemployment in the 1830s and 1840s and again in the 1880s and 1890s when they were joined by the shipbuilding workers, bakers and printers. Indeed, some categories of workers appeared to experience a perpetual slump, depression being apparently the norm for the coopers who hardly allowed a decade to pass in which their spokesmen failed to lament – with or without statistical evidence – the bad state of their trade.[51]

On its own, the evidence of trade-union spokesmen provides one with only impressionistic accounts and figures of doubtful reliability which point to a wide range of possible rates of unemployment for different trades – rates calculated on the available evidence varying from seven per cent for the printers in the 1880s to a massive one hundred per cent for the shipwrights in the early 1890s.[52] All in all, however, taking account of the unreliability of surviving data, the available figures generally indicate that unemployment levels in slump periods could be between fifty and eighty per cent. How accurate is this figure? The more one investigates the surviving data, the more difficult interpretation becomes. At times, the trades seemed to contradict themselves, painting a picture of gloom and doom in public statements while their union records presented a less grim scenario.[53] Were craft spokesmen speaking in the presence of press reporters exaggerating their misfortunes for public effect? Or was the more positive picture in union records simply a matter of a union secretary omitting even point-scoring detail so as to spare himself interminable minute writing? As always, the truth probably lies somewhere in between. Even if trade-union records exaggerated the misfortunes of the craftsmen, in another sense they understated the seriousness of their situation, because they took account only of union members and ignored the plight of the infinitely greater number of non-union men. In 1886, for

instance, when the local bakers' union complained that twenty-
five of its 105 members were idle, it was ignoring the other two
hundred local bakers who were not unionised. Similarly, when
in 1897 the cabinet makers' society noted high levels of unemployment among what it calculated to be the city's thirty cabinet
makers, it completely failed to take into account the other ninety enumerated in the census since they were outside union
ranks.[54]

Probably the greatest impediment to investigating nineteenth-
century unemployment levels is the failure of contemporary artisans to define precisely what they meant by the term unemployment or, as they put it, idleness. The historian can, however,
tentatively distinguish between two types of unemployment. The
first type, experienced by the weavers and redundant coopers
of the 1830s and 1840s, and the nailers of the 1880s, could be
described as terminal unemployment. These crafts' livelihood
had dried up, and without the lifeline of subsidised emigration
they either melted into the ranks of the casual labourers or found
refuge in the workhouse.[55] For other classes of workers,
unemployment could more properly be termed cyclical and,
though well-nigh undocumented in trade-union records, actually
varied widely in duration, from between one and thirteen weeks
at a time for coopers in 1892 to over a year for ironmoulders
in 1886.[56]

The inbuilt boom-slump pattern of many trade cycles – or,
as Thompson put it, 'cycles of hardship and short commons' particularly affected employment and income levels.[57] Predictably,
employment in the building trades was to a large extent determined by the weather, a rainy season causing earnings to fall
by as much as fifty per cent.[58] In other cases, demand varied
less with the weather than with the seasons. Thus, that section
of coopering which was linked with the butter trade was at its
busiest in the summer months, and came to a virtual standstill
between November and March, so that the making of extra
brewery casks had to be introduced to tide the firkin makers over
the slack season.[59] As was the case elsewhere in Ireland and
Britain, tailors and shoemakers experienced similar seasonal fluctuation, the Corkmen depending for much of their income on
the custom of the gentry during the autumn hunting season.

Consequently, tailors' working time could vary from two days per week in winter to a full week of twelve to fourteen-hour days in summer, and any fall in the hunting season demand could cut weekly earnings from thirty to twelve shillings. For the factory-based footwear workers the situation was reversed, the winter months providing more employment since the Cork factories manufactured few light summer goods.[60]

Seasonal variations in trade fortunes were, moreover, frequently interwoven with dependence on contracts. The navy's provision contract was the mainstay of the coopering trade, and its progressive dismantling from the mid-1850s onwards detrimentally affected the coopers' employment prospects. However, the greatest dependence on contract work in Cork as elsewhere was in the shipbuilding sector. This dependence led from the early 1880s onwards to a scramble for government contracts, leading in 1885 to the placing of the Passage Docks on the admiralty lists. The resulting contracts, however, with the exception of the building of HMS Bann between 1885 and 1886, were not of much consequence, and the erratic pattern of boom and slump continued, seriously weakening the shipwrights' bargaining position and making them susceptible to sporadic wage cuts. Even when wage rates in the industry actually rose in the long term (i.e. by some fifty per cent between 1850 and 1900), real earnings were seriously eroded by chronic unemployment, so that the 1864 comment of the *Cork Examiner*'s proprietor, John Francis Maguire, that 'he did not know any town in Ireland subject to greater vicissitudes of poverty and distress than was Passage' was equally applicable right through the latter half of the century.[61] Similarly, the building trades' fortunes (already determined by the weather) were susceptible to the availability of contracts provided either by private building schemes or by the municipal corporation. Thus in the 1860s the stonecutters were deeply concerned by the city fathers' decision to build new iron bridges rather than the traditional stone structures, and from the 1880s onwards the building trades in general exerted considerable pressure on the town council to provide employment in the form of public works, demolition, painting, street flagging and house building.[62]

Artisans tended to blame their problems on the breakdown

of traditional trade regulations, particularly those concerned with the settlement of wages. Traditional wage regulation had taken different forms from one trade to the next, but generally involved some degree of consultation between masters and men. In the mid-1820s the Cork cabinet-making trade, like its Dublin equivalent, adopted the method known as the London Union Book of Prices, a payment system originally framed by a committee of London masters and journeymen. During the same period the journeymen shoemakers' wage rates, determined by a weekly meeting of their trade society, were then presented to the masters for approval. Since the mid-eighteenth century, in line with the practice in England, the coopers and others followed the so-called 'court settlement' system. Seen by Price as the last vestige of 'the mediation of social relations through the law' before the final disintegration of eighteenth-century social reciprocities and obligations, this system required annual consultation between magistrates, masters and journeymen before determining at the Easter Quarter Sessions Court

> what wages or sum of money every mason, carpenter, slater, cooper, or other artificer shall take and be paid by the day or by the certain denomination, piece or parcel of work, or job, either with or without meat and drink, during the year following.[63]

Even in their heyday, of course, these methods were not without their own inherent flaws: the Cork master shoemakers increasingly resented the trade society's control of wage rates, while the working coopers disliked the court settlement system because it favoured masters over journeymen insofar as it allowed the former to force a reduction in wages while preventing the latter from seeking an increase – an issue leading to a major strike in the trade in 1821. It is not clear what system was operated by the cabinet makers before the adoption of the London Union Book of Prices, except that it was viewed (with typical nostalgia) as being vastly superior to the new system, which was considered to lower former rates by between thirty and forty-five per cent.[64]

In reality, however, there were no clear-cut breaks between old and new systems, and elements of traditional wage settlement machinery survived in fossilised form well into the late nineteenth century. In the mid-1840s it was still customary each spring for the journeymen stonecutters to hold a special meeting which, in order to settle wages for boys and old men, drew up for submission to each master a list of names with attached weekly rates from five to eighteen shillings 'as their merits and demerits are ascertained'.[65] The tailor's 'log', formalised in the 1830s and lasting into the twentieth century, was another such survival of the old system, involving as it did a degree of consultation between masters and men. Similar formal co-operation between employers and journeymen in the coopering trade continued until late in the century. In order to protect earnings while offsetting a glut in firkin manufacture the 'idle week' was enforced, during which a journeyman was prohibited from working on firkin making, but was paid a certain rate by the master cooper while he remained idle.[66] In general, however, most of the regulation systems began to disintegrate in the decades between 1820 and 1840, their breakdown being accompanied by the journeymens' complaints of deteriorating conditions. When the London Union Book was jettisoned by the master cabinet makers during the 1830s the journeymens' bargaining power was seriously impaired as uniform wage regulation disappeared, rates were cut, and a 'great want of harmony' developed between masters and men. Similarly, by the mid-1840s the wage-bargaining capacity of the working shoemakers was totally defunct and wage regulation was solely in the hands of the masters.[67] In the coopering trade the traditional court settlement system began to disintegrate sometime in the 1820s so that two decades later journeymen's incomes were less than half the 'court rate' of 1821.[68]

In some trades, however, the disintegration of traditional regulations and the consequent weakening of the journeymen's bargaining power is also suggested by the increasing preponderance of piecework over timework. In some cases, of course, piecework predominated because journeymen preferred it and because it suited the nature of a craft, the bakers being paid by the batch – i.e. 320 two-pound loaves – sawyers per one-hundred feet sawn, shoemakers on the basis of each pair of shoes made, while printers, too, preferred to be paid by the job.[69] Most artisans, however, very reluctantly accepted piecework though it was only the better organised trades like the engineers who in 1893 were sufficiently strong to force the employers to accept time-work. Other trades were less successful: in shipbuilding all work except caulking and coppering was paid on piece rates and the journeymen's attempts in the early 1880s to enforce a day-rate system for repair work proved unavailing. Similarly in the coopering trade those who, by the 1890s, worked exclusively on time-work were regarded with envy by the piece-workers, whose rates had been eroded in the course of the century.[70]

The breakdown of the formal wage regulation machinery in the first half of the nineteenth century was not, of course, the only factor in the deterioration of wages and working conditions. Changing patterns of demand, the flooding of the market by imported goods, and an inability to adapt to modern production methods also played their part. Thus, the post-war slump from 1816 onwards together with the famine conditions of 1817, precipitated the near collapse of several areas of local manufacture, leading to unemployment-related starvation among many city workers.[71] However, despite the multiplicity of reasons for this distress, it was largely blamed by the journeymen on the disintegration of 'traditional' regulation machinery. Forgetting the inherent faults of former systems which, in spite of their relatively recent origins they insisted on regarding as 'traditional', the artisans' complaints up to mid-century echoed the hopeless quest for a lost – and largely imaginary – golden age. In 1826 the assimilation of the Irish and English currencies, which led to a wage reduction of one penny in the shilling, sparked off a wave of trade-union agitation for a return to the old rates,[72] while in 1840 a cooper's lament for the defunct court wage settlement system exuded this nostalgia for the past fuelled by the distress of the present:

> You may talk of your free trade system as you will of the conventional rules, but during the old law there was never so much hardship dealt out to the journeymen as now. I tell you that the coopers of Cork are an ill-used body of men: they never combine but to get bread for their starving families.[73]

By the latter half of the century, as the passage of time removed the individuals who personally remembered the 'traditional' system, nostalgic references to the past became less frequent. But a losing battle continued to be fought for another aspect of the traditional trade structure – i.e. the control of apprentice numbers. Among all the skilled trades, this had long been a prerequisite for the artisan's firm bargaining position in the labour market. In the 1820s and 1830s only members' sons could enter the ropemaking trade, the slaters and hatters allowed only two apprentices to each master, while the shoemakers permitted each journeyman to have only one apprentice, preferably his son. Fifty years later the artisans still clung to the same closed shop systems. The local printers' society gave preference to members' sons as apprentices, allowing only one apprentice to each six journeymen employed. In coopering the recognised number of boys was settled at a maximum of three per master, and all boys except the eldest son of a cooper had to be indentured, the society maintaining its preference for members' sons into the 1890s.[74]

From the mid century onwards, however, the ever-decreasing ability to enforce such limitations was proof that the traditional rampart of the closed shop was crumbling. Thus, during the 1850s the badly organised cabinetmakers were much affected by the incursions of boy labour while at the same period the coopers' society found it necessary to organise an all-out, though ultimately ineffective, campaign against local masters' indiscriminate employment of apprentices.[75] Among the printers the progressive erosion of rules on apprentice limitation can be traced through the decades: in 1845, nine of Cork's twelve offices were run exclusively on boy labour; it was calculated that apprentices accounted for thirty-five per cent of the printing workforce in 1850 and thirty-eight per cent in 1860; while by the 1880s the printers' society found itself increasingly powerless to deal with the bigger printing houses which ran their concerns almost exclusively on boy labour.[76]

In the nineteenth-century context, moreover, the artisan was under threat from the interrelated issues of mechanisation and importation. The latter had always figured prominently in the organised trades' list of grievances, so much so, in fact, that in the 1830s and 1840s the first true politicisation of the Cork trade unions was linked with the rise of economic nationalism in the shape of prototype 'buy-Irish' campaigns.[77] In those earlier years complaints had centred mainly on the flooding of the local market with foreign-produced textiles, hats, shoes and gloves, and sporadic protests of a similar nature continued to be made over the following three decades.[78] It was in the 1880s and 1890s, however, when the newly established trades council provided a platform for the articulation of labour grievances, that the most sustained complaints were made against importation. Reflecting a similar tendency in the Dublin context, crafts like the coopers, coachmakers, ropemakers and cabinet makers blamed their decline on the flood of imported goods.[79] From the late 1880s, in particular, the coopers' employment prospects were threatened as butter buyers, fishcurers, gunpowder manufacturers and breweries increasingly imported casks from Denmark, England and Scotland.[80] From the 1860s onwards, the under-capitalised corkcutters sank under the tide of cut corks from France, Spain and Portugal; the employment prospects of the local nailors fell by over ninety per cent between 1877 and 1886 in the face of foreign competition; and even the printers – the trade least affected by the economic slump of the 1880s – suffered from the increasing use of foreign-printed work in the book trade, in advertising and in electioneering literature.[81] It was in the footwear trade, however, that the effects of foreign competition were most sharply felt, even after the local factory-based footwear trade had been launched with the express purpose of countering importation. From the mid century onwards, British footwear manufacturers offered large discounts to Irish shopkeepers buying their wares, enabling the imported goods to undercut and displace the more expensive local products. Estimates of the level of footwear importation varied widely, but the main offenders were deemed to be the general goods stores, the 'monster houses' and the boot warehouses being established in the city since the 1870s. These boot warehouses were frequently run by small capitalists who answered the market demand for cheap footwear and who were themselves merely agents for English footwear firms at Bristol, Leicester and Kettering, transacting little or no business with Irish footwear producers, either handcraft or factory-based.[82]

The inability to compete with imported goods was directly related to the incapacity to adapt working methods to meet changing demands. Early in the century the first sector to fall before the tide of modernisation had been the domestic textile trade which by 1826 was collapsing in centres as far apart as Cork, Bandon, Dublin and Drogheda.[83] In Cork small masters were reduced to the level of journeymen, extreme distress spread among the unemployed, and attempts to alleviate the situation through relief works and subsidised emigration schemes proved futile.[84] Further attempts from the early 1830s to the mid-1850s to revive the dying textile sector through movements to patronise local manufacture proved equally unavailing, since the decline of the industry had gone too far to be reversed. Most weavers who worked in slum tenements or in wretched suburban cabins operated looms reputedly thirty years behind those of Manchester, were unable to afford costly raw materials, and had little or no opportunity to secure a consistent market. By 1850 most Cork weavers had apparently emigrated to Manchester, the remaining sixty gingham weavers earning scarcely four shillings each for an average 120-hour week, while thereafter textile production had passed from the hands of the traditional skilled handloom weavers to the semi-skilled labour of the emerging factory system.[85]

The same combination of redundant production methods and inability to meet changing market demands affected other sectors in the second half of the century. Tanning, which in the 1830s had been one of the city's principal industries, fell behind when it failed to innovate technologically and, by the 1870s, had been completely undermined by the competition of the mechanised British industry. Similarly, the local distilling industry lost valuable ground by sticking with the traditional pot still at a time when competitors were turning increasingly to patent-still production.[86] Shipbuilding, which had flourished in Cork harbour in the 1850s, fell into decline from the 1860s onwards. Blamed variously on the frequency of trade disputes, lack of capital and absence of business acumen on the part of the shipyard owners,

this decline was also seen by contemporaries as the result of failure
to adapt from wooden to iron shipbuilding. This was particularly
so in the case of the traditional shipbuilding centre at Passage
West in the lower harbour, where the adaptation to iron shipbuilding, apparently came too late to save the industry. Modern
research suggests, however, that the shipyards nearer to the city
adapted very successfully to iron shipbuilding and that the fundamental source of decline was, rather, the tailing-off of Cork's
transatlantic trade and the consequent loss of local contracts for
the construction and repair of deep-sea vessels.[87]

Other industries failed to make even this belated transition
from traditional to modern production methods and as a result
collapsed on the threshold of the new century. One such trade
– ropemaking – possibly traced some of its problems to the
decline of shipbuilding, of which it was partly a subsidiary. Its
main shortcoming, however, was a lack of the capital needed to
establish a large-scale rope and twine manufactory which could
compete with imported goods and allow the Cork ropemakers
to break into the English market.[88] Similarly, it was the local
corkcutting trade's lack of the capital necessary to adapt to
mechanised production and meet the high costs of raw materials
which hastened its demise. Ironically, when mechanisation was
introduced in the 1880s, its main effect was the displacement of
the skilled craftsmen by unskilled workers, so that by 1892 the
ranks of the traditional artisans were decimated, many emigrating
or themselves falling into the ranks of the casual labourers.[89]

The coopers, too, though less obviously than the corkcutters
and ropemakers, faced the problem of redundant skills. One of
the trade's mainstays – the manufacture of butter firkins and
provision casks – was being shaken from the mid-1850s onwards
by the substitution of iron binding in the place of the traditional
wooden hoops, and by the 1880s was increasingly threatened by
the growing preference in both English and Irish markets for
butter boxes. Consequently, by the mid-1890s, firkin makers were
the lowest-paid workers in the trade, with very insecure employment prospects. In fact, when one local firm of butter merchants
changed from firkins to boxes in 1899, over forty men were
immediately thrown out of work, falling back on the scanty

unemployment fund of their trade union.[90] The coopering trade, in fact, provides an example of the multiplicity of factors which led to craft decline in the course of the nineteenth century. Not alone was the trade detrimentally affected by the competition of machine-produced alternative products, but it also suffered from the decline of other related areas on which its prosperity depended. Closely linked from the mid-eighteenth century with the butter and provision trades, coopering was hit indirectly from 1814 onwards by the post-Napoleonic War peacetime slump and by the competition of the American salt provision trade, and more directly from 1842 by tariffs on imported cask timber.[91] In the mid-1850s further misfortune hit the coopers when Cork's share of the navy provision contract was cut, and two decades later when a portion of the navy's salt pork contract, hitherto monopolised by Cork merchants, was given to Dutch and Danish firms.[92] At the same time, the employment prospects of coopers engaged in the butter trade further contracted as the demand for Cork butter fell with the opening of the British market to French, Dutch and Danish butter and with the simultaneous appearance of the new product, butterine.[93] The consequent depression in coopering was felt not just in Cork but throughout Munster. In 1887 a cooper tramping to Cork from Kilfinane in the County of Limerick reported that employment 'was bad all over the country and . . . there was not an apprentice at the trade'. In the city itself, the majority of unionised coopers were either idle or employed on casual work, and special levies were put on all working members for the support of the idle men while the lack of society funds necessitated the temporary suspension of all emigration aid.[94] By the early 1890s, then, the Cork coopers depended more and more on brewery and distillery work, and their employment prospects in this quarter were increasingly threatened by the increasing monopolisation of the market by Guinness of Dublin, a firm which was not only increasing its share of the Irish and export trade in beer, but which had been making considerable inroads into the Cork city market since setting up a sales agency there in 1859. Moreover, the employment prospects of the coopers in the alcohol industry were further affected by the amalgamation of local Cork

distilleries. Whereas seven distilleries had operated in the city
in the early nineteenth century, this was cut to four by the 1870s
and further reduced to two by 1890, so that the number of
distillery-employed coopers was cut by over sixty per cent during the last three decades of the century.[95] Though this shrink-
age of traditional areas of employment was partially counteracted
by moving into new fields of production – lard kegs for the provision trade and casks (some machine-made) for use in the west
Cork fishing industry – the coopers were unable to compete with
modern production methods and changing market demands.

Though the disastrous consequences of failure to mechanise
were obvious to all, modernisation was itself a mixed blessing.
Throughout the industrialised countries of Western Europe,
artisans waged a 'desperate struggle to preserve their skills against
machinery' and although the pace of change proceeded less
violently in Ireland than in other more developed economies,
its results were far from negligible.[96] Machinery and new techniques progressively eroded traditional work patterns, eventually
replacing one set of craftsmen with another and changing the
identity of the occupational community. In the printing trade,
for instance, where the growing use of machinery in the 1890s
led to an increase in wages and in overall numbers employed,
these benefits were counterbalanced by the phasing out of an
entire category of workers – the pressmen – whose *raison d'être*
disappeared on the heels of mechanical innovation.[97] Local
shipbuilding experienced similar difficulties, the belated move
to iron shipbuilding in the Passage yard completely changing
the character of the industry by displacing the local shipwrights
by iron shipbuilders brought in specially from Scotland.[98] Most
trades, therefore, were either extremely suspicious of, or totally
hostile to modernisation of production methods in general, and
especially to the introduction of machinery. In the 1830s and
1840s, for instance, the local sawyers launched a bitter and ultimately futile campaign against the introduction of steam-driven
sawmills. Half a century later this issue of sawmill mechanisation was still a source of conflict in the city's building trade and,
combined with grievances regarding wages and apprentice labour,
led to a major carpenters' strike in 1892 and again in 1896.[99]

In 1892 a long-standing rule of the carpenters' society prohibiting the working of any timber cut by steam-driven machinery was modified following a meeting between the local trades council and the Master Builders' Association but the precise interpretation of the agreement's clauses continued to cause trouble. Similarly, the mechanisation of the local corkcutting trade in the 1880s facilitated the employment of labourers at cheaper rates than the traditional hand-cutters. As a result, the latters' ranks shrank dramatically, many men emigrating or turning to the only other employment they could find – that of unskilled casual labourers.[100]

Other trades, like the french polishers, cabinet makers and – as seen earlier, the coopers – found the introduction of machinery directly responsible for rising redundancies, but those who most felt the ill-effects of mechanisation were the trades whose work was touched by the sewing machine.[101] From the 1860s onwards, upholsterers, bookbinders, shoemakers and, above all, tailors complained of their progressive displacement by unskilled and semi-skilled workers, many of them female, who were employed as machinists at low rates of pay which seriously undercut the earning capacity of the male craft workers. Though the untrustworthy nature of the census figures makes these complaints difficult to substantiate, the available statistics do, indeed, suggest that from the mid century onwards, mechanisation enabled the female workforce in some of the formerly craft-dominated manufacturing sectors to increase considerably. In the clothing sector, where women had numerically dominated the workforce since the 1840s, increasing mechanisation made little statistical change, although the female share of the workforce did rise from seventy-seven per cent in 1851 to eighty-three per cent in 1901. Over the same period, the proportion of female labour in the shoemaking sector rose from four to fifteen per cent, from zero to twenty-two per cent in the upholstery business, and from twenty-nine to seventy per cent in the bookbinding trade.[102]

It was the footwear and tailoring industries which best illustrated the dual problem facing traditional crafts in the nineteenth century, i.e. the disastrous results of failure to offset foreign competition by adopting mechanised production and, at the same time, the capacity of mechanical innovation to undercut and eventually displace traditional craft workers. As E. P. Thompson noted in the English context: 'The old skill and the new almost always were the prerequisite of different people . . . The rewards of the march of progress always seemed to be gathered by someone else.' The process of change which had reduced English shoemakers to the status of outworkers from the mid-1820s onwards operated to produce the same results in Cork three decades later.[103] Large-scale bootmaking firms had existed in the city since the 1850s but these were really 'putting-out' firms, employing large numbers of handsewing outworkers. Seeking to cut costs by the increasing use of prepared uppers and cheap sole-leather produced by the sweated footwear trade in English centres, they waged a losing battle against the competition of cheap footwear imported from the same quarters. Despite the obvious need to mechanise in order to save the local footwear industry, the first major structural change in the trade did not occur until the early 1880s. This first move towards technological production methods came with the establishment of the Cork Boot Factory (originally the brainchild of the local trades council) which launched the manufacture of machine-made boots in the city, and by the late 1880s four such factories had been set up. This move, however, did not so much shore up the local footwear trade as change its entire character. There was very little overlap between the new entrepreneurs and the older master shoemakers, while the factories introduced a completely new group of workers, the semi-skilled boot rivetters and finishers, described by the handsewers as 'a totally different body from the tradesmen of Cork'. It is not clear how quickly the rivetters displaced the handsewers for the census of the period failed to distinguish between handworkers and factory workers in the footwear industry, but the approximate change in the numbers of unionised men in each group between 1880 and 1900 gives some indication of the revolution within the industry. Whereas in 1880 some seventy-seven per cent of those unionised were handsewers, by 1904 the figures had been reversed and seventy-six per cent of the unionised workers were factory-based rivetters and finishers.[104]

That this wholesale mechanisation occasioned little recorded controversy was not due to any real welcome for machinery but to the lack of effective organisation among the handsewers. Though the factory-based workers proved less docile than the handsewers, they, too, found their working conditions and bargaining strength undermined by further mechanisation when one boot factory, that of Dwyer and Co., attempted to free themselves from trade-union restrictions by operating on 'scab' and boy labour – a process facilitated by the introduction of lasting and finishing machines and the consequent easy sub-division of labour. The union's helplessness in the face of such a policy was evident in the virulence of their condemnations of Dwyers' as 'a shop of machinery and boys . . . accommodators, sweaters [and] refractory members' and a decade of conflict ensued between management and union until the workforce was unionised in 1896.[105]

Tailoring, reflecting contemporary conditions in Britain, France and Germany, revealed a similar pattern of change. Since the 1860s, the making of vests was largely in the hands of female outworkers, while by the end of the century trousers were made mainly by boy labour, both in the tailoring workshops and in the homes of the outworkers.[106] In the early 1870s the tailors' union tried to offset the undercutting effects of mechanisation by imposing special charges (usually at half the rate of hand-sewing) for preparing garments for the machine, but such measures were to an extent self-defeating as they pushed smaller economising employers to depend even more on the combination of machinery, non-union tailors, and sweated female outworkers so as to meet the competition of imported and locally produced ready-made clothing.[107]

This process of displacement by machinery involved the local tailoring trade in three major disputes over five decades. The first such strike in 1859, basically involving wage claims, was brought to a speedy end not only by the inevitable availability of strike breakers but also by the master-tailors' threat to bring in machinery to permanently displace the striking journey-men.[108] This uneasy settlement led eventually in 1870 to the second major tailoring strike which revolved around the three issues of wages, non-union and sweated labour, and the mechanisation of the trade. The strike began in one city establishment and spread quickly to the other houses, eventually involving 240 members and lasting ten weeks. Earlier in the year the city masters, under pressure of business, had acceded to the operatives' demand that the threepence-halfpenny log, in force since the 1840s, should be raised to fourpence. But when business slackened the rise was withdrawn and a new log substituted, prepared by twelve of the Cork masters and approved by some of the masters of Dublin and London. Though this purported to be a fourpenny log, it was rejected by the operatives' society because, unlike their own log, it allowed for the further mechanisation of the trade. The tailors' society, seeing in the sewing machine an instrument to cut labour costs and to replace society men by sweated female labour, had imposed fines on employers who used sewing machines. The employers, for their part, claimed that machinery would actually increase the amount of work available by enabling the manufacture of cheap ready-mades during the slack season when other work was not in demand.[109] After a number of weeks the journeymen accepted a nominal fourpenny log which, however, allowed for the introduction of further machinery into the trade, and continued as a source of conflict over the following decades.[110] Though the log had risen to fourpence-halfpenny by 1878, eight years later in recognition of the prevailing depression, the tailors' union allowed some employers revert to the fourpenny log, so that thenceforth two logs ran concurrently in the city. The fourpence-halfpenny or first-class log was paid by the well-established and thriving employers who each employed on their own premises an average of fifty tailors. The fourpenny or second-class log was paid by the smaller, struggling employers, each with an average in-house workforce of seven to nine tailors, but heavily dependent on the labour of an unspecified number of sweated outworkers.[111]

The third major tailoring dispute regarding mechanisation erupted in early 1893 when five of these 'second-class' employers were called upon to pay the first-class log, and following a brief compliance, three of this number locked out their men and were joined in the lock-out by eight other employers of the second class. The results of the strike were typically inconclusive. Though some masters conceded the operatives' demands, the majority persisted in their lock-out into the late 1890s, running their concerns on blackleg labour and paying at the old second-class rates.[112] While the lock-out masters became the folk villians of the unionised tailors, who claimed that they had amassed large fortunes at the expense of the journeymen, their cost-cutting mechanisation really reflected their vulnerability as employers in a handcraft under siege from factory-based production. They, like their journeymen, had been placed in a double bind: if they used machines and sweated outworkers, they displaced the working craftsmen; if they did not safeguard their own struggling business concerns through mechanisation, they and the journeymen went to the wall together. Indeed, subsequent events indicated that even mechanisation could not save the small employer, for of the eleven minor masters involved in the 1893 dispute, four had gone bankrupt a decade later. Even among the more substantial master tailors and clothiers, the casualty rate was high: between 1890 and 1912 fourteen went bankrupt – all men of considerable standing in the trade, and some of whom had been in business for many years.[113]

Thus, throughout the nineteenth century, the combined trends of modernisation and depression pushed many skilled artisans further and further into a position of beleaguerment. Responses to this development varied from craft to craft and from decade to decade. For some artisans the remedy lay in more efficient control of both the trade's customs and access to the employment market – ends to be achieved through the setting up and development of trade unions. For others, the only road to prosperity was through political means, particularly through the achievement of some measure of self-government for Ireland. These two groups and methods frequently contradicted one another, but together they also helped to push artisans out of traditional obscurity and localism onto a more public stage and into contact with developments outside the boundaries of their craft and their native city.

NOTES

1   *Royal Commission on Friendly and Benefit Building Societies, Report of the Assistant Commissioners (Ireland),* HC 1874 (C – 995), xxiii, pt. II, p. 31.

2   R. J. Morris, 'The labour aristocracy and the British class structure', in Anne Digby and Charles Feinstein (eds.), *New Directions in Economic and Social History* (London, 1989), p. 178; Fergus D'Arcy, 'The National Trades' Political Union and Daniel O'Connell, 1830–1848', *Éire/Ireland,* vol. xvii, no. 3, 1982, p. 8.

3   Mary Daly, *Dublin, the Deposed Capital,* p. 63.

4   *CE,* 29 Mar. 1886, 8 Aug. 1888, 26 Aug., 2 Sept. 1892; *Labour Gazette,* 1894–98.

5   *CE,* 24 Mar., 17 May 1847.

6   *CE,* 15 Mar. 1847.

7   *CE,* 25 Jan. 1847.

8   *CC,* 5 Jan., 7 Dec. 1847; *CE,* 5 July 1845, 13 Jan. 1847.

9   *CE,* 18 Jan. 1847.

10 *CE,* 15 Mar. 1847.

11 *Southern Reporter* (cited hereafter as *SR*), 21 Mar. 1848.

12 *CE,* 1 Dec. 1843.

13 *CE,* 4 Feb. 1846, 25 Jan., 19 May 1847; Chief Secretary's Office Registered Papers (cited hereafter as CSORP), Z/1474, 9 Feb. 1847.

14 *CE,* 19 Aug. 1841, 5 Mar. 1845, 21 Sept. 1846, 25 Jan., 15 Mar. 1847, 21 Mar. 1848.

15 Manufacture, which in 1841 employed 40·88 per cent of males and 30·89 per cent of females in paid employment, employed only 19·15 per cent of males and 28·09 per cent of females by 1901. *Census of Ireland,* 1841–1901.

16 In the engineering sector, the term 'engineers' includes a wide variety of skilled craftsmen, including turners, fitters, millwrights, patternmakers, most of whom were employed either in the transport sector, the ship-building industry, or the city's small but fairly prosperous engineering shops. Although numbers in the building sector rose in the course of the century, and accounted for proportionately more male city workers in 1901 than they had done fifty years earlier (9·17 per cent of the male workforce in 1901 as opposed to 7·95 per cent in 1841), the internal structure of the building industry changed considerably in the course of the century. John Lee, 'Aspects of the development and decline in the building industry in Cork City 1850–1899', (Unpublished MA dissertation, National University of Ireland, 1988); *Labour Gazette,* 1894–1898.

17 *CE,* 23 Sept. 1881, 23 Mar. 1886, 23 Mar. 1897.

18 *Minutes of Evidence before the Select Committee on Irish and Scottish Vagrants,* HC 1828, iv, 14; *Yearly and Financial Report of the Amalgamated Society of Tailors,* 1874–1894; *Quarterly Report of the United Kingdom Society of Coachmakers,* 1874–1900; *Monthly Report of the National Union of Boot and Shoe Rivetters and Finishers,* 1888–90.

19   Adrian Pimley, 'The working-class movement and the Irish revolution, 1896–1923', D. G. Boyce (ed.), *The Revolution in Ireland 1879–1923* (London, 1988), p. 193.

20   *CE*, 28 June, 6, 7 July 1870, 1 Jan., 26 Oct., 9 Nov. 1871; CSORP, 1870: 14005, 15232; Seán Daly, *Cork: A City in Crisis*, pp. 79–108; Maura Cronin, 'Work and workers in Cork City and County', O'Flanagan and Buttimer (eds.), *Cork: History and Society. Interdisciplinary Essays on the History of an Irish County* (Dublin, 1993), pp. 742–3.

21   *CE*, 2, 3, 5, 9, 11, 17 Aug., 13 Sept. 1882.

22   Brendan McDonnell, 'The Dublin labour movement 1894–1907' (Unpublished Doctoral thesis, National University of Ireland, 1979), p. 145.

23   *CE*, 1 Jan., 26 Oct., 9 Nov. 1871; 10, 29 Aug., 2 Sept., 28 Oct. 1872; CSORP, 1870: 16317.

24   *CE*, 13 Sept. 1882, 22, 23, 25, 26, 28, 29, 30 Apr., 1, 2, 3, 5 May 1890; *Report on changes in the rate of wages and hours of labour in the United Kingdom* (cited hereafter as *Report on Wages*), HC 1890–91, lxxviii, App. 1, 104.

25   *CE*, 9, 14, 20, 21 May, 5, 6, 20, 25 June 1890. The wages structure among the labourers was quite complex: of the 230 men in the society in 1890 between 50 and 60 received thirteen shillings weekly, some 120 received fourteen shillings, between 15 and 20 earned fifteen shillings, and 70 earned from fifteen to eighteen shillings, different rates being paid by different builders. The builders' labourers, whose society numbered some 230 members by 1893, were the only unskilled group to consistently assert their position. The most serious strike, that of 1890, was largely a wage strike aimed at securing a general rise of two shillings a week plus overtime pay. The seven-week strike ended in a compromise fourteen-shilling rate, with the promise of a further shilling from March 1891. But even this compromise wage settlement was not allowed to stand for long, and over the next half decade at least one strike per year among the builders' labourers sought to retain the fifteen-shilling rate and prevent the employment of non-unionists by economising builders.

26   *CE*, 9, 14 May 1890, 6 May 1891.

27   E. P. Thompson, *The Making of the English Working Class* (Harmondsworth, 1963), p. 273.

28   *CE*, 23, 28 Jan., 11 Feb., 4 Mar., 1 July 1857, 2, 16 Apr. 1858, 20 July, 23 Sept. 1881, 6, 10 Mar. 1883. From the 1850s onwards employment prospects in the baking trade were also seriously affected by the arrival on the market of boys trained in the workhouses and industrial schools.

29   *CC*, 10 Dec. 1833, 15 Feb., 8 July, 6, 11, 20 Nov. 1834.

30   *CE*, 14, 21 May, 2 June 1858, 10, 11, 12, 14, 19 Jan. 1859. The strike was also apparently due to the master tailors' opposition to the city trade societies' recent resolution against working on Church holy days, and it went ahead not because the masters proved totally non-compliant (they had actually abandoned the wage cut) but because the holiday issue was

not settled to the journeymens' satisfaction: 'Holidays, as a general rule, are to be kept: but in cases of necessity, one or more men may finish or make alterations, provided the work is in a hurry.'

31 *CE*, 13 July 1853.

32 *CE*, 7 Mar. 1851, 24 Jan. 1855; *Typographical Protection Circular*, 1850, p. 60; *Typographical Society Monthly Circular*, Feb. 1860, p. 2, Sept. 1860, p. 1.

33 *CE*, 12 Jan. 1853, 19 Jan., 20, 23 Apr., 7 May 1855, 29 Apr. 1859, 1, 2, 3 July 1863, 30 May 1894, 7 Sept. 1897; Cork Coopers' Society Minute Books, 7 Jan. 1875, 4, 5 May 1886, 21 Apr. 1887, 10 May 1888, 6 Sept. 1898; Cork Plumbers' Society Minute Books, 6 Feb. 1875, 19 Feb. 1878, undated entry between 9 July 1891 and 30 Sept. 1892, undated entry following that for 28 Mar. 1894; *United Operative Plumbers' Association Quarterly Return*, Dec. 1892, p. 4.

34 Dick Geary, *European Labour Protest*, p. 17.

35 *CC,* 18 Feb. 1830.

36 Fergus D'Arcy's work on building trade rates in Dublin may in the future be replicated in the Cork context, but at the time of writing sufficient continuous documentary evidence is not available. See Fergus D'Arcy, 'Wages of labourers in the Dublin building industry, 1667–1918', *Saothar*, 14, 1989, pp. 17–35, and 'Wages of skilled workers in the Dublin building industry, 1667–1918', *Saothar*, 15, 1990, pp. 21–38.

37 *United Operative Plumbers' Association of Great Britain and Ireland, Quarterly Report*, 1876, 1880–86; *Statistical Tables and Reports on Trade Unions* (cited hereafter as *Reports on Trade Unions*, [C–5104] HC 1887, lxxxix, 715, pt. II, 179–206; [C–6990] HC 1893-4, cii, 85, 190; [c-7436] HC 1895, xciv, 55, 116, 181–214; *CE*, 3, 24 Feb., 10 Mar. 1893. The engineers' and plumbers' rates were from six to eight per cent higher than those paid to their Dublin counterparts, and from eight to twenty-one per cent higher than in Belfast.

38 *Reports on Trade Unions*, [C–5104] HC 1887, lxxxix, 715, pt. II, 325, 341; 135 [C–5505] HC 1888, xvii; [C–6990] HC 1893–94, cii, 85, 19); *Annual Report of the General Union of Friendly Operative Carpenters and Joiners*, 1886–89; *Annual Report of the Amalgamated Society of Carpenters and Joiners*. 1866–1900; *Quarterly Report of the General Alliance of Operative House Painters*, 1877–82; *Friendly Society of Operative Cabinet Makers: Trade Report and Financial Statement*, 1875–1877; *Alliance Cabinet Makers' Association, Annual Report*, 1878–1900; *Yearly Account of the Income and Expenditure of the Journeymen Cabinet Makers', Carvers' and Woodturners' Friendly Society*, 1844–88; *CMC*, 1 Oct. 1802; *SR*, 19 Sept. 1840; Fergus D'Arcy, 'Dublin artisan activity, opinion and organisation 1820–50' (Unpublished MA dissertation, National University of Ireland, 1968), pp. 168–72.

39 Data on wages are taken from various newspaper reports, trade-union documents and parliamentary enquiries. Wage increases from 1850 to 1900 varied widely: twenty-five per cent among the cabinet makers, from twenty-five to forty per cent among the engineering trades, twenty-eight to fifty per cent in the shipbuilding sector, fifty-five per cent in the case of the

printers, fifty per cent among the building trades and from fifty to sixty-six per cent among the bakers.

40 Dick Geary, *European Labour Protest,* p. 53, notes that real wages in Britain rose by some eighty-four per cent between 1850 and 1900.

41 It must be noted that prices were subject to severe fluctuation depending on the season and the availability of any given commodity. Potato prices rose to one and twopence per twenty-one pound weight in 1895, lowest quality meat to sevenpence halfpenny in 1875 and bread to tenpence in 1855. For discussions on food prices in Cork during the nineteenth century, see John O'Brien, 'Agricultural prices and living costs in pre-famine Cork', *JCHAS* lxxxii, 1977, and Maura Murphy, 'The working classes of nineteenth century Cork', pp. 38–9.

42 Giving evidence before the *Poor Enquiry,* HC 1836, xxx, App. C to First Report, 27–8, a Cork weaver pointed out how tripes, heads and legs had become scarce since cattle and pigs were exported on the hoof, while Daphne D. C. Pochin Mould, *Discovering Cork* (Dingle, 1991), pp. 261–2, describes how hearts and 'skirts' came to be salted and exported to Scotland and thus removed from the diet of the poor.

43 Cork had several thriving second-hand clothes markets patronised by working people, one such, the Coal Quay, being immortalised in the 1970s by the folksinger Jimmy Crowley. Both the increasing demand for footwear (as bare feet became less acceptable) and the meeting of that demand are evident in the proliferation of cheap footwear warehouses in Cork and other towns from the 1860s onwards. See below, pp. 38–39.

44 On the funeral provisions made by the Cork working class in the nineteenth century, see Maura Murphy, 'The working classes of nineteenth century Cork', pp. 40–1.

45 O'Flanagan and Buttimer (eds), *Cork: History and Society,* pp. 730–31.

46 *Poor Enquiry,* HC 1836, xxx, App. C to First Report, 24–5, 28; *Third Report of Her Majesty's Commissioners for Inquiring into the Housing of the Working Classes in Ireland* (cited hereafter as *Housing Enquiry*) [C–4547] HC 1884–85, xxxi, Qs. 23713; Cork Archives Institute, Public Health Committee Minutes 13 June 1898, Cork Corporation Committee on Working Class Dwellings, 2 Feb. 1909.

47 *Poor Enquiry,* HC 1836, xxx, App. C to First Report, 27–8; *CE,* 5 May, 20, 22, 25 Sept. 1843; *SR,* 19 Sept. 1843; Cork Coopers' Society Minute Books, 9 Dec. 1886.

48 See below pp. 35–36.

49 *Minutes of Evidence taken before the Royal Commission on Labour* (cited hereafter as *Royal Commission on Labour*), Group C, [C–7063–vc] HC 1892–93 xxxviii, 82–3.

50 *CE,* 25, 27 May 1870, 6 June 1893; *Yearly Report of the Amalgamated Society of Tailors,* 1868–1900; *Quarterly Report of the Amalgamaged Society of Tailors,* 1874–1875; 1885; 1887; *Reports on Trade Unions,* [C–5104] HC 1887, lxxxix, 715, pt. II, 410.

51 *CMC*, 21 Jan., 1 Feb. 1832; *CE*, 18 Sept. 1843, 13 Jan. 1853, 17 Apr., 12 June 1862, 16, 29 Jan. 1874; Cork Coopers' Society Minute Books, 16, 30 Sept. 1886, 3 Mar., 5 Oct. 1887, 24 Sept. 1895.

52 Cork Typographical Society List of idle members 1869–1900; *Quarterly Report of the Associated Shipwrights' Society*, June 1893–June 1894. Until the publication of the *Labour Gazette* in the early 1890s there was no regular commentary on unemployment figures among either skilled or unskilled workers in the United Kingdom.

53 In periodic press reports union spokesmen mentioned the depletion of unemployment and benefit funds, but a study of surviving union balance reveals surprisingly little, showing few fluctuations from year to year.

54 *CE*, 23 Sept. 1886, 23 Mar. 1897; *Census of Ireland*, 1881–1901.

55 *SR*, 4 Nov. 1826, 10 Mar. 1827; *CC*, 6, 17 April 1830; *CMC*, 21 Jan., 1 Feb. 1832; *CE*, 29 Mar. 1886, 8 Aug. 1888; *Poor Enquiry*, HC 1836, xxx, App. C to First Report, 27–8. Attempts were made in the 1820s and 1830s to relieve the condition of the Cork cotton weavers by emigrating them to Manchester. No such relief schemes were extended to the local coopers, only twenty-two per cent of whom were employed by 1832. Even this percentage was only partially employed, with an average of four months' work in the year.

56 Cork Coopers' Society Minute Books, 26 July 1883, 3 Mar. 1887, 28 Nov. 1892; *CE*, 28 Oct. 1886. Neither the manuscript minute books of local societies nor the more regular and comprehensive printed records of the amalgamated unions documented this subject in any detail. The minute books of the local coopers' and plumbers' societies regularly mentioned unemployment as a problem, but usually without giving any figures.

57 E. P. Thompson, *The Making of the English Working Class*, p. 444.

58 *CE*, 5 May 1843. See Mary Daly, *Dublin, the Deposed Capital*, pp. 55, 63, 80, for similar problems in the Dublin building trade.

59 Cork Coopers' Society Minute Books, 3 Mar. 1887, 2 Feb. 1888, 6 Feb. 1893, Jan. 1899 – undated entry preceding 6 Jan. 1899; James S. Donnelly, Jr., *The Land and the People of Nineteenth Century Cork* (London, 1975), p. 139; Seán Daly, *Cork: A City in Crisis*, p. 296.

60 *Royal Commission on Labour*, [C–7063] HC 1892–93, xxxviii, 82–3, Qs. 14641–2; *CE*, 1, 10 Nov., 11 Dec. 1882; 20 Apr. 1886; 10 Mar., 23 Nov. 1887; *CDH*, 18 Nov. 1887; R. Q. Gray, 'Class structure and the class formation of skilled workers in Edinburgh 1850–1900.' (Doctoral thesis, University of Edinburgh, 1972), p. 71; Mary Daly, *Dublin, the Deposed Capital*, p. 60.

61 Colman O Mahony, *The Maritime Gateway to Cork: A History of the Outports of Passage West and Monkstown from 1754–1942* (Cork, 1986), pp. 25–7, 56–60, 88–91; *CE*, 21, 29 Oct., 1 Nov. 1886, 4 Feb. 1891, 26 Feb., 10 June, 26 Aug., 8, 9 Sept., 17 Oct., 29 Nov. 1893, 27 Feb. 1894, 19 Nov. 1896, *Labour Gazette*, Feb. 1894, p. 43, Apr. 1894, p. 107, May 1894, pp. 138–9; *Quarterly Report of the Associated Society of Shipwrights,* June 1893–June 1894; CSORP, 1883: 1375; *Reports on Trade Unions*, 277 [C–8232] HC 1896 lxxx, pt. I, 88–9;

Weekly wages were cut in 1886 by three shillings to thirty shillings for new work and thirty-three shillings for repair work.

62 *CE*, 21 Apr., 25 June 1858, 22, 26 Sept., 2 Oct 1862, 12, 24 Feb., 11 Mar. 1886; *CC*, 23 Sept. 1862. See below, pp. 136–8.

63 J. D. Clarkson, *Labour and Nationalism in Ireland* (New York, 1925), pp. 40–2, 75; *Cork Morning Intelligencer* (cited hereafter as *CMI*) 8 Mar. 1821; *SR*, 2 Feb. 1826; Richard Price, *Labour in British Society: An Interpretative History* (London, 1986), p. 21; *Poor Enquiry*, HC 1836, xxx, 28. In 1821 the newspapers referred to court settlements of wages for coopers, curriers, masons, carpenters, plasterers and shoemakers.

64 *CMI*, 18, 29 May 1821; *SR*, 22 Feb. 1826.

65 *CE*, 10 Oct. 1845.

66 Cork Coopers' Society Minute Books, 30 Apr. 1886.

67 *SR*, 27 Feb. 1841; *CC*, 6 Feb. 1849.

68 *CMI*, 1 Oct., 31 Dec. 1802; 8 Mar. 1817; 19, 29 May 1821; *SR*, 15 Sept. 1840, 27 Feb. 1841. The court price of 1821 was twenty shillings per week while a cooper's average weekly earnings in 1846 were from seven to ten shillings.

69 *CC*, 23, 26, 30 Nov. 1855; *CE*, 29 June 1870, 28 Apr. 1871; 3, 24 Feb., 10 Mar. 1893; *Report on wages*, [C–7567] HC 1894, lxxxi, Pt. III, 181–214; *Royal Commission on Labour*, [C–6894–ix] HC 1893–94, Qs. 28798; Cork Typographical Society Minute Books, 3 Oct. 1896; R. Q. Gray, 'Class structure in Edinburgh', pp. 86–8. Weekly earnings for shoemakers during the period 1850–70 averaged between twelve and sixteen shillings; those for printers showed wider differentials, from eighteen to forty-two shillings, though averaging around thirty shillings. As Gray points out, the Edinburgh printers generally preferred piecework to 'stab' or time-rates because the former made allowance for extra payment for such additional work as footnotes, passages in foreign languages and complex text layout. Though no detailed evidence is available on the Cork printers' preference for piecework, their outlook appears to have been much the same as that of their Edinburgh equivalents.

70 *CE*, 11 June 1855; 7 Oct. 1882, 21 July 1887; Cork Coopers' Society Minute Books, 13 Dec. 1871; 17 Jan., 25 June 1883; 6 July 1886; 9, 16, 23 Sept. 1896.

71 Andy Bielenberg, *Cork's Industrial Revolution 1780–1880: Development or Decline?* (Cork, 1991), pp. 16–19, 25–9, 35–6; State of the Country Papers 1817: 1835/15 (cited hereafter as *SOC*); British Museum Additional Manuscripts No. 38270, f. 450. Cork Archives Institute, Cork Petition to Parliament *re* Unemployment, 1822. From 1817 onwards foreign competition damaged the local linen and sailcloth industry, heavy import duties on timber affected the timber merchants and carpenters, and the decline of local shipbuilding since the 1780s threw shipwrights and dockside labourers out of work. Several food riots occurred in the city in 1817 and in the following year it was reported that almost two hundred unemployed carpenters were on the borders of starvation.

72 *CMC*, 13, 15 Feb., 31 Mar. 1818; *SR*, 10, 12, 15, 19, 24 Jan. 1826; CSORP.OR 1828: C/10.2. In 1826 the shoemakers struck unsuccessfully to maintain the wage rate paid since 1810, while the tailors demanded and won the same concession. The various workers in the breweries and distilleries made similar demands, which these establishments, long considered the most generous employers, readily conceded. These limited concessions and – more importantly – the refusal of the other employers to concede led to a further wave of protest in 1828.

73 *SR,* 15 Sept. 1840.

74 *Poor Enquiry,* HC 1836, xxx, App. C to First Report, 27; *CE*, 15, 18 Mar. 1882; Cork Coopers' Society Minute Books, 7 Jan. 1875, 4, 5 May 1886, 21 Apr. 1887, 10 May 1888, 6 Sept. 1898. On the disintegration of apprenticeship restrictions in England, see. E. P. Thompson, *The Making of the English Working Class*, p. 279.

75 *CE,* 23 Oct. 1850; Cork Coopers' Society Minute Books, 7 Jan. 1875, 4, 5 May 1886, 21 Apr. 1887, 10 May 1888, 6 Sept. 1898. Of the 175 cabinet makers in the city in 1850, only a handful were in the cabinet makers' society, and these were greatly outnumbered by apprentices. Many of the smaller houses in the city were run exclusively on boy labour, and even one of the major establishments had sixty-five apprentices to eighteen journeymen. From the 1870s onwards, the recognised number of boys in the coopering trade was settled at a maximum of three per employer and all boys except the eldest son of a cooper had to be indentured. A master employing ten men was allowed one apprentice while the employer of upwards of ten men was allowed two apprentices, the third apprentice possibly being the permitted eldest son. The society maintained its preference for members' sons into the 1890s. The effectiveness of this rule, however, is far from clear, but its constant reiteration by the society suggests that it was very difficult to enforce.

76 *CE*, 15, 18 Mar. 1882; *Half-yearly Report of the National Typographical Association,* Jan–June 1845; 1860; *Typographical Protection Circular,* Feb. 1850, p. 60; *Proceedings of a Meeting of Delegates from the Typographical Societies of the United Kingdom*, 1861; *Census of Ireland*, 1861. In 1850 the ratio of apprentices to journeymen in the city was thirty-two to fifty-eight, whereas by 1860 it was forty-nine to seventy-nine. In 1882 Guy Brothers, one of the biggest printing houses in the city, was run largely on boy labour in spite of the vociferous protests of the printers' union.

77 See below, pp. 130–32.

78 Thomas Sheahan, *Articles of Irish Manufacture: Or Portions of Cork History* (Cork, 1833) p. 187; *CMC*, 11, 13 June 1832. For the fluctuating fortunes of the textile trade in the Cork region, see Bielenberg, *Cork's Industrial Revolution,* pp. 8–40.

79 Brendan McDonnell, 'The Dublin labour movement', pp. x, xxxiii; *CE*, 28 Sept., 7, 19 Oct., 15 Dec. 1881; 24 Apr. 1882; 3 Mar. 1885; 28 Apr. 1887; 9 Mar., 20 July, 7 Sept. 1894; 8 May, 27 Sept. 1895; *Quarterly Report*

of the United Kingdom Society of Coachmakers, 1880–1900; *Alliance Cabinet Makers' Society Monthly Report*, Jan.–Dec. 1895; *Alliance Cabinet Makers' Society Annual Report*, 1894, pp.192–3; *Labour Gazette*, 1895–98 *passim*.

80   *CE*, 11 Mar. 1892; 6, 12 June 1895; Cork Coopers' Society Minute Books, 8 June, 20 Aug. 1886, 17 May 1888, 7 Dec. 1892.

81   *CE*, 19 Oct. 1881; Cork Typographical Society Minute Books, 1887–1900, *passim*. Some 100 nailors worked in the city in 1877, by 1881 thirty were working and by 1886 this number had fallen to six.

82   *CE*, 31 Aug. 1881, 14 Apr. 1882, 21, 22 Oct. 1886, 5, 21 Apr. 1887, 21 Oct. 1898; Bielenberg, *Cork's Industrial Revolution*, p. 83; Cork Archives Institute, Cork Bankruptcy Court Records, 1890–1916. Some contemporaries claimed that £10,000 worth of foreign footwear came into Cork every year, others that a single city establishment imported £20,000 worth of footwear annually. One such importing firm was that of the McNay Brothers, three of whose creditors at time of bankruptcy were Irish firms – Woods of Dublin, Hearnes of Waterford and Bennis of Limerick – while thirty-eight were England-based.

83   For an analysis of the demise of the textile trade in Bandon, see Andy Bielenberg, 'The growth and decline of a textile town: Bandon 1770-1840', *JCHAS*, vol. 97, 1992, pp. 111–19.

84   *SR*, 16 Mar., 29 Apr., 9, 16 May, 15 June, 15 Aug., 4, 9, 11 Nov. 1826, 10, 15, 20, 25 Feb. 1827; *CC*, 6, 17 Apr. 1830. In this period weavers' weekly earnings reputedly fell to between four and six shillings.

85   *CMC*, 17 Aug., 19 Nov. 1832; *SR*, 9 Mar., 9 Apr., 9 May 1841, 3 Aug. 1848; *CE*, 8, 13 Dec. 1841, 28 Aug., 9 Oct. 1850. Maura Cronin, 'Work and workers', pp. 737–8.

86   Bielenberg, *Cork's Industrial Revolution*, pp. 70–1, 82–3.

87   Bielenberg, *Cork's Industrial Revolution*, pp. 108–114; Colman O Mahony, 'Shipbuilding and repairing in nineteenth-century Cork', *JCHAS*, vol. xciv, no. 253, Jan.–Dec. 1989, pp. 74-87; *CE*, 24 Apr., 29 Sept. 1882, 21, 24, 25, 27 Jan. 1887; M. J. Gough, 'History of the physical development of Cork City' (Unpublished MA thesis, National University of Ireland, 1973), p. 222.

88   *CE*, 19 Oct. 1881.

89   *CE*, 19 Oct. 1881, 14 Feb., 29 Apr. 1884, 17 Feb. 1887, 26 Aug., 2, 9 Sept. 1892, 19 Sept. 1895, 17 June 1898.

90   *CE*, 14 Sept. 1855, 24, 28 Mar., 9 Apr. 1856, 2, 11 May 1894, 6 June 1895; Cork Coopers' Society Minute Books, 9 Dec. 1886, 28 Nov. 1892, 6 Feb. 1893, 25 Apr. 1894, 14 June, 24 July, 30 Nov. 1895, 17 July, 1 Oct. 1896.

91   *CE*, 20 May 1844, 6, 27 Jan. 1845; *Hansard's Parliamentary Debates*, Third Series (cited hereafter as *Hansard* 3), 1844, lxxiv, 1259–69; lxxvi, 133, 1560-62. For a general account of the butter and provision trades in Cork, see Louis Cullen, *An Economic History of Ireland since 1660* (London, 1972), pp. 54–9, 85, 87–8; William O'Sullivan, *An Economic History of Cork from the Earliest Times to the Act of Union* (Cork, 1937), pp. 165–70.

92   *CE*, 14 Sept. 1855, 24, 28 Mar., 9 Apr. 1856, 19 Sept. 1891, 18 Mar. 1895.

In the 1880s between 300 and 400 coopers were still employed in navy provision work, but this number had contracted sharply by the 1890s.

93 Butterine was an artificial butter made from animal fat churned with milk and water, or from milk churned with some sweet butter and the yolks of eggs.

94 Cork Coopers' Society Minute Books, 30 Sept. 1886, 3 Mar., 5, 14 Oct. 1887, 5 May 1888; James S. Donnelly Jr., *The Land and the People of Nineteenth Century Cork*, pp. 149–54.

95 Andy Bielenberg, *Cork's Industrial Revolution*, pp. 58, 61–76. *CE*, 22 Mar. 1895, 3 Mar. 1896, Cork Coopers' Society Minute Books, 14 Mar., 18 Aug. 1895. Guinness's share of the total Irish beer output rose from seven per cent in 1837 to 29 per cent in 1871 and 75 per cent by 1900. By the 1890s forty coopers were directly employed by the Cork breweries, though many more did brewery work in outside shops belonging to independent master coopers. In the 1870s the city's four distilleries directly employed a total of over fifty coopers: the two distilleries of the 1890s directly employed twenty coopers between them.

96 Dick Geary, *European Labour Protest*, p. 72; E. P. Thompson, *The Making of the English Working Class*, p. 486.

97 *Royal Commission on Labour,* 1893–94, 17058–62. For similar trends in nineteenth-century Britain, see R. Q. Gray, 'Class structure in Edinburgh', pp. 86–92.

98 *CE*, 21, 24, 25, 27 Jan. 1887; Colman O Mahony, *The Maritime Gateway to Cork*, p. 88.

99 *CC*, 7 Feb., 31 Mar., 5, 10, 12, 19, 22 May, 7 July 1835; *CE*, 2, 11 Mar., 12 May 1842; 4, 5 Dec. 1888; 10, 11 June 1892; 8, 18 June, 17, 19 Sept., 27, 30 Oct. 1896.

100 *CE*, 6 Nov. 1883, 29 Apr. 1884, 2 Sept. 1892.

101 *CE*, 7 Sept. 1894; 8 May, 27 Sept. 1895; 23 Mar. 1897; Alliance Cabinet Makers' Society Monthly Report, Jan.-Dec. 1895; Alliance Cabinet Makers' Society Annual Report, 1894, pp. 192–3. The modern sewing machine, first patented in 1846 by Elias Howe, and more advanced versions designed by A. B. Wilson and Isaac Singer appearing from 1854 onwards, became increasingly common in commercial garment production from the late 1850s onwards.

102 *Census of Ireland,* 1841-1901. The breakdown of these occupations was as follows:

Clothing:	1851 – 546 males, 1814 females	
	1871 – 543 males, 2409 females	
	1901 – 426 males, 2166 females	
Upholstery:	1851 – 68 males, 0 females	
	1871 – 142 males, 20 females	
	1901 – 120 males, 36 females	
Shoemaking:	1851 – 1230 males, 56 females	
	1871 – 762 males, 95 females	
	1901 – 415 males, 75 females	

Bookbinding:1851 – 20 males, 8 females
1871 – 32 males, 18 females
1901 – 34 males, 69 females.

In the case of upholstery, the degree of domination of the trade by females may also be obscured by the fact that males are listed in most census tables under the combined categories of cabinet makers and upholsterers, so that, in fact, most listed males were probably cabinet makers rather than upholsterers. In the clothing industry, the picture is further complicated by the multiple categorisation of female workers as tailoresses, milliners, dressmakers, staymakers, shirtmakers and seamstresses.

103   E. P. Thompson, *The Making of the English Working Class*, pp. 264, 274; R. Price, *Labour in British Society: An Interpretative History* (London, 1986), p. 27; John Foster, *Class Struggle and the Industrial Revolution*, p. 104.

104   The four major boot factories of the late 1880s were: the Cork Boot Factory, Watercourse Road; Dwyer and Company's Lee Boot Factory, Great George's Street; D. Ryan and Sons, the Glen Tannery; and St. Finbarr's Boot Factory, South Main Street. As is obvious in the case of Ryan's factory, some at least of the new establishments were connected less with traditional shoemaking than with the tanning industry, while some smaller factories, like that of B. King and Sons, North Main Street, had apparent connections with traditional boot and shoemaking firms of the older type. *Guy's Directory of Munster*, 1886–1900 (Cork 1886); *CE*, 1 Sept. 1881, 5 Apr. 1887; *Southern Industry*, May 1889, p. 11; *National Union of Boot and Shoe Rivetters and Finishers, Monthly Report*, Nov. 1889, p. 8. In 1880 there were some 120 men in the handsewers' society while in 1885 the rivetters' union branch had only thirty-five members; in 1904 the handsewers had only fifty-four union members while the rivetters had over 170.

105   *National Union of Boot and Shoe Rivetters and Finishers, Monthly Report*, Sept. 1892, p. 6, May 1894, p. 8. By the early twentieth century, Dwyers' boot factory had, along with the many other manufacturing and distributing concerns established by the family, become a model paternalistic employer.

106   Dick Geary, *European Labour Protest*, p. 34; *CE*, 22 Aug. 1855, 18, 19 May 1893, 27 Sept. 1895, 8, 15 May 1896. In the mid 1850s, the labour of female outworkers was already being used in the making of vests, five tailors employed by Arnold of Winthrop Street being engaged in an assault on such an outworker in 1855.

107   *CE*, 18, 19 May 1893.

108   *CDH*, 16 Feb. 1859; *CE,* 23 Oct. 1860.

109   *CE*, 27, 30 May, 11 June, 6 July, 2 Aug. 1870.

110   *CE*, 1, 2, 4, 6 Aug. 1870. For a very comprehensive treatment of the tailors' strike of 1870, see Seán Daly, *Cork: A City in Crisis*, pp. 144–56.

111   *CE,* 6 Feb. 1886, 23 Aug. 1887, 3, 4, 8, 10 Apr., 31 May, 10 June, 25 Aug. 1893; *Yearly and Financial Report of the Amalgamated Society of Tailors*, 1878, 1887.

112   *CE*, 31 May, 1, 6, 9, 10, 22, 30 June, 12, 27 July, 10, 24 Nov. 1893.

113   *Cork Bankruptcy Court Records*, 1892/27A, 1895/ no ref. no., 1898/113, 1899/148, 1902/181, 1906/217, 247, 230, 1910/311, 1911/297, 1912/303; *CE*, 9, 10, 31 May, 1, 6, 9, 10 June, 10, 24 Nov. 1893.

2

FROM LOCALISM TO A
WIDER AWARENESS

One of the most remarkable developments in recent political history is the growth of sympathy between working men of the two countries [i.e. Ireland and Britain] . . . The quay labourers in Cork or Waterford, in Belfast or in Dublin, have today a keener personal interest in the fate of the workmen in Bristol or in Hull than their fathers had in the affairs of the neighbouring county.[1]

It was through experience of trade unionism that the artisan progressed towards awareness of a wider world than that which existed within the municipal boundaries of Cork City. This path, however, was difficult and tortuous, extending from the first decades of the nineteenth century or earlier, to the threshold of the twentieth century, and even then not quite reaching its destination. It could well be argued that the above assessment by *The Cork Examiner* in 1893 was over-optimistic, and that even by the late 1890s Cork trade unionism was no less introverted than it had been in the mid eighteenth century, when the attention of the House of Commons was drawn to the existence of

several unlawful combinations kept up by and amongst the workmen and artificers in the several trades and manufactures of the . . . city of Cork, to the great detriment of the trade of the said city.

The precise foundation date of the different trade societies of
Cork is impossible to pinpoint, but at least eight unions including
the coopers, tailors and bootmakers dated from the period
1750–1800, while the bakers' and printers' societies were among
those founded in the first decade of the nineteenth century.[2]
Just as in contemporary Britain most unions consisted of 'a single
trade in a single town', so in Cork all these early trade societies
were locally based, apparently unconnected with their counterparts in other towns, and inward-looking, conservative and fearful
of change.[3]

Such introversion derived from the artisans' need to defend
themselves against outsiders' incursions into the local labour
market. Right through the century skilled workers' wage levels
and their bargaining power during strikes had been eroded by
the ready availability of surplus rural labour. But while the vast
number of underemployed agricultural labourers had always provided a fund of cheap labour and strike breakers for city
employers, artisans of small-town origin were even more to be
feared.[4] Skilled but badly organised, and accustomed to working in their home areas for far less than the union rates which
applied in the city, these small-town artisans were readily available
to undermine both the wage levels and working conditions of
city trades.[5] Traditionally, the skilled trades responded to this
problem by seeking to exclude all non-local artisans from the
city labour market, making no apparent distinction between the
non-union men and those who belonged to small-town societies.
Thus in the 1830s the coopers tried (though with little success)
to prevent the incursions of country coopers into the city, and
would not even contemplate allowing them join the local trade
society. Thirty years later, the local stonecutters' society had
steeled itself to admit outsiders but imposed a heavy entrance
fee, requiring a payment of three and five pounds respectively
from any Limerick and Dublin stonecutters who came to work
in Cork.[6] Little had changed by the 1890s when the local
carpenters' society flatly refused to work with society men from
Queenstown, ten miles down the harbour, and the plasterers
would not admit to the city labour market their unionised
counterparts from the twenty-mile distant town of Fermoy.[7]

Despite this intense localism, however, in the course of the century and particularly from the 1830s onwards a gradual move was evident from labour organisation on a purely local basis to involvement with a wider network throughout the British Isles. Even in earlier decades, it must be stressed, isolation was not total, wider contacts being long facilitated by the traditional tramping system. Described by Hobsbawm as 'the artisan's equivalent of the Grand Tour', the tramping system involved unemployed craftsmen travelling in search of work, being assisted by local trade societies in the towns through which they passed. Whereas not all Cork trades favoured tramping, particularly because it lent itself to fraud, others preserved the system to the end of the century.[8] In the late 1870s, the local bakers' society held it as a point of honour never to refuse aid to a tramp while in the 1890s the coopers paid one-and-sixpence out of their scanty funds to each tramp calling to the society rooms.[9] The degree to which the tramp system forged links between local artisans and those in other centres is suggested by the considerable number of tramps who were relieved locally and by the length of the circuits covered by them. While rudimentary transport methods certainly hampered travel before the mid century, even in the 1830s a tramping artisan could cover an average of fifty miles a week, not merely seeking work, but spreading news (and sometimes, apparently, unionisation) among the artisans of the towns through which he passed.[10] A decade later, the improvements in cross-channel steamer travel, which led to a decided increase in the number of tramps in the port towns, opened up the artisan's potential circuit and and exposed him to further contact with his peers from British centres. The Cork branch of the ironmoulders' union, for instance, apparently relieved a total of eight hundred tramps in 1847 and 1848, and while this is an exceptionally high figure (the average number of tramps relieved by the coachmakers' society around the mid century being three per month), it does suggest the degree of outside contact facilitated by the tramping system.[11] These tentative outward moves were also facilitated by the changing structure of the trade unions themselves, as purely local foundations were gradually supplanted by bodies having links with wider organisations.

Such links were not unknown in the earlier decades of the nineteenth century, for although the oldest unions in the city traced
their origins to local societies of the mid- and late eighteenth century, even some of these earlier bodies had connections outside
the city. In the 1830s, the local hatters and glovers had Dublin
links, while the coachmakers and possibly the brushmakers worked in conjunction with their counterparts in Britain.[12] It was
from the late 1830s, however, that the outward moves became
most obvious. While transport improvements presumably help
to explain this development, it was also at least partly due to
the influence of the O'Connellite popular movements in support of Parliamentary Reform and Repeal of the Union. These
movements, by generating a wave of artisan political activity in
almost every sizeable Irish town, gave rise to a sense of common
political interest among the trades of different centres. This sense
of common identity was particularly obvious in the proliferation of trades political demonstrations in different Irish towns
and cities. Because on these occasions the parading of trade
patriotism and solidarity (real or imagined) required the display
of an elaborate banner, the exchange of such banners between
the trades of different centres helped to reinforce the trade communication network already operating through the traditional
tramping system. Thus, the Cork tailors' society and other city
unions agreed to lend their banners to the Mallow trades for use
in the Repeal demonstration of 1843, two years later the Cork
societies lent their banners to the Cahir trades marching in
Thurles, while in 1862 the situation was reversed when the Cork
tailors borrowed the Limerick tailors' banner for another public
demonstration.[13]

More importantly, during the same period several apparent
attempts were made by various trades to establish Irish-centred
amalgamations based on permanent co-operation between the
trade societies of the different towns. Whether such arrangements
involved centralisation or merely informal co-operation is not
clear now, though both types of arrangement apparently existed.
An Armagh-based stonemasons' amalgamation of the early 1840s
was as centralised as existing communications permitted, while
the separate trade of stonecutters throughout the country

seemingly belonged to a looser federation, the Cork society in 1845 being described simply as 'in union with' those of Dublin. Similarly, the Cork United Society of Ladies' and Gentlemen's Shoemakers in the same years was apparently a loose union of the shoemakers of the city with those of the town of Youghal.[14] This idea of Irish-centred amalgamation survived into the later years of the century. In 1873 the Cork bakers' society joined the Dublin-based Bakers' Union of Ireland, which ambitiously aimed to raise wages and abolish night-work by organising the trade in all thirty-two counties. Branches were, in fact, established in fourteen centres in County Cork as well as in the city, and although the successes of the new union were short-lived and the city branch had by 1876 apparently reverted to organisation on a purely local basis, the attempted federation was an indication of the trends of the future.[15] In 1890, almost two decades after the collapse of this early body, the Cork bakers' society again experimented with the principle of federation, on this occasion joining the Belfast-based Irish Bakers' Federation set up in imitation of a similar federation in Scotland. Almost as ineffective as its predecessor in achieving its objectives of higher wages and the abolition of night-work, this latter body at least survived, being transformed in 1895 into a more tightly organised amalgamated union. Though considerable local autonomy still existed for individual branches, the principle if not the practice of broad-based co-operation had been recognised.[16]

The most significant outward move for local trade unionism, however, was the series of attempts from the 1830s onwards to establish English-based amalgamated unions in Ireland. The idea of amalgamation between craftsmen of different centres had been growing apace in Britain from the mid-1830s onward. It was a phenomenon most common among the vibrant crafts, like those in the building industry whose fortunes had not been detrimentally affected by the industrial revolution, or those like the engineering trades which were actually born of the technological innovations of the period.[17] As these British amalgamations turned to Ireland, their main efforts centred on Belfast and Dublin, and radiated thence to eastern Ulster, Leinster, the midlands and eventually to Munster, where Waterford, Cork,

Clonmel and Limerick were the main foci of attention. The Birmingham-based United Operative Stonemasons' Society, for example, which in 1835 began to set up Irish lodges, had by 1837 established a branch in Cork.[18] The Ironmoulders' Friendly Society of England, Wales and Ireland set up a branch in the city in 1839, while around the same time the journeymen coach-makers of the city, organised since early in the nineteenth century in their own locally-based society, joined the United Kingdom Society of Coachmakers.[19] In 1845 the Cork hatters were affiliated to the Hatters' Society of Great Britain and Ireland, and the printers opted briefly for amalgamation with the National Typographical Association.[20] In 1847 a local branch of the United Society of Boiler Makers and Iron Shipbuilders was established, followed in 1851 by a branch of the Amalgamated Society of Engineers.[21] The dramatic progress of this latter organisation may be partly explained by reference to improvements in cross-channel communication which provided officials of British unions with ready access to Ireland, either for the establishment of new branches, canvassing of support for striking union members in Britain, or for the settlement of disputes in Irish centres.[22] Tailing off in the mid-1850s, the trend towards amalgamation revived in the late 1860s and early 1870s, reflecting the growing assertiveness and cohesion of British unions, the development of an increasingly favourable public attitude towards unionism, and the legal recognition of trade unions under the Trade Union Act of 1871.[23] In this new organisational drive by British unions in Ireland, the most successful amalgamations affecting Cork artisans occurred when the Liverpool-based United Operative Plumbers' Association of Great Britain and Ireland established a lodge in the city in 1868, and when the local tailors' society, together with twenty other local tailors' societies throughout the island, fused in 1873 with the Amalgamated Society of Tailors.[24] Among the carpenters a similar trend towards amalgamation was evident in the closing years of the century. The Amalgamated Society of Carpenters and Joiners which had established branches in Belfast and Dublin in 1866, extended its organisation to Cork in 1886. After a number of false starts in the 1870s, another amalgamated carpentry union, the General

Union of Friendly Operative Carpenters and Joiners established a Cork branch in 1895, while in the same year a branch of the National Union of Operative Plasterers was set up in the city.[25]

Among the unskilled and semi-skilled workers, extensive unionisation was delayed until the last two decades of the nineteenth century, though some attempts to establish locally based societies had been made in the early 1870s following a wave of spontaneous labour unrest in the city.[26] In 1870 the Butter Market porters had organised themselves in the short-lived Saint Dominick Society, while around the same time a number of other organisations of the unskilled came into existence: the Cork Labourers' Society catering for the general labourer, the Cork Grocers' and Wine Merchants' Working Men's Benevolent Benefit Society, and the Cork Working Men's Association which was initially a Fenian front organisation but later came to concentrate its attention on labour matters, particularly among the waterside men.[27] Some of these societies had died out by the 1890s but the Grocers and Wine Merchants' Porters' Society survived (with a mercifully abbreviated title), and a number of new societies came into existence. These were the Coal Carriers' Union, the Cork Carriers' Society, the City of Cork Quay Labourers' Protective and Benefit Society, and the Builders' Labourers' Society, all of which catered for clearly defined classes of local labour.[28]

A slightly broader basis of organisation among the non-craft occupations was evident in the form of the Amalgamated Society of Pork Butchers which catered for the butchers and curers working in the large bacon factories of the Munster towns. Cork was apparently the first centre to establish such a society late in 1889, followed by Waterford and Limerick. In early 1890 it was decided that

> the three societies representing Cork, Waterford and Limerick be amalgamated for our common good, without injuring employers in any way, and that we will be considered in future as one body, acting in concert for our mutual good, without harassing anybody.

The amalgamated society soon entered a major dispute with the large bacon-curing firms of the Munster cities, and though the outcome for the union was not entirely successful, the solidarity of the union members and the support of the other trade societies ensured that the settlement was to some extent in their favour.[29]

Apart from these new societies established on either a local or provincial basis, the Cork labour scene was profoundly affected in 1890 by the 'new unionism' which had been developing in Britain since the mid-1880s. In contrast to the older craft unions, these 'new unions', which catered mainly for unskilled and semi-skilled workers, had lower entrance fees, depended largely on the weapon of the aggressive strike to attain their objectives, and, cen-tred as they were among the sailors, dockside labourers and railwaymen, catered within their ranks for mixed categories of workers.[30] Their impact on large numbers of Cork workers, who had hitherto been at best sporadically unionised, at worst totally unorganised, was swift and dramatic. By March 1889 the Sailors' and Firemen's Union, founded in Sunderland in 1887, had a Cork branch, recruiting mainly among the employees of the Steam Packet Company. Later in 1889 the Merseyside-based National Union of Dock Labourers established a branch in the city, again drawing its membership from the Steam Packet Company's employees and subsuming the local Quay Labourers' Society. At the same time the British-based Amalgamated Society of Railway Servants set up a branch in the city. Though it had to compete for some time with a hostile separate Irish society established in February 1890, the two societies eventually merged in late 1890 and thereafter Cork remained in the amalgamated union.[31]

These 'new unions' of the 1890s had their limitations. It has been pointed out that in Britain their impact reached only a cer-tain sector of the non-craft workers, since they

> depended far more on their foothold in certain industries and large works, than on their ability to recruit indiscriminately . . . [They were] alliances of local closed shops, composed of regular employees rather than associations of mobile, footloose labourers ready to turn their hand to almost any task, which constitute an essential element in the myth of the new unionism.[32]

What was true of Britain was equally true of Ireland. Almost all the 'new unions' of the late 1880s and early 1890s, whether

based on local or amalgamated principles, catered for clearly
defined classes of workers. Most of these workers, though referred to as 'unskilled', did, like the butchers or dockers, possess
a considerable skill or experience in their particular line of work,
and they were considered far superior to the truly unskilled casual
labourer. Most of the 'new unions' set up in Cork around 1890,
therefore, recruited neither among the unskilled nor (with the
possible exception of the builders' labourers and railwaymen)
among the lowest wage earners, and it was not until the foundation of the Irish Transport and General Workers' Union in the
first decade of the twentieth century that the casual unskilled
labourers were unionised.[33]

Yet, whatever their limited impact, it was the unions of the
unskilled that shook, however briefly, the narrow localism of Cork
labour. Practically every recorded strike among the city's craft
workers in the course of the century was run on a local footing,
without affecting equivalent artisans in other towns. Unskilled
labour unrest, on the other hand, had the effect of a bush fire,
beginning in one business concern and spreading out from there
to affect a multiplicity of areas. The labour disturbances in Cork
in 1879, for instance, had spread within a week to Mallow,
Youghal, Kanturk, Fermoy, Queenstown and Kinsale – towns
within a radius of between ten and thirty miles of the city.[34] In
1881 the sequence was reversed, when striking farm labourers
from Castletown Kinneigh, some thirty-five miles south-west of
Cork, marched into the city and successfully called upon the urban labourers to strike.[35] It was, however, particularly during
the dramatic events of 1889 and 1890 that the volatility of unskilled labour unrest, and its capacity to spread, became most
apparent. In 1889 a strike by railway goodsmen employed by
the Great Southern and Western Railway Company (GSWR)
spread within days among the goods guards, signalmen and
porters all along the Cork–Dublin line, while in the following
year a strike by goodsmen in the city's GSWR terminus radiated
out to the company's workers in Queenstown and along the
Limerick–Waterford line, and was only with difficulty prevented
from affecting the workers on the Cork–Bandon railway.[36] In
the same year, the pork butchers' strike (though less contagious

than that of the railwaymen) spread within three days from
Limerick to Cork and Waterford, while some ten months later
a strike by Cork dockers and seamen affected their counterparts
in the British centres of Milford Haven, Bristol and Liverpool.[37]

The wildfire nature of unskilled labour unrest and unionisation can be explained in a number of ways – the ready-made
network of contagion available to transport workers on sea and
land, the phenomenon of the sympathetic strike which was an
essential part of the 'new unionism', and the euphoria (usually
short-lived) which accompanied the formation of infant union
branches in occupations hitherto unorganised. Labour unrest
among the skilled crafts proved less contagious, strikes still continuing to operate on a purely local basis even when local societies
became part of amalgamated unions. Yet, for all that, the widening vistas were there, so that by the 1890s local unions had been
largely supplanted by those allied with British amalgamated
unions. Whereas the city had less than half a dozen amalgamated
branches in 1880, the number had risen to twenty-two in 1895.
Expressing the development in different terms underlines the
transformation even more forcibly: whereas in 1880 over seventy-
nine per cent of all unionised workers in Cork city had belonged to locally based societies, by 1895 seventy-three per cent
belonged to amalgamated union branches (Table 4).

The establishment of such amalgamated branches obviously
opened up communication between the artisans of the southern
city and their counterparts in the British centres in which the
union headquarters were located. Thus, in Cork the unionised
masons and plasterers were put in direct contact with Birmingham, the coachmakers and plumbers with Liverpool, the
engineers with London, and the ironmoulders, boiler makers,
tailors and carpenters with Manchester. Moreover, the amalgamated network, even more than the contemporary attempts to
form Irish federations, facilitated contacts between trade members
in a wide variety of centres throughout Ireland itself. In the late
1830s the Birmingham-centred stonemasons' amalgamation formally linked Cork to seven other Irish centres – Belfast, Dublin,
Galway, Ennis, Limerick, Cahir and Waterford. By the 1870s

TABLE 4: MEMBERSHIP OF LOCAL AND AMALGAMATED
UNIONS IN CORK CITY 1880—1895[38]

	Branch Membership	
	1880	1895
Amalgamated union branches		
United Society of Boiler Makers and Iron Shipbuilders	12	30
United Kingdom Society of Coachmakers	79	79
Amalgamated Society of Engineers	111	145
United Operative Plumbers' Association of Great Britain and Ireland	10	39
Amalgamated Society of Carpenters and Joiners	0	240
Amalgamated Society of Tailors	238	220
General Union of Friendly Operative Carpenters and Joiners	0	21
Alliance Cabinet Makers' Society	0	42
Ironfounders Friendly Society of England, Wales and Ireland	0	15
National Union of Boot and Shoe Rivetters and Finishers	0	42
Amalgamated Society of Railway Servants	0	228
National Amalgamated Sailors' and Firemen's Union of Great Britain and Ireland	0	340
Amalgamated Society of Pork Butchers of Cork, Limerick and Waterford	0	ND
Irish National Federal Union of Bakers	0	208
National Union of Dock Labourers of Great Britain and Ireland	0	30
Mutual Association of Coopers of Great Britain and Ireland	0	100
Associated Shipwrights' Society	0	83
National Association of Operative Plasterers	0	36
Amalgamated Society of Millsawyers and Woodcutting Machinists	0	ND
Operative Stonecutters of Ireland	0	110
Amalgamated Society of Lithographic Printers of Great Britain and Ireland	0	ND
Ropemakers' society (title unknown)	0	ND
Subtotal	450	2,008

TABLE 4 (Cont.)

	Branch Membership	
	1880	1895
Local societies		
Cork Brewery Workmen's Society	150	ND
Cork Bakers' Benevolent Society	200	0
Builders' Labourers' Society	0	240
Ancient Corporation of Carpenters	200	0
Cabinet Makers' Society	60	0
Cork Society of Coopers	200	0
Corkcutters' Society	20	20
Cork Farriers' Society	32	20
French Polishers' Society	24	0
Cork Operative Society of Masons and Bricklayers	160	152
Working Millers' Society	40	0
Co-operative Nailmakers of the City of Cork	50	0
Amalgamated Society of Painters and Paperhangers	120	70
Cork Society of Plasterers	100	60
Cork Ladies' and Gentlemen's Bootmakers' Union	120	55
Cork Harbour Shipwrights and Passage Shipwrights	110	0
Cork Typographical Society	116	121
Total	2,152	2,746

ND = No details

the Amalgamated Society of Engineers had connected Cork to nine other towns – the Ulster centres of Belfast, Lisburn, Londonderry and Newry, the Leinster centres of Drogheda, Dublin and Dundalk, and the Munster centres of Limerick and Waterford. In the early 1880s the Amalgamated Society of Carpenters and Joiners put the trade in Cork into direct contact with twelve other Irish towns, while perhaps the widest network of all was in the tailoring trade where in the late 1880s the Amalgamated

Society of Tailors had associated Cork with a total of thirty-three Irish centres in all four provinces.[39]

The advantages of membership of such a wide trade network were obvious. In the first place, it perpetuated and refined the traditional tramping system by formalising the links between unionised artisans in different centres in the British Isles. Tramp relief rates were agreed between local branch and central executive, the figures varying with the union and the centre in question. In the late 1840s, for instance, the ironmoulders generally allowed eleven shillings and ninepence for mileage and supper and three shillings and twopence halfpenny for five-and-a-half nights' bed and beer, while the Cork coachmakers' branch in 1856 sought the raising of tramp relief to one shilling and threepence and a bed. The amalgamated structure could also operate as an official bush telegraph, whereby the deaths of artisans on tramp were communicated to headquarters and thence to the families of the deceased.[40] Most significantly, the tramping circuit was considerably widened, particularly for trades like those in the engineering sector, who could cross by steamer from Cork or Waterford to south Wales and thence do the rounds of the industrial centres of northern England and southern Scotland.[41] Some amalgamated unions, moreover, ensured the efficient working of the tramping system by publishing regular accounts of the exact state of trade and employment prospects in each centre in which a union branch existed, and by accurately documenting the whereabouts of tramping union members.[42] Indeed, such printed annual and monthly reports, combined with the personal contacts with individual artisans who passed through the city as part of the tramping network, helped to open up local unionism to outside influences. Whether these printed reports were widely perused by all the paid-up members of the local union branch or read only by the branch officers is impossible to ascertain, but they helped to draw the union committees, if not the general body of artisans in Cork, Dublin and Belfast as well as many smaller Irish towns like Waterford, Kilkenny, Sligo and Clonmel out of narrow localism into awareness of trade-union growth in the United Kingdom as a whole.

Amalgamation also strengthened a local trade's position *vis-à-vis* employers. The printed reports disseminated information on trade disputes in affiliated centres, pinpointing anti-union employers and identifying union members who had broken ranks by strike breaking or working under price. For instance, the stonemasons' amalgamation reports in 1837 named two Cork members who sub-contracted for work at half the recognised local rate; the Typographical Society's report in 1860 gave a detailed list of named blacklegs in the *Cork Daily Herald* office strike; the union returns of the United Kingdom Society of Coachmakers in 1868 gave a comprehensive report of the anti-union activities of Julian's coachmaking establishment in Cork; and from 1852 onwards until the early 1870s local members expelled for 'acting against the union' were regularly listed in the reports of the Amalgamated Society of Engineers.[43] But by far the greatest advantage of amalgamation was that, while a local society involved in a trade dispute had to rely mainly on its own limited resources, the amalgamated branch had the moral and financial support of a much wider federation. Artisans were fully aware of this advantage of amalgamation and therefore it was no coincidence that when a Cork tailoring strike in 1870 collapsed through lack of funds, the local society almost immediately afterwards fused with the Amalgamated Society of Tailors. Significantly in the next major local tailoring dispute of 1893, it was the backing of the amalgamated executive and branches which made possible a sustained if not unduly successful campaign.[44]

From the mid century onwards, pro-union commentators were greatly encouraged by this amalgamation trend between the artisans of the sister islands, and particularly by the increasing tendency of local trade societies to support striking unionists in British centres. In 1852 the Cork branch of the Amalgamated Society of Engineers organised a collection for the locked-out engineers in Lancashire and London, while towards the end of the century local society minute books make periodic reference to subscriptions raised for strikers in various centres in Britain.[45] One trade-union spokesman in 1866 painted this apparent progress towards brotherhood in glowing terms:

We have at length succeeded in accomplishing an amalgamation between the Irish and English workmen. In the past we have seen with regret that Irish workmen have not in all cases met with that cordial reception and treatment at the hands of their English co-workers, which every man is entitled to at the hands of his fellow-men, irrespective of country or creed. But now the Irish workers have joined us in large numbers and in good faith, we have every confidence that the advantage will be mutual, and that past differences, arising from whatever cause they may, will be buried in oblivion.[46]

This statement, to say the least, proved excessively optimistic. In spite of the advantages of amalgamation, Irish artisans remained essentially localist in outlook, particularly in the first half of the century when most Irish foundations by British amalgamated unions, though established in a flurry of enthusiasm, proved transient. Irish branches of the Manchester-based Friendly Society of Journeymen Cabinet Makers, Carvers and Woodturners (founded in 1833) lasted only three years, and although a reorganisation drive occurred in Dublin and the north-east in the late 1840s, the trade in Cork was not again organised on an amalgamated basis until the London-based Alliance Cabinet Makers Society established a branch there in 1880.[48] Similarly, the Cork printers remained affiliated to the National Typographical Association for only four years in the 1840s, the local branch of the boiler makers' union lasted only from 1847 to 1853, while the ironmoulders' branch survived somewhat longer, from 1839 to 1853.[48]

The later Cork ventures by British amalgamations had a higher survival rate. Despite fluctuations of fortune, the local branch of the coachmakers' union founded in the 1840s survived into the twentieth century, as did the Amalgamated Society of Engineers' branch established in 1851.[49] This capacity to survive was still more obvious in the case of amalgamated branches established in the later years of the century, yet even then an amalgamated branch's survival was not guaranteed. For example, the shipwrights' attempts at amalgamation were erratic. In 1864 they were apparently allied with the loose and largely ineffective federation known as the United Kingdom

Amalgamation of Shipwrights, but then seemingly reverted to a local basis of organisation. It was not until the mid-1890s that, deciding that 'in these days of mammoth firms with large capital the days of local societies have gone by', they joined the Glasgow-based Associated Shipwrights' Society.[50] Similarly, the local branch of the Amalgamated Society of Carpenters and Joiners collapsed in 1877 after half a decade's troubled existence, and even when it was re-established in the mid-1880s it had a hard struggle for survival until it became firmly established in the early 1890s. Even less happily, the rival General Union of Friendly Operative Carpenters and Joiners had two false starts – one in the late 1870s and another in the 1890s – on each occasion perishing quietly through lack of funds and local support.[51]

The vulnerability of amalgamated branches during the entire course of the nineteenth century can be explained in a number of ways. Firstly, in spite of the financial backing of the central executive, amalgamated branches could prove almost as vulnerable as local societies to periods of severe slump which decimated branch funds and precipitated organisational collapse. For many unions this was as true in the late nineteenth century as it had been in the earlier decades. Because of the dearth of trade-union records for the first half of the century, Andrew Boyd's premise that many trade unions collapsed during the famine years of the mid-1840s is difficult to substantiate in the Cork context, but it does seem a valid supposition when one considers just how transient many trade societies proved in the depressed periods of the later nineteenth century.[52] For example, during the 1880s and 1890s the numbers in the Cork Alliance Cabinet Makers' branch fluctuated sharply from year to year, the depressed state of the local cabinet-making trade weakening its finances, until in 1892 it was cut off from the union for non-payment of union dues. Though the Cork branch was re-admitted in 1894 with a greatly increased membership, it was again defunct by 1901. In the case of the Cork branch of the coachmakers' union, changing membership numbers similarly reflected the fluctuations of local trade fortunes: averaging a membership of one hundred in the 1870s, it was reduced to fifty-five in the depressed 1880s, rising again to ninety in the 1890s.[53] Moreover, amalgamated branches could, in some cases, be even more unstable than local societies: since some of them – particularly in the newly emerging engineering occupations – were established and manned by non-locals, their foundations were totally undermined by the departure of the members from the city. This happened in the case of the Cork branch of the Manchester-based boiler makers' union in the late 1840s. Set up by immigrant Scottish boiler makers, it collapsed when a large proportion of its members, mostly Glasgow men, left Cork after an unsuccessful strike in 1853.[54]

Financial troubles consequent upon trade depression were the occasion not only of local destabilisation, but also of considerable friction between branch and head office. The printers were unique in maintaining good relations with the headquarters of their union in England, but in most other cases, distance, money problems and mutual lack of understanding led to confrontation between local amalgamated branches and the British parent union.[55] Perhaps the most unfortunate experience was that of the Birmingham-based United Operative Stonemasons' Society in the late 1830s, which proved incapable of disciplining its Irish lodges. The latter distinguished themselves by a consistent reluctance to obey union rules and pay union dues until total financial chaos eventually convinced headquarters to cut off the Irish branches. The lack of any real empathy between the English and Irish branches was revealed when the Armagh branch, indignant at its ejection from the union, threatened in retaliation to send its members to England as strike breakers;

> Irish blood will not be trampled on; you have often taken the advantage is [sic] and treated us as though we were a parcel of blacks, but we will whiten some of your jobs for you with Irish Volunteers, for they are not all down yet.[56]

Little had changed by the 1880s when similar squabbles broke out between the British executive and the Cork branch of the Amalgamated Society of Tailors. The executive consistently and unsuccessfully harried the branches in Cork City and county because of the unsatisfactory nature of their financial reports and because they insisted on holding their meetings in a room whose rent the executive considered to be exorbitant. Bitterness increased when, in 1837, the Cork secretary spent the branch funds on drink and the union executive refused to send any further money to Cork until the funds had been reimbursed. Four years later the squabble still raged as the local branch was still defending the secretary and was blankly refusing to pay back the money to headquarters.[57]

While much finance-related friction concerned such incidental misspending of funds and non-payment of dues, the later amalgamated unions had a further in-built guarantee of trouble – i.e. the practice of 'equalisation'. This allowed a union executive, when the funds of individual branches rose above a certain level, to appropriate the surplus money and distribute it among other branches whose funds were low. While equalisation was obviously advantageous to weaker branches, it was considerably resented by the more prosperous, who tended to see it as high-handed action by a remote central authority which failed to take sufficient account of local circumstances, as when the Cork branch of the Amalgamated Society of Engineers, for instance, saw its funds cut by almost two hundred pounds in 1894 to meet the equalisation requirements of the union.[58]

Lack of understanding between Irish amalgamated branch and British executive was further exacerbated by the periodic conflicts which arose regarding local strike action. What local union members saw as vitally important issues were dismissed by the distant and uninvolved executive as petty and wasteful of union funds. In 1843 when the Cork branch of the Ironmoulders' Friendly Society struck against a wage cut, the executive roundly denounced the branch's failure to resort to less extreme measures, while in 1872 the Coachmakers' Society executive sharply criticised the Cork branch for striking for a reduction in working hours. In the Cork dock strike of 1891 the local branches of the seamen's and dockers' unions received particularly severe censure from their respective executives for their strike action and though the executives did stand by the men in the settlement talks, several of the offenders were penalised by receiving no strike pay.[59]

Basically, in matters of finance, principle and identity, there was little compatibility between the expectations of the local artisan and the aims of the amalgamated union's executive. It was no coincidence that trade union banners in Cork gave as much prominence to the symbolism of local identity as to the insignia of trade solidarity. Banners from the 1830s included pictures of prominent places of employment, later banners represented well-known local beauty spots and buildings, while right through the century the arms of the city figured on a great number of banners.[60] The sense of trade identity was, in fact, essentially local, and it was this desire for local autonomy which proved the greatest deterrent to the advance of amalgamation. As John Boyle pointed out in the context of Dublin and Belfast, the smoothest establishment of amalgamated branches occurred not only in those cases where local society members unanimously agreed to fusion with the British union, but also where a trade was previously unorganised and no local rival union existed to bar the way of the new amalgamated body.[61] In the Cork context, therefore, the most trouble-free amalgamations occurred among previously unorganised occupations – the ironmoulders (1847), plumbers (1868), bootrivetters (1885), seamen (1889) and dockers (1889) – and among the coachmakers (1840s), engineers (1851), tailors (1873) and coopers (1892), who agreed as bodies to join their respective amalgamated unions. On the other hand, when an amalgamated branch was set up in opposition to a local society, either by outsiders or by local journeymen who had quarrelled with their own society, trouble was guaranteed and the amalgamated branch doomed from the start. Such a situation occurred in 1894 when the eighty-strong local Plasterers' Society was rocked by an internal dispute concerning the raising of society fees and the alleged misspending of the funds. The dissenters withdrew from the society and, to the number of fifty-five, joined the Birmingham-based National Association of Operative Plasterers. The fortunes of the amalgamated branch in Cork, however, were not happy: its members were regarded with implacable hostility by the local society, which in 1897 pressurised a number of employers to dismiss them so that by 1899 the branch had collapsed.[62]

When contending local and amalgamated protagonists were evenly matched, such confrontations could drag on for years.

This was most common among the building trades, as was clear in the case of the Dublin Regular Society of Carpenters, who waged a long battle with the organisers of the Manchester-based Amalgamated Society of Carpenters and Joiners (ASCJ) for almost a quarter century.[63] A parallel dispute of equal duration occurred in Cork between the same amalgamated branch's organisers and the local Ancient Corporation of Carpenters. In 1871 a city branch of the ASCJ was established by a Welsh carpenter working in one of the local dockyards, but the two hundred-strong local society resisted all overtures to join the new body, and had veritably squeezed it out of existence by 1877. A further attempt to establish a Cork branch in the mid-1880s met with the same reception, for, pleading the depressed state of the building trade as justification, the local society and the trades council pressurised employers and workmen alike against any dealings with the amalgamated branch. On this occasion there was no mistaking the intense localism around which the squabble revolved. The Ancient Corporation of Carpenters, ignoring the fact that most of the amalgamated branch members were themselves natives of the city, denounced them as belonging to a 'society imported from England' whose funds, paid to an English executive, never helped projects of local or national benefit.[64] Six years later, this particular quarrel had been patched up, and the local body fused with the amalgamated society, but even then the internal troubles of the carpenters were not over. A splinter group of the old body still remained independent and later formed the local nucleus of another amalgamated union, the General Union of Friendly Operative Carpenters and Joiners. Though the majority of the local unionised carpenters had by now joined the ASCJ, this did nothing to increase their tolerance of rival bodies, for when the General Union again attempted to establish a local branch in the early 1890s, they persecuted it vigorously, the General Union's organiser describing the

> open hostile opposition of the Cork branch of the Amalgamated Society of Carpenters and Joiners, who tried in every way to prevent us from opening a lodge . . . by intimidating the men who are favourably inclined towards joining us – in fact,

by using every means both foul and fair – more of the former
than the latter . . .

The ASCJ branch used all the well-tried methods which had been
used against itself in former times – sending deputations to local
builders against the employment of General Union men,
picketing the meeting rooms of the new body, and finally,
withdrawing from the 1895 Trades Union Congress when the
General Union's local representative was allowed to attend. Even
the request by their own amalgamated union executive (which
had obviously mellowed in its attitude since the 1870s) that the
Cork branch establish friendly relations with the General Union
men was met with an adamant refusal so that, as in the case
of the plasterers, local opposition proved too strong and by late
1896 the Cork branch of the General Union had collapsed.[65]

If attempted unionisation of individual trades revealed the in-
herently localist outlook of the Cork artisans, so, too, did successive attempts from the 1850s onwards to establish a city trades
council. Periodically, it is true, outside influences were at work
and some transient links were forged with similar bodies in other
centres. For instance, the first short-lived trades council established in 1857 apparently had some connection with the tailors and
bakers of Queenstown, Bandon, Mallow and Fermoy, while an
equally ephemeral body established in 1864 was directly modelled
on a Dublin trades council set up some months previously.[66]
The establishment of this trades council of the mid-1860s was,
in fact, part of a general movement towards trades council formation in a number of different Irish towns. Just as the O'Connellite years had fostered a common political identity among the
trades of various centres, so the laying of the foundation stone
of the Dublin O'Connell Monument in 1864 provided an occasion for the trades of different centres to meet and discuss the
formation of local trades councils.[67] Similarly, some outside influences were evident in 1881 when the trades council established in that year saw itself as a larger variation of that set up some
months previously in the County Cork town of Kanturk, and
ambitiously planned to spread its influence over the entire province of Munster so that it would eventually become an all-Ireland

body. During the first year of its existence the council's outward push seemed likely to succeed as it co-operated with the trade societies of smaller centres to establish branches in eleven towns in County Cork and in two centres in the neighbouring county of Tipperary. But just as most of the earlier and less stable councils had proved inward-looking, that of the 1880s soon lost its impetus for recruitment outside the city. While contemporaries justifiably blamed the disturbances accompanying the land agitation for hindering the establishment of county branches, the real impediment in the way of such organisation was the continuing defensiveness of the city artisans in the face of erosion of their local conditions of work by closer contacts with what they rather ungraciously termed 'barbarian hordes of rustic mechanics'.[68]

These same fears also produced a disquieting ripple of anti-Semitism which spread through the ranks of the Cork trades council from the late 1880s onwards. An immigrant German Jew who opened a furniture factory became the butt of trade-union hostility, firstly because he employed non-union labour, and secondly because his production of cheap, glue-stuck furniture threatened to destabilise the market for the established local cabinet makers. The same objections were raised against immigrant Jews involved in the cheap clothing trade, with added accusations that Jewish areas were breeding grounds for disease. Although the trades council claimed (not wholly inaccurately) that its attacks were levelled against Jewish undercutting rather than against their race and religion, there was no doubt that such arguments were heavily laced with the crude sentiments of localism, racism and religious bigotry.[69]

If these fears of the enemy both within and without the city were so all-pervasive, it was hardly any surprise that the trade unionists of Cork showed considerable disinterest in wider labour contacts. They had never paid any recorded attention to the British Trades Union Congress since its formation in Manchester in 1868, and an attempt by Michael Austen, one of the few outward looking members of the local trades council, to send delegates to the congress at Liverpool in 1890 were pointedly ignored by the rest of the council. Though it must be admitted that, in view of the lack of attention given to Irish affairs by the

British TUC, and that Cork labour's disinterest was perhaps a sensible enough attitude, it proved almost equally indifferent to native efforts. In 1889 some more adventurous Dublin trade unionists pioneered the establishment of the Irish Federated Trades and Labour Union to supplement the work of the too remote British Trades Union Congress. The brainchild of T. J. O'Reilly, the Dublin Trade Council's secretary, this new body was modelled on the rank-and-file organisation of Parnell's parliamentary party. It ambitiously sought 'an affiliation of the trades throughout not only Ireland but the United Kingdom' to hasten the abolition of sweated and boy labour, to improve working conditions, and to promote increased technical education and the formation of more trades councils and women's trade unions. Cork sent six delegates to the first conference, but it was clear that the mainstream of Cork trade unionists regarded the new body's programme as peripheral to their real interests.[70]

When, on the initiative of the Dublin Trades Council, the Irish Trades Union Congress was eventually set up and met for the first time in Dublin in 1894, the Cork trades did participate and were represented at all subsequent congresses.[71] The number of Cork delegates in any particular year understandably depended on the location of the congress, the highest representation being at that held in Cork itself in 1895, when forty delegates attended the proceedings.[72] This high attendance, however, which was obviously due to the practical matter of ease of access, was expressed not in the rhetoric of labour solidarity but in the lofty terminology of traditional local pride. This preponderance of local pride over labour consciousness had already been evident when, invited to the first congress in Dublin in 1894, the Cork trades council president had airily volunteered the opinion that

> personally, he did not much care about interfering in the matter, but it would be a curious thing if they were not represented . . . They ought to send one or two gentlemen, at least, to represent the council, and to show that they were trade unionists at heart, as well as they were in the metropolis, or in any part of Ireland.[73]

The Cork delegates obviously survived this 1894 congress with their sense of localism unimpaired, for scarcely had the proceedings terminated and Cork been selected as the 1895 venue when the trades council began to prepare itself for the event, not because of any commitment to the wider cause of labour but because 'the honour of Cork was at stake'.[74]

Such attitudes hardly provided a sound foundation on which to build an infant trades congress, and once Cork's turn as host city had passed, both moral and financial support for the congress dribbled away. Whereas in 1895 sixteen local trades together contributed over ninety pounds, only two trades subscribed to the 1897 congress with a pathetic total contribution of ten shillings. Indeed, even in the heady enthusiasm of the Cork congress in 1895, trade society officers experienced great difficulty in collecting the required levy from branch members. Only when the local Typographical Society was threatened with exclusion from the congress was a concerted effort made to collect the levy and even then the members were willing to pay only half the required sum, the balance being taken from the society chest.[75]

However, the Cork artisans' lack of moral and monetary support for the infant Irish Trades Union Congress, like its previous disinterest in the British congress, was neither unreasonable nor unique. Support for the Federated Trades and Labour Union back in 1889 had been given grudgingly enough in other quarters, too, the Belfast trades council agreeing to co-operate only after some hesitation, and then helping to scuttle the venture by quarrelling with the Dublin trades council.[76] From a purely practical standpoint, moreover, the infant congress of the 1890s added to the existing financial demands pressing on unionised artisans. Frequently called upon for extra payments to meet a decline in funds, the death of a society member or the expenses of a political demonstration, they correctly saw the congress as but another expense weighing on the trade society and its members. Besides, in the intervals between its annual meetings the congress hardly impinged on the everyday business of the local trade society, still less on that of the individual artisan. The quarterly meetings of the Congress Parliamentary Committee, which operated as a pressure group between congresses, and on which the Cork trades had their own representative, were little more than talking shops at which trade grievances were discussed without any real solutions being attempted, much less arrived at.[77]

The same degree of disinterest characterised the organised Cork trades' attitude towards the issue of independent labour representation in parliamentary and local government. This was hardly surprising. Although the city's corporation had been opened to limited popular representation by the Irish Municipal Reform Act of 1840, it was still quite remote from the greater part of the city's working classes, and contact between it and the trade societies remained extremely infrequent over the greater part of the century. During the 1840s the corporation was mentioned in trade circles only in connection with its perceived failure to support contemporary manufacture revival, while for the greater part of the 1850s there was no communication whatever between the two bodies. Even during the following decade, moreover, when trades and city fathers clashed, the issues between them were based not upon any matters of political principle but on the corporation's hesitancy to consider the material interests of the city trades. In the mid-1860s the corporation had roused the ire of the trades in general, and the stonecutters in particular, by its plan to rebuild two city bridges using ironwork instead of the traditional stone. The controversy proved sufficiently serious to force concessions on both sides. In the case of St. Patrick's Bridge, the main bridge in the city, stonework was agreed upon and the stonecutters reciprocated by pledging against strikes or wage-rise demands for the duration of the contract. In the case of the second bridge, the North Gate Bridge, the corporation favoured the less expensive ironwork, and with this the stonecutters had to be content, though not without expressing their general dissatisfaction with the town council's action.[78] During the early 1860s sporadic contact was made between artisans and municipal authorities when some members of the corporation linked up with the organised trades in their campaign against night-work and Sunday-work in the baking trade. At this stage, however, as during the following two decades, trade contact was with individual town councillors rather than with the corporation as a body, the latter development being impossible until the trades had provided themselves with a permanent central organisation through which they could articulate their needs.

This centralisation was finally provided in the early 1880s with the establishment of the trades council or United Trades Association. Thereafter, the trades council became the main platform for the publicisation of trade grievances against employers, unskilled labour and – above all – the local municipal corporation. As in the past, however, the matters at issue between the trades and the city fathers remained at a very practical level, and there was very little consciousness on the part of the trades that their grievances might be articulated more forcibly through independent labour representation at the level of local government. Thus, when in 1891 the Dublin Trades Council invited other trades councils throughout the island to a meeting concerning labour representation in parliamentary and local government, the Cork trades council was patently uninterested. In fact, although three delegates were eventually sent from Cork, this was achieved only after Trojan efforts had been made to scrape together a sufficient attendance at the weekly trades council meeting to decide on the delegation.[79]

However, with the passing of the Local Government Act of 1898, which assimilated the local and parliamentary franchises and abolished property qualifications for candidates, direct labour representation in local government became a real possibility in Cork as elsewhere. The resulting sixfold increase in the local municipal electorate ensured that of the twenty labour candidates put forward in the municipal elections of January 1899, nine were elected from within the three predominantly working-class wards of the city.[80] But while the rhetoric of the labour campaigners during and after the election of 1899 suggested that traditional local and party-political allegiances were being put aside in favour of a new labour solidarity, little had really changed. Even a superficial scratching of the surface revealed that behind most labour orators there lurked an old-style localist, and that despite the undoubted widening of attitudes among unionised Cork artisans in the course of the century, the focus of their attention and their loyalties was still centred within the city bounds. Whatever increase had occurred locally in the number of amalgamated unions, whatever attempts were made to extend trades-council membership outside the city, or whatever vistas had been opened up by the concept of a trades-union congress and independent labour representation, widening horizons remained constricted by traditional defensive localism. It is in this context, therefore, that one must view the scathing comment made in 1891 by the immigrant English coachmaker, Charles Kelf, as he observed the Cork trades council's closed-shop attitude to unionised artisans outside the city:

> The [Cork trade] societies are mostly local and everything is looked at from a local standpoint . . . The Fermoy branch of the Democratic Labour Federation applied to be affiliated to the Cork Trades Council. The Council was agreeable to the affiliation but when I asked whether the members of the Cork societies would work by the side of the Fermoy men providing they obtained employment in Cork and worked for the trade union rate of wages, I was told certainly not. They could not think of allowing any but Cork men to work in Cork, except in very rare cases if they were short of men, and then they would have to join the local society and pay from two pounds to five pounds entrance fee. But I may say the Cork men will go to Fermoy and work whenever they get the chance, and only a short time ago three members of the Painters' Society went and blacklegged the Fermoy men on strike, and their action was defended in the Trades Council by the delegate of their society, who stated that their society had nothing to do with men of other towns and only looked after its own members. And I think that a fair specimen of the ethic of trade unionism in Cork.[81]

NOTES

1   *CE*, 16 Oct. 1893.
2   J. D. Clarkson, *Labour and Nationalism in Ireland*, pp. 40–42; Andrew Boyd, *The Rise of the Irish Trade Unions* (Tralee, 1972), p. 14; Seán Daly, *Cork: A City in Crisis*, pp. 281–310. The other eighteenth-century unions were the paperstainers, carpenters, masons, cabinet makers, shipwrights and stonecutters.
3   Dick Geary, *European Labour Protest*, p. 45.
4   *CE*, 25 Sept. 1891, 4, 17 May 1893; *Labour Gazette*, June 1894. Agricultural labourers from the Skibbereen and Kanturk areas poured into the city in the lean years of the early 1890s, strike-breaking and doing skilled men's work at lower rates of wages.

5 The bakers, coopers and printers were particularly vulnerable to this competition from country tradesmen. See Maura Cronin, 'Work and workers', pp. 726–7.

6 By the 1880s the Cork Coopers' Society allowed the coopers from Ballincollig (five miles west of the city bounds) to work in the city, but only under the strictest conditions. *Poor Enquiry*, HC 1836, (35) xxx, App. C to First Report, 27–8; *CE*, 9 July 1860, 14 Jan. 1885; *Proceedings of the Select Committee on Sunday Closing Acts, Ireland*, HC 1888, xix, Qs. 8490; Cork Coopers' Society Minute Books, 15 May 1889, 1 Mar., 21 June 1896.

7 Webb Trade Union Collection, section A, vol. iii, ff. 46–7 (London School of Economics); *CE*, 4, 18, 25 Sept., 2 Oct. 1891.

8 In the later years of the century the Amalgamated Society of Tailors preferred relieving unemployed members in their local area to spending money on tramp relief. E. J. Hobsbawm, *Labouring Men: Studies in the History of Labour*, Chapter 4, 'The Tramping Artisan', pp. 34–63. See also Maura Cronin, 'Work and workers', pp. 750–2 for a general discussion on tramp relief among Cork trade societies. For details of payouts to tramps and a fascinating account of the fraudulent use of the tramping system, see Belinda Loftus, *Marching Workers: An Exhibition of Trade Union Banners and Regalia* (Belfast, 1978), pp. 11–12.

9 The printers, plasterers and cabinet makers also continued to support the tramping system until the end of the century. *CE*, 7 Nov. 1879; Cork Coopers' Society Minute Books, 9 May 1895, 26 Feb., 10 Sept, 1896, 9 Aug. 1898; Cork Typographical Society Minute Books, 12 Sept. 1896; *National Association of Operative Plasterers, Annual Reports*, 1894–97; *Alliance Cabinet Makers, Annual Report*, 1882–86.

10 *CC*, 30 Nov. 1833. One journeyman baker who had covered 160 miles between five county Cork towns in 1833 was significantly brought up on combination charges.

11 *Half-yearly Report of the Friendly Society of Ironmoulders*, 1846–1850; *Quarterly Report of the United Kingdom Society of Coachmakers*, 1851–1860.

12 Seán Daly, *Cork: A City in Crisis*, pp. 281–310; *CMC*, 12, 13, 16 Mar. 1832; J. D. Clarkson, *Labour and Nationalism*, pp. 110, 112–13; William Kiddier, *The Old Trade Unions: From Unprinted Records of the Brushmakers* (London, 1930), pp. 63, 161-3. Of the thirty-one trades marching in the Cork Repeal procession of March 1832, twenty-seven were certainly locally based.

13 *CE*, 5, 9, 12 June 1843, 22 Sept. 1845; *CDH*, 2 Jan. 1862.

14 *CE*, 5, 9, 12 June 1843, 22 Sept. 1845; *CDH*, 2 Jan. 1862.

15 *CE*, 23, 25 Aug., 16 Sept. 1873, 4, 5, 16 Dec. 1876. The Co. Cork towns organised in 1873 were Bantry, Charleville, Clonakilty, Dunmanway, Fermoy, Kanturk, Kinsale, Macroom, Mallow, Midleton, Millstreet, Mitchelstown, Rosscarbery and Youghal.

16 John Boyle, *The Irish Labour Movement in the Nineteenth Century* (Washington, 1988), p. 98; *CE*, 1, 25, 26 Aug. 1873; 4, 5, 15 Dec. 1876; 9 Oct., 15 Nov. 1890, 29 May, 3 June 1895; *Bakers' Record and General Advertiser*, 19 Apr.,

19 July, 6, 16, 30 Aug., 13, 20 Sept. 1890, 7 June 1895; *Report on Trade Unions,* [C-8644] HC 1897, xcix, 275, 2-3. Along with the Cork City branch, others were established at Aghada, Carrigtwohill, Castlemartyr, Cloyne, Midleton, Whitegate and other unnamed towns. In 1894 another Irish amalgamation, the Operative Stonecutters of Ireland, was founded with 512 members country-wide. Numbers rose to 700 in the following year and fell slightly to 621 in 1896.

17 Henry Pelling, *A History of British Trade Unionism* (Harmondsworth, 1971), p. 43.

18 *United Operative Stonemasons' Fortnightly Report,* 26 June 1835, 22 July 1836, 3 Feb., 13 Mar., 28 Apr., 21 July 1837.

19 In 1812 a thirty-two member local coachmakers' society was either established or reorganised in the city, its rules being revised in 1823. A decade later the several local coachmakers' societies of England amalgamated to form the United Kingdom Society of Coachmakers and at some stage between then and the late 1840s the Cork coachmakers' society joined the amalgamation with forty-one members. Cork Coachmakers' Minute Book 1812, pp. 3-8; *Cork Branch Rules and Regulations 1823,* Panel 2A, Vehicle Building and Automotive Museum, Holyhead Rd, Coventry; *United Kingdom Society of Coachmakers, First Quarterly Report,* Panel 3, Vehicle Building and Automotive Museum; F. S. Winchester, *A Short History of the National Union of Vehicle Builders 1834-1959* (Manchester, 1959), pp. 1-2.

20 *CE,* 9 June 1845; *Half-yearly Report of the National Typographical Association,* Jan.-June 1845, Jan.-July 1846.

21 D. C. Cummings, *A Historical Survey of the Boiler Makers and Iron Shipbuilders' Society from August 1834 to August 1904* (Newcastle-on-Tyne 1904), p. 38; *Annual Report of the Amalgamated Society of Engineers,* 1851. By 1851 there were fifteen other Irish branches of the Amalgamated Society of Engineers, seven in Ulster, three each in Munster and Leinster and two in Connacht.

22 As early as 1852 a deputation from the Amalgamated Society of Engineers came to Cork to canvas the local branch's support for the striking engineers in England, and in 1864 and 1872 the United Kingdom Society of Coachmakers sent delegates to Cork to settle disputes and forward the Nine-Hours movement. In 1870 the London Operative Society of Tailors sent its secretary to Cork to settle a major tailors' dispute. *CE,* 31 Mar., 2 Apr. 1852, 7 July 1870; *Quarterly Report of the United Kingdom Society of Coachmakers,* Sept. 1864, p. 1; June 1872, p. 1.

23 Andrew Boyd, *The Rise of the Irish Trade Unions,* pp. 67-9; Henry Pelling, *A History of British Trade Unionism,* pp. 59-86. The Trade Union Act of 1871, which legalised trade unions fully and enabled them to safeguard their funds by registering under the Friendly Societies Act of 1855, was somewhat negated by the Criminal Law Amendment Act of the following year which prevented any form of picketing.

24 *Quarterly Report of the Amalgamated Society of Tailors,* Nov. 1873, pp. 1-7.

25 *Amalgamated Society of Carpenters and Joiners, Monthly Report,* 1866-93; *CE,* 12, 18 Apr. 1875, 22 Mar. 1877, 23 Sept. 1886; *CDH,* 11, 12 Apr. 1873; Andrew

Boyd, *The Rise of the Irish Trade Unions*, p. 49. The amalgamated union branches in 1880 were at Belfast, Ballymena, Lisburn, Londonderry, Portadown, Newry, Hollywood, Armagh (Ulster); Dublin, Carlow, Drogheda, Dundalk (Leinster); Waterford and Clonmel (Munster); and Sligo (Connacht). The Cork amalgamated branch in the 1870s never attracted more than ten members, while in the 1880s the average membership was twenty-one. *Annual Report of the General Union of Friendly Operative Carpenters and Joiners*, 1866–1900; *Monthly Report of the General Union of Friendly Operative Carpenters and Joiners*, May–Oct. 1895; *CE*, 16 Oct., 18 Nov. 1894; *Monthly Report of the National Association of Operative Plasterers*, Nov. 1894, p. 16, Sept. 1897, p. 17; *National Association of Operative Plasterers, Auditor's Report*, 1894–99.

26   See above, p. 23.

27   Seán Daly, *Cork: A City in Crisis*, pp. 5, 90, 314.

28   *CE*, 12 Dec. 1889, 18 Mar., 9 May 1890; *Reports on Trade Unions*, [C–8232] HC 1896, xciii, 277, 60; [C–8644] HC 1907, xcix, 277, 16–17, 132–3.

29   *Limerick Chronicle*, 25, 28 Jan. 1890; Emmet O'Connor, *A Labour History of Waterford* (Waterford, 1989), pp. 91–2.

30   For an account of the 'new unionism' in Britain, see Henry Pelling, *History of British Trade Unionism*, pp. 93–122.

31   *CE*, 22 Mar., 9 Dec. 1889; *Seafaring*, 30 Mar. 1889; *National Amalgamated Seamen's and Firemen's Union of Great Britain and Ireland Annual Report*, 1889, p. 11; *Amalgamated Society of Railway Servants of England, Ireland, Scotland and Wales, Report and Financial Statement*, 1889–92; *Amalgamated Society of Railway Servants, General Secretary's Report*, Feb. 1890.

32   H. A. Clegg, Alan Fox, and A. F. Thompson, *A History of British Trade Unions since 1889* (Oxford, 1964), p. 87.

33   Emmet O'Connor, *A Labour History of Ireland 1824–1960* (Dublin, 1992), pp. 68–9, 75–7; *CE*, 12 Dec. 1889, 31 Mar., 9, 14 Nov. 1890; *Seafaring*, 6 Apr. 1889, p. 13, 1 June 1889, p. 12, 7 June 1890, p. 13. Builders' labourers earned an average of fourteen shillings a week; railway porters and signalmen from sixteen to twenty-one shillings; goods porters and foremen sixteen shillings. Further up the scale, seamen earned between seventeen-and-sixpence and twenty-eight shillings a week, and dockers earned an average of twenty-three shillings – rates not much lower than those earned in many skilled trades.

34   *CE*, 6, 7 July 1870; CSORP 1870, 6/4005, 15232.

35   *CE*, 2 Aug. 1881.

36   *CE*, 9, 11, 12, 14, 16 Dec. 1889, 22, 23, 25 Apr. 1890.

37   *CE*, 27, 28 Jan., 1, 6, 12, 19 Nov. 1890; *Seafaring*, 8 Nov. 1890, p. 3.

38   Where figure 0 appears in the table, this indicates that a branch which had formerly existed was defunct by the given date. 'No details' indicates the existence of a branch, but no membership figures are available.

39   *United Operative Stonemasons' Financial Report*, 26 June 1835; 22 July 1836; 3 Feb., 13 Mar., 28 Apr., 21 July 1837; *Annual Report of the Amalgamated Society of Engineers*, 1877; *Yearly and Financial Report of the Amalgamated Society of Tailors*,

1889. *Amalgamated Society of Carpenters and Joiners, Monthly Report,* 1866-93; *CE,* 12, 18 Apr. 1875, 22 Mar. 1877, 23 Sept. 1886; *CDH* 11, 12 Apr. 1873; Andrew Boyd, *The Rise of the Irish Trade Unions,* p. 49. The Amalgamated Society of Carpenters and Joiners had Irish branches in 1880 at Belfast, Ballymena, Lisburn, Londonderry, Portadown, Newry, Hollywood, Armagh (Ulster); Dublin, Carlow, Drogheda, Dundalk (Leinster); Waterford and Clonmel (Munster); and Sligo (Connacht). The branches of the Amalgamated Society of Tailors in 1889 were in the Ulster centres of Armagh, Ballymena, Belfast, Cavan, Coleraine, Cootehill, Dungannon, Enniskillen, Keady, Lisburn, Londonderry, Lurgan, Newry, Omagh, Portadown and Strabane; the Leinster centres of Ardee, Drogheda, Dublin, Dundalk, Kells, Kilkenny, Kingstown and Parsonstown; the Munster centres of Clonmel, Cork, Limerick, Midleton, Queenstown, Skibbereen, Tralee, Waterford and Youghal; and the Connacht centres of Galway and Sligo.

40 In December 1844 the ironmoulders' report recorded the death in Cork of A. Blamer of Liverpool on 31 July previously. *Half-yearly Report of the Ironmoulders' Friendly Society,* 1844, p. 28; 1848, p. 31; *Quarterly Report of the United Kingdom Society of Coachmakers,* Mar. 1856, Suppl., p. 2.

41 Whenever the Boot and Shoe Rivetters' and Finishers' Union reported favourably on the state of trade in Cork, there was an inrush of hands from other centres, leading to a glut of workers on the local market. *Monthly Reports of the National Union of Boot and Shoe Rivetters and Finishers,* Aug. 1888, p. 5; July 1890, p. 7; May 1898, p. 5. See also: *Annual Report of the Societies in the House Furnishing Trade,* 1834-38, *Quarterly Report of the United Kingdom Society of Coachmakers,* 1848-1900; *Annual Report of the Amalgamated Society of Engineers,* 1851-1900. For a brief account of the detrimental effects of the tramping system on local trade fortunes, see Maura Cronin, 'Work and workers', pp. 750-2.

42 *Monthly Report of the National Union of Boot and Shoe Rivetters and Finishers,* 1885-1900. *National Association of Operative Plasterers,* 1894-97.

43 *United Operative Stonemasons' Society, Fortnightly Returns,* 28 Apr. 1837; *Typographical Society Monthly Circular,* Feb. 1860, p. 2; *Quarterly Report of the United Kingdom Society of Coachmakers,* Dec. 1868, p. 2; *Annual Report of the Amalgamated Society of Engineers,* 1852-72.

44 *CE,* 15 May, 10, 12 June 1893; *Yearly and Financial Report of the Amalgamated Society of Tailors,* 1893, 1894; Cork Coopers' Society Minute Books, 30 Oct. 1873; Seán Daly, *Cork: A City in Crisis,* p. 146. A large portion of the £446 spent on the strike of 1893 was given by the executive of the union, and in the settlement negotiations the local strikers were strongly backed by the delegate of the amalgamated union.

45 Henry Pelling, *A History of British Trade Unionism,* p. 51; Cork Plumbers' Society Minute Books, 1 Sept. 1890; Cork Typographical Society Minute Books, 18 Nov. 1893, 3 Apr. 1897, 14 May 1898.

46 *Amalgamated Society of Carpenters and Joiners, Monthly Report,* July 1866.

47 *Annual Report of the Societies in the House Furnishing Department,* 1834-39. *Yearly Account of the Income and Expenditure of the Journeymen Cabinet Makers', Carvers'*

   and Woodturners' Friendly Society, 1844–88. *Alliance Cabinet Makers' Association, Annual Reports*, 1878–1901.

48 *Half-yearly Report of the National Typographical Association*, Jan.–June 1845, Jan.–
   July 1846; *Typographical Protection Circular*, 1849, p. 4, 1850, p. 60; D. C. Cum-
   mings, *Historical Survey of the Boilermakers*, p. 38; *Annual Report of the United
   Society of Boiler Makers and Iron Shipbuilders*, 1877–1900; *Half-yearly Report of the
   Friendly Society of Iron Founders of England, Ireland and Wales*, 1839–48, 1884–1900.

49 *Quarterly Report of the United Kingdom Society of Coachmakers*, 1851–1900; *Annual
   Report of the Amalgamated Society of Engineers*, 1851–1900.

50 *CE*, 11 Oct. 1864, 26 Feb. 1890; *Financial Report of the Associated Shipwrights'
   Society*, 1893, pp. xi, 126; Reports on Trade Unions [C–9013] HC 1898,
   ciii, 127, 32–3; Seán Daly, *Cork: A City in Crisis*, p. 308; David Dougan,
   The History of the Ship Constructors' and Shipwrights' Association 1882–1963
   (Newcastle-on-Tyne 1975), pp. 14–18.

51 *Amalgamated Society of Carpenters and Joiners, Monthly Report*, 1866–93; *Annual
   Report of the General Union of Friendly Operative Carpenters and Joiners*, 1866–1900;
   Monthly Report of the General Union of Friendly Operative Carpenters and Joiners, 1895.

52 Andrew Boyd, *The Rise of the Irish Trade Unions*, p. 43.

53 *Alliance Cabinet Makers' Association, Annual Reports*, 1878–1901; *Quarterly Report
   of the United Kingdom Society of Coachmakers*, 1880–1900.

54 D. C. Cummings, *A Historical Survey of the Boiler Makers*, p. 38.

55 Even when the Cork printers broke their affiliation with the Typographical
   Association in 1849, they still sent periodic trade reports to the Association, supported striking printers in other centres, and had an arrangement for the mutual relief of tramps.

56 *United Operative Stonemasons' Fortnightly Report*, 26 June 1835, 22 July 1836,
   3 Feb., 13 Mar., 28 Apr., 21 July 1837, 28 Aug. 1839, 2, 16 Jan., 12 Mar.
   1840; R. W. Postgate, *The Builders' History* (London, 1923), p. 125.

57 *Quarterly Report of the Amalgamated Society of Tailors*, July 1874, Apr. 1875, Feb.,
   Apr. 1887, Feb. 1891.

58 *Annual Report of the Amalgamated Society of Engineers*, 1893–95.

59 *Half-yearly Report of the Ironmoulders Friendly Society of England, Ireland and Wales*,
   June 1843, p. v; *Quarterly Report of the United Kingdom Society of Coachmakers*,
   June 1872, p. 1; *Seafaring*, 8 Nov. 1890, p. 3, 4 July, 22 Aug. 1891, p. 12.
   On the seamens' and dockers' strike issue, which was complicated by
   political issues, see also p. 114, 188.

60 *CMC*, 21 Mar. 1832; *CE*, 22 May 1843, 9 June 1845, 10 Oct. 1864, 22
   Aug. 1871, 22 Nov. 1875, 7 Oct. 1880, 11 Apr. 1881; *CDH*, 11 Oct. 1890.
   In 1890 the Queenstown and Passage shipwrights marched in public procession under a banner 'on one side of which [was] depicted a liner steam-
   ing out of Cork Harbour, and on the reverse a sailing vessel and views
   of Passage and Queenstown'.

61 John Boyle, *The Irish Labour Movement in the Nineteenth Century*, (Washington,
   1988), p. 39.

62 *CE*, 16 Oct., 19 Nov. 1894; *Monthly Report of the National Association of Operative*

Plasterers, Nov. 1894, p. 16, Sept. 1897, p. 17; *National Association of Operative Plasterers, Auditors' Report,* 1894–99.

63 John W. Boyle, *The Irish Labour Movement,* p. 95; Emmet O'Connor, *A Labour History of Ireland,* p. 45; Brendan McDonnell, 'Dublin labour movement', pp. 45–51.

64 *Amalgamated Society of Carpenters and Joiners, Monthly Report,* 1866–93; *CE,* 12, 18 Apr. 1875, 22 Mar. 1877, 23 Sept. 1886. The Cork amalgamated branch in the 1870s never attracted more than ten members, while in the 1880s the average membership was twenty-one.

65 *CE,* 5 Apr., 4 June 1895; *Monthly Report of the General Union of Friendly Operative Carpenters and Joiners,* May 1895, p. 17, June 1895, p. 10, Oct. 1895, p. 19; *Report of the Second Irish Trade Congress, held at Cork, 1895,* pp. 17–20.

66 *CE,* 29 July 1857, 28 Nov. 1864. On the Dublin United Trades Association, see John Boyle, *The Irish Labour Movement,* pp. 54–61.

67 Emmet O'Connor, *A Labour History of Waterford,* p. 78; Arthur Mitchell, *Labour in Irish Politics 1890–1930* (Dublin, 1974), p. 14. The move towards forming a trades council in the 1860s was also influenced by a local event – the unveiling of the Fr. Mathew Memorial in 1864, at which eighteen of the city's trade societies had attended, this short-term co-operation spurring them to consider a more permanent organisation. *CE,* 14 Sept., 28 Nov. 1864.

68 *CE,* 1 Jan., 21 Feb., 10 Mar., 11 July, 2, 3, 10 Sept., 17, 18 Oct. 1881. The County Cork branches were in Bantry, Clonakilty, Fermoy, Kanturk, Mallow, Millstreet, Mitchelstown, Passage, Queenstown, Skibbereen and Youghal. The County Tipperary branches were in Clonmel and Tipperary town. These country branches paid affiliation fees to the city body, though some apparently resented this. Although it seems that several of the county branches continued to function even after the city branch turned in upon itself in the early 1880s, their history is shrouded in obscurity.

69 *CE,* 3, 10, 12, 15, 16 Mar. 1888, 14 Oct. 1893, 22 Aug. 1894, 1 May, 25 Oct. 1895.

70 *CE,* 9 Aug. 1890; Arthur Mitchell, *Labour in Irish Politics,* pp. 16–18; Brendan McDonnell, 'The Dublin labour movement', p. xix.

71 For an analysis of the Irish Trades Union Congress in its early years, see John Boyle, *The Irish Labour Movement,* pp. 144–153; Emmet O'Connor, *A Labour History of Ireland,* pp. 57–61.

72 *Report of the Irish Trades Congress,* 1894–98 (National Library of Ireland, microfilm); Cork Typographical Society Minute Books, 7 Apr. 1894; Cork Coopers' Society Minute Books, 31 May 1895. As both the trades council and the individual trade societies paid the fares and expenses of their respective delegates, they were more likely to send delegates to congresses held in Munster than to those held in Dublin or Belfast. Thus, the Cork delegation at successive congresses numbered five in Dublin in 1894, forty in Cork in 1895, eleven in Limerick in 1896, nine in Waterford in 1897 and four in Belfast in 1898.

73 *CE*, 6 Apr., 1894.

74 *CE*, 9 Apr., 22 June 1894.

75 Cork Typographical Society Minute Books, 10 Nov. 1894, 16 Mar., 6 Apr. 1895. It is difficult to estimate the true level of contributions for although those of locally based societies are separately listed, amalgamated branches' subscriptions are hidden by being included in the total subscription figure of the relevant union.

76 John W. Boyle, *The Irish Labour Movement*, pp. 132–35.

77 *Report of the Second Irish Trades Congress*, 1895, p. 33. John Henry Jolley, member of the Typographical Association and president of the trades council, was elected to the Parliamentary Committee in 1895.

78 *CE*, 21 Apr., 2 June 1858, 22, 26 Sept., 2 Oct. 1862; *CC*, 23 Sept. 1862.

79 John W. Boyle, *The Irish Labour Movement*, pp. 138–40; *CE*, 14, 17 July, 25 Sept. 1891. Two parliamentary candidates put forward by the Dublin-directed movement of 1891 were successful, Eugene Crean being elected for Queen's County and Michael Austen for West Limerick. Ironically, while both men were members of the Cork trades council (with whom they were *personae non gratae* because of their anti-Parnellite stand), no labour candidate was started for Cork itself. It must also be stressed that neither Crean nor Austen were purely labour candidates, but primarily nationalists and anti-Parnellites with a genuine though secondary commitment to labour.

80 As a result of the 1898 act, the Cork municipal electorate rose from under two thousand to thirteen thousand, of whom three thousand were women. The Dublin municipal electoral increase was from eight to thirty-eight thousand. In Cork, the predominantly working-class wards were the North-central Ward (returning one labour representative), and the North-west and West Wards, which returned four labour representatives each. Emmet Larkin, *A Labour History of Ireland*, p. 61; *Dod's Parliamentary Companion*, 1898; *CE*, 1, 5, 12 Dec. 1898; *CC*, 18 Jan. 1899.

81 Webb Trade Union Collection, sect. A, vol. iii, ff. 46–7 (London School of Economics).

3

PASSIVITY TOWARDS POLITICAL PARTICIPATION

If unionisation was seen by artisans as providing the first rampart against economic decline and the first avenue towards widening horizons, so involvement in nationalist politics was envisaged as performing a similar function. By the eve of the twentieth century, the average Cork artisan was undoubtedly a political animal who attended public meetings, participated in political demonstrations, sometimes voted, and almost always identified with one or other political grouping in the city.

Where the roots of this politicisation are ultimately to be found is difficult to decide. The long-held view that popular politicisation began with O'Connell's mass movement for Catholic Emancipation in the 1820s is being effectively challenged by recent research which traces popular political participation to the disturbed years of the later eighteenth century and to the growing sectarianisation of Irish life in the two decades after the Act of Union.[1] That the populace in Cork City and county shared in this process of politicisation can hardly be doubted, for although the overall development of local popular awareness in this period still awaits its historian, signs of growth are clearly visible from the late eighteenth century onwards. Agrarian disturbance in the county in the 1760s and, more particularly, in the 1780s, periodically intersected with politics, preparing the way for more overt political agitation and recruitment in the excited atmosphere of the 1790s. Revolutionary organisers in that decade seemingly had high hopes of recruiting the county's peasantry through the medium of an Irish language newspaper and claimed a total membership of between sixty and seventy thousand United Irishmen in the county as a whole. Though such views may have grossly exaggerated reality, they do, along with (often inaccurate) contemporary newspaper reports of rural disaffection, suggest the speed with which politically related issues were penetrating the countryside.[2] Politicisation at popular level was also advancing in Cork City, though we can, as yet, only guess to what extent. By 1796 Thomas Paine's writings were reputedly 'in everyone's hands and in everyone's mouth' while United Irish recruitment was actively pursued in the course of the 1790s, with contemporaries claiming that by 1798 a four thousand-strong organisation had been established in the city with another twelve to thirteen thousand sympathisers. Though this movement collapsed following arrests and general repression in 1798, informers described how remnants of it still survived underground in 1805.[3]

At a less seditious and more overt level, there were many indications, particularly in the city, that politicisation was accelerating not only among the merchants and larger manufacturers, but also within that wide and amorphous grouping known to contemporaries as 'the populace'. The debate over the Act of Union, for instance, had mobilised considerable political activity within Cork merchant circles, petitions both for and against the measure including a large number of names prominent in the business life of the city. In the years following the Union, local personality clashes and mercantile–landed rivalry all furthered this already well-developed merchant politicisation. It is significant that one of the more radical newspapers of the city in this period was entitled the *Cork Mercantile Chronicle* and that electoral politics were run, apart from the recurring Catholic question, on the issue of local business prosperity. The days of the merchant-politician had arrived, and as one election squib of the 1820s in favour of the candidate, Gerard Callaghan, expressed it –

> Then come forward my boys, and give Gerard your voice,
> 'Tis the mercantile man who must be your choice,

Delay not support for the son of the man
Who has laboured and prospered among you.[4]

While such mercantile interests crossed the political and religious divide, the re-emergence of the Catholic Emancipation issue and the related question of a royal veto on Irish Catholic episcopal appointments ensured the progressive sectarianisation not only of mercantile politics, but also of politics within a much wider sector of the population. Bartlett has noted how Catholic merchants, in particular, increasingly harnessed the support of those beneath them on the social scale. This was particularly evident in the Cork context where, reflecting the pre-reform electoral system throughout the island, there existed within the socially varied electorate a considerable number of artisans and labourers who, as freeman and forty-shilling freeholder voters, provided both a malleable voting force and a link between the mercantile interest and the voteless but increasingly politicised population.[5] The political harnessing of both voters and voteless continued through the second and third decades of the century with the periodic appearance of merchant-dominated political clubs designed to mobilise a Catholic voting force.[6] Such mobilisation of popular opinion suggests both pre-existing politicisation and the readiness of 'the people' to become further involved. For instance, during the veto controversy, which threatened to divide the Catholic side in politics, a meeting of the local pro-veto Catholic Board was disrupted by 'the tumult of the lowest populace' who turned the affair into a demonstration in favour of Daniel O'Connell's anti-veto stance.[7]

Elections, of course, provided the main occasion for demonstrations of popular political interest. It mattered little whether a city or county election was in question, for the polling for both was carried out in the city, thus involving not only the relevant electorate but also the urban populace. While the successive elections of the period between 1807 and 1830 would never produce the level of excitement generated by those of 1832 onwards, most manifested a progressively increasing popular involvement. From 1812 onwards – when the county election produced such uproar that an election song described Cork City as

> . . . one huge troubled ocean,
> Where in truth there's no hearing one's ears from the
> noise[8]

– elections became affairs in which sectarian issues, personality clashes and popular love of excitement combined to produce scenes of tumult. Thus, by the 1820s popular politicisation in Cork was well under way, to be further accelerated not only by rural disturbances but also by the organisation in both county and city of highly efficient machinery to collect the Catholic Rent.[9] Well might O'Connell warn his middle-class Cork supporters in October 1830 that unless they actively took the lead in politics, the populace would march on and leave them behind.[10]

To what extent was the Cork artisanate touched by this progressive politicisation? Recent research suggests a considerable level of political activity among the artisans in late eighteenth-century Dublin, but this era is as yet relativey unploughed in the Cork context.[11] There are hints that artisans were directly involved in both the local revolutionary movement of the late 1790s and the remnants of that movement that struggled on underground into the early years of the nineteenth century, while a not insubstantial portion of the pre-1832 city electorate was composed of artisans.[12] During the 1820s, moreover, there was some evidence of craftsman participation in the rival popular organisations forming at either side of the political-sectarian divide, individual Protestant artisans certainly belonging to local Orange Lodges while their Catholic counterparts joined the Catholic Association and acted as collectors of the Catholic Rent.[13] However, there is no evidence to date which might link the trade societies with pre-1830s political activity. The artisan voters were frequently masters rather than journeymen, their position as freemen and members of the coopers' guild entitling them to vote, while the underground activists of the late eighteenth-century revolutionary movement possibly operated as individuals rather than as members of a trade. Moreover, even in the heightening tensions of the late 1820s, the city's trade and mortality societies – the only bodies which could be considered exclusively working class in composition – do not appear to have become involved in the rival campaigns concerning Emancipation. Indeed, the only recorded reference to anything approaching collective political activity on the part of a trade was the participation of the journeymen coopers of the city in a demonstration to honour George IV in 1821, on which occasion their behaviour was sufficiently 'decent, orderly and well-conducted' to persuade the master coopers to supply them with 'a very liberal quantity of porter'.[14] For the present, the artisan and labourer were resigned, if not content, to operate politically under the umbrella of their social betters, and distinctive political activity by journeymen had to await the 1830s.

That this was so is hardly surprising. It was at this period that the so-called 'age of reform' dawned in Britain, characterised by a tendency to effect gradual social change through cautious parliamentary legislation, not only with due sensitivity to the needs of the establishment but also in response to popular 'pressure from without'.[15] Within the Irish context it was the period when O'Connell's mass political campaigns succeeded in directly drawing into the political arena the masses of both country and town, whose politicisation had been proceeding over the previous decades. Finally, (and partly as a result of the O'Connellite campaigns) vital changes occurred in the immediate local context of Cork politics. The traditional 'politics of ascendency' which had involved a power struggle between urban mercantile Protestantism and landed aristocratic Protestantism, giving way in the 1820s to a new pattern of political conflict shaped along sectarian lines, now passed through a further stage: sectarian issues were henceforth to overlap with the political issues surrounding the Repeal of the Act of Union of 1800, and into the ensuing conflict were injected the political energies of the working classes on both sides of the sectarian political divide.[16]

The launching in autumn 1830 of O'Connell's Repeal campaign was the prelude to this new scenario in which working-class and particularly artisan political activism became an essential feature. While Protestant working men eventually rallied to the anti-Repeal cause under the banner of the local Protestant Operative Association, organised labour became inextricably bound up with the Repeal Movement. It was, in fact, the trade

societies that first responded to O'Connell's call and initiated
the campaign in Cork, beginning with a public dinner supported
largely by the trades and the smaller manufacturers, and
culminating in a series of pro-Repeal meetings whimsically
described by the contemporary press as 'a fit of the ague, sweeping
through all the trades and professions, down to the very
sweeps'.[17] Even when in late 1831 O'Connell temporarily
shelved Repeal in favour of the more attainable objective of parliamentary reform, the trades of the city refused to abandon the
cause, and continued to press O'Connell for a revival of the campaign through the medium of letters and meetings, culminating
in March 1832 in a grand procession which even hostile observers
admitted was

> a most astonishing and very grand spectacle. The trades passed
> with costly emblems of their respective employments, in regular
> and most systematic order. From the regularity in which they
> moved, the numbers could be easily taken . . . The crowds of
> spectators, taking trades and all, must have been from twenty
> to thirty thousand. The utmost decorum and regularity was
> observed throughout – not a row or disturbance during the day
> or night.[18]

Such disciplined and self-conscious participation in a political
demonstration was to become the model for the future manifestation of trade political expression during the remainder of the
century. The active presence of trade societies in political life
became even more obvious in the summer of 1832 when, following the example of Waterford, a manufacture revival movement
was launched in Cork City centred on the Cork Irish Manufacture Association. Ironically, this campaign was originally unconnected with the trade societies and was intended to be non-
political, deriving from the conviction of some lower-middle-class
individuals involved in relieving victims of the current cholera
epidemic that the long-term allieviation of poverty required the
promotion of employment.[19] However, it soon attracted the attention of the organised trades who, while seen by the revival
promoters merely as auxiliaries, actually found in the revival
movement a launching pad for a more distinct artisan role in
public life.

It was not, of course, the artisans alone who were propelled into politics during the manufacture revival campaign. They were just one among several hitherto politically submerged socio-economic groups which now seized their chance to challenge the local merchant élite at a time when traditional structures were being rendered fluid by franchise Reform and O'Connellite politics. In contemporary Britain the Parliamentary Reform campaign of the early 1830s drew into the popular political arena a diverse group of publicans, shopkeepers and small employers.[20] Now in the Cork context, this scramble for a political role led to the establishment of a number of new political organisations drawing their membership from social groups as diverse as retailers, minor manufacturers, journeymen and labourers, for whom they provided an alternative forum for the expression of economic and political opinions.

The first such group to emerge in mid-1832 was the Cork Trades Association for the Encouragement of Irish Manufactures. This Trades Association, open to subscribers of one penny per week, was deliberately tailored as a respectable working-man's counterpart of the Irish Manufacture Association. Indeed, the prohibition of subscriptions of more than a shilling per week reflected its desire to remain distinct from the middle-class leadership of the revival movement which, in fact, it soon supplanted to become the chief local pressure group for manufacture revival.[21] More importantly, along with the *Cork Mercantile Chronicle*, it also became the centre of the local campaign for radical political reforms, pushing in the 1832 election for Repeal of the Union, abolition of tithes, triennial parliaments, the ballot, enfranchisement of the five-pound householders, popular election of grand juries and municipal officers, abolition of slavery, and abolition of stamp duties.[22] A second such radical popular forum appeared in 1837 when the Trades Association established as an offshoot the People's Hall which by 'bringing the honest elector and the unrepresented thousands together' sought to accelerate 'the extension of civil right' to the working classes.[23] In the case of each of these popular associations the artisan connection was vital, the Trades' Association's rules being drawn up in 1832 by a committee representing the trades' and labourers'

clubs in the city while the People's Hall later provided accommodation for trade union meetings and was partly funded by
a number of trade societies.[24] By 1841 when another Irish
manufacture movement was launched with the establishment of
an employer-dominated local Board of Trade, this trend towards
the formation of independent artisan pressure groups had gone
a stage further. The by now inevitable alternative organisation
appeared in the shape of the Mallow Lane Board of Trade, located
in one of the main working-class areas on the city's north side.
Differing significantly from its predecessors in the 1830s in that
it was an exclusively artisan body drawing its membership from
among the city's trade societies, it set about investigating the
state of the various city trades. Most significantly, it attempted
to establish among the trade societies the principle of mutual
patronage, instituting a public pledge in support of Irish manufacture, establishing a short-lived market for the display and sale
of locally produced goods, and constantly pressurising the local
middle and upper classes to support the cause of the artisan.[25]

If the original *raison d'être* of all these bodies was the revival
of local manufacture, they were soon carried along on the wave
of popular political enthusiasm to become (at least in their own
estimation) the main local pressure groups for the political
measure of Repeal of the Union. This role of Repeal watchdog
was particularly evident in the election of 1832 when the Cork
Trades Association acted as mobiliser of the popular side, drawing up a Repeal election pledge to be taken by candidates, electorate and non-electors alike. Moreover, it took it upon itself to
vet the popular candidates in defiance not only of the local liberal
élite but also of O'Connell himself. Members insisted on debating
one candidate's suitability even after he had been approved by
O'Connell, and deliberately humiliated the second candidate and
his backers in the Chamber of Commerce when he sought the
Trades Association's approval for his candidature. Moreover, the
reality of the association's power was evident when, against considerable odds, it secured a Repeal pledge from the two candidates.[26] Between elections the association continued in its
self-appointed role as 'guardian of the rights of the great majority of the electors'. Acting as vigilante over the behaviour of the

city and county representatives in parliament, it checked on their voting records, pressurised them to forward the Repeal cause in the House of Commons and on at least three occasions called them to task for what it considered neglect of their duties.[27]

However, one must not exaggerate either the contemporary effectiveness of these 'alternative' pressure groups nor their role as mouthpieces of a distinctive artisan political consciousness. Firstly, their power was limited: control of local politics ultimately lay with the liberal merchant élite in the Cork Chamber of Commerce; candidates, once elected, proved less amenable to popular pressure than they had been at the hustings; and manipulation of an electorate only recently integrated into a proto-democratic system proved difficult in the extreme, as evidenced by the defeat of the popular candidates in the city election of 1835.[28] Secondly, with the exception of the Mallow Lane Board of Trade of 1841, these popular associations were not exclusively artisan in composition, but were dominated by a lower-middle-class element comprising retailers and pawnbrokers who were less interested in forwarding artisan interests than in displacing the merchant political élite.[29] Yet, despite the limitations of these popular pressure groups of the O'Connellite period, their role in working-class (and particularly artisan) politicisation must not be dismissed lightly for they provided a publicly acceptable forum of expression for groups and individuals whose opinions had hitherto been largely hidden from the public. Even when hijacked by politically ambitious lower-middle-class cliques, the popular associations still provided this vital forum, so that instead of the traditional token artisan who had been condescendingly allowed to speak on the early manufacture revival platforms, trade and labour societies were facilitated in becoming collectively active in public life, petitioning parliament, canvassing voters, and participating in political processions. By the mid-1840s it was clear that there had been considerable advances in the politicisation of both the Protestant and Catholic lower classes at local level. Among the Protestant workers a clear sense of political consciousness had been shaped by the Orange Order and the Protestant Operative Association, while on the Catholic side the Irish manufacture movement (originally intended as non-political) and the Repeal issue in particular had drawn the artisan into public life to a degree inconceivable two decades previously.[30] This newly articulated political consciousness of both Protestant and popular sides was composed of several strands, the former based on 'the maintenance of religion, loyalty and good order' and the latter on a combination of local loyalties, naïve hopes of economic regeneration under Repeal, and a romantic and ill-defined pride in being Irish.

In 1845, the first signs of potato failure and rising food prices heralded a period of intense distress for Cork's lower classes, and in the same year O'Connell and Young Ireland quarrelled over the Queen's Colleges' Bill and the theoretical question of the justification of force in politics.[31] By July 1846 the two sides finally parted company, the followers of Young Ireland in January 1847 founding a new body, the Irish Confederation, a branch of which was established in Cork City in the following September under the title of the Desmond Club. In this quarrel between Old and Young Ireland, the Cork trade societies, like their counterparts in Dublin, were almost totally identified with O'Connell and Old Ireland. At least, the Cork Trades Association (never, admittedly, an exclusive trades preserve) made the ultimately symbolic gesture on its withdrawal from the confederate-orientated People's Hall, of bringing with it the statue of O'Connell which had graced the building since its inception.[32] Not surprisingly, the local Desmond Club was almost exclusively non-artisan in composition, and had little contact with or understanding of organised skilled labour. Though a few token journeymen were eventually added to the club's committee, there was a distinct sense in which they were regarded by the mainstream membership as interesting but somewhat peculiar specimens of working-class life, and their occasional speeches at meetings were not apparently deemed worthy of publication in the local press. The wide gulf between the trades and the confederates was revealed most clearly by the latters' attitude to unionisation: the Desmond Club's leadership, drawn largely from the ranks of the retailers and young professionals, was openly opposed to trade unionism, urging the journeymen tailors in 1847 to submit to an impending wage cut and thus 'win the confidence of [their] employers by their reasonable behaviour.[33]

Between mid-1847 and early 1848, however, three further events occurred which accelerated both the general trend towards nationalist extremism and the increasing politicisation of the trade societies. The first event was the death of O'Connell in May 1847, which left a certain vacuum in leadership and which also cut some of the emotional ties with Old Ireland. The second was the 'bloodless' February Revolution of 1848 in France, which replaced the monarchy with a republic and prompted among the politically aware classes in Ireland a popular enthusiasm for militant republicanism. The third (which actually preceded the second by three weeks) was the secession from the Irish Confederation of John Mitchel and others who argued (though sometimes not very clearly) for a more militant approach to social and political issues.[34] Popular politics in Cork, as elsewhere in the country, were dramatically affected by these developments.[35] From February 1848, in particular, the Desmond Club began to court working-class support, and when it reorganised itself as the Citizens' Club in April 1848, there was a frantic drive to recruit the support of the hitherto O'Connellite artisans. As a token of reconciliation, the statue of O'Connell was restored to its old position in the People's Hall, and while the spokesmen of the newly named club were the same individuals who had dominated its predecessor, the artisans were given a real voice, twelve of the thirty-one committee places being reserved for representatives of the trade societies.[36]

Clubs organised on the model of the Citizens' Club proliferated from May 1848 onwards, encouraged by the visit of Thomas Francis Meagher to the city, and by John Mitchel's arrest and conviction for treason-felony. By late July 1848 there were seventeen Confederate Clubs in the city with an estimated membership of over four thousand.[37] In an atmosphere of popular disaffection where the manufacture and sale of pikes went on briskly and young men carrying guns passed openly through the streets, the clubs both echoed and intensified the growing militancy among the city's workers, arranging lectures on military tactics and organising rifle drilling.[38] The skilled artisans were drawn along in the growing expectations of rebellion. On

Meagher's visit to the city in May 1848 over thirteen trades
marched out to greet him, bearing not only the banners they
had carried in the O'Connell demonstration of 1845, but also
tricolours of green, white and orange, and joining in the as-
sembled crowd's euphoric response to Meagher's dramatic call
to arms. Moreover, although the Confederate Clubs were by no
means exclusively artisan bodies, they were sufficiently identified
with the artisans to be confused by hostile observers with the
'Union of Trades'.[39]

The events (or, more correctly, non-events) of 1848 need little
attention here. The largely middle-class leaders of the Confederate
Clubs, typical 'revolutionaries afraid of revolution', though adept
at inflammatory speech-making, were most uneasy about the
popular excitement they had generated, and when the city and
county were proclaimed in July 1848 leaders and rank-and-file
parted company. While rumours of a successful rising in Tipperary
and Kilkenny spurred the club rank-and-file on to prepare for
rebellion, several leaders resigned immediately while the arrest
or emigration of others threw the clubs into disarray and a show
of force by the army and fleet completely crushed the affair.[40]

This fiasco of 1848 in Cork, as in Dublin, ushered in a period
of political apathy among the trades. The Repeal Movement was
dead and the short-lived Irish Democratic Association which
sought to perpetuate the revolutionary enthusiasm of 1848 had
as pathetic a showing in Cork as elsewhere, for although it did
count a number of artisans among its one hundred strong
membership, it received no support from the organised trades
and disappeared from the public scene in the early 1850s.[41] It
is true that during the early 1850s the Tenant League and the
Independent Irish Party occasioned much political excitement
in the Cork region, but, true to the general urban pattern of
the 1850s, city elections were fought out vigorously on the issues
of local rivalries rather than of land and religion.[42] But the
political movements of this period, unconnected as they were with
the issue of manufacture revival, made no attempt to recruit support through the medium of the trade societies, which, in turn,
stood aloof from local and national politics. When the old Cork
Trades Association sank into utter oblivion after a few faint

pipings in the 1853 election, the trades were left without a distinctive political cause to support.[43] Thereafter, the last vestiges of distinctively artisan political activity in the city evaporated and, over the following decade, the organised trades apparently eschewed party politics to concentrate, instead, on union organisation, discussed in the previous chapter.[44]

It was not until the 1860s that the artisans, both as individuals and as members of trade societies, again took a distinctive part in local politics, drawn in on this occasion not by the mild Repealism of the O'Connellite tradition but by militant republicanism. In Cork the first signs of this resurgent militarism were seen in April 1858 when placards were posted through the city in support of the Indian Mutiny. Later in the same year, the arrest and trial of the Skibbereen-based Phoenix Society leaders, who had linked up with the newly-established city branch of the Irish Republican Brotherhood, brought the revolutionary movement into the public eye.[45] The popularisation of separatist and anti-English sentiments during this time is difficult to trace with accuracy. Just as disloyal language among the lower orders had caused considerable alarm on the part of the authorities in the heady days of 1848, so there was similar evidence in the early 1860s of passive popular sympathy for the underground revolutionary movement.[46] In 1861 anti-English feeling was manifested at the opening of the new St. Patrick's Bridge when many in the crowd allegedly refused to doff their hats for the playing of 'God Save the Queen'. Two years later the same popular disaffection facilitated local Fenians in fomenting a riot in protest against celebrations of the Prince of Wales' wedding, while in 1864 a similar riot erupted when a soirée of local orangemen was disrupted by a mob singing 'Up with the Green'.[47] By the mid-1860s, popular anti-English sentiment was rife in the city, a local police constable confiding to Dublin Castle that

> if the governmental authorities made Ireland a second Eden, it would not tend to smoulder [sic] the spirit of disaffection that exists in the breasts of the artisan and labouring classes in this city.[48]

Many sources, moreover, indicate not just passive working-class sympathy but active membership of the underground movement.

Whereas in later years the republican movement was apparently flooded by retailers, salesmen and small-scale businessmen, the membership of earlier years came from somewhat lower on the social scale.[49] In the 1880s, James Stephens described the Fenian organisation of two decades previously as comprising 'the farmers' sons, the mechanics, the artisans, the labourers and the small shopkeepers', while modern historians have compared the list of Dublin Fenian suspects to 'a trades directory' including 'all social grades, from labourers to law clerks'.[50] Contemporary evidence corroborates this assessment in the Cork context, the informer, Warner, claiming in 1865 that 'all the shopmen, small traders, those employed at the breweries, distilleries and the factories, etc., are to a man sworn Fenians'. It is not now clear whether the artisan share of this popular support for Fenianism dates back to the foundation of the movement in Cork City, for in the early years shopkeepers and clerks appear to have been the main organisers while the trade societies did not openly associate themselves with the movement. By the mid-1860s, however, the intermeshing between the artisanate and Fenianism was clear to all, artisans accounting for forty-six per cent of all identified local members of the brotherhood, while about thirty-one per cent of the local leadership was also drawn from among the artisans. Among the rank-and-file members, the other predominant groups were labourers, drapers' assistants and clerks, while among the leaders publicans and shopkeepers were also prominent, but only the artisans dominated both leadership and rank-and-file.[51] It was, therefore, not surprising that in 1869 the Castle was advised by a Cork-based intelligence source that detectives sent to the city should be

> members of the Constabulary, and *Tradesmen* if such can be procured, men who whilst employed at their trade, can best obtain the most valuable information. If tradesmen can't be had, the others can be of little more use than those already here.[52]

It was the McManus Funeral of 1861 which, in Cork as elsewhere, publicly launched Fenianism and, after the doldrums of the 1850s, again drew the trade societies into the public realm of politics. Invited to participate in the funeral demonstration, eleven city trades gave a 'hearty response', subscribing money towards the event, and participating in the funeral procession through the city in scenes repeated by the Dublin Fenians and trade societies a few days later.[53] The first public political demonstration in which the trade societies had taken part since 1848, the McManus funeral proved the starting-point for a whole series of similar manifestations of Fenian sympathy over the following seventeen years.[54]

In Cork as in other centres, however, the ongoing artisan participation in Fenianism does not necessarily imply any direct link between the revolutionary movement and the trade societies.[55] While, for example, the coopers and tailors of the city were reputed to be strongly Fenian in sympathy, there is no tangible evidence of the direct involvement of their respective trade societies in the underground movement. Moreover, prominent members of a trade society could be active Fenians without at all committing the trade society as a whole to Fenianism, the local typographical society, for instance, successfully banning all political discussion within its ranks even though its secretary and a number of members were active in the brotherhood.[56] On the other hand, the latent Fenian sympathies of the artisans, and their willingness to parade them under the banner of the trade, was evident in the number of Fenian-related public demonstrations in which the trade societies of the city participated in the 1860s and 1870s. Over the seventeen years from 1861 to 1877, the Cork trades took part in ten demonstrations of a Fenian character, nine in Cork city itself, and one in Dublin. Even where such demonstrations were initially intended as non-political, the Fenian element stepped in to mould the affair into a show of sympathy for militant separatism. To some extent the O'Connell Centenary in Dublin in 1875 was manipulated in this way, while the 1864 demonstration in Cork to mark the unveiling of the monument to Father Theobald Mathew, the 'Apostle of Temperance', met a similar fate. In fact, on this latter occasion, the trades themselves, in response to Fenian urging and in defiance of the demonstration organisers' admonitions, insisted on wearing green sashes and carrying, as well as their trade banners, several green banners with nationalistic emblems.[57]

Trade-society participation in the demonstrations of the Fenian period was, admittedly, never quite as enthusiastic as it had been in the O'Connellite years. Whereas the great Repeal demonstrations of the 1830s could bring out between thirty and forty trades, the greatest number of trades marching in a nationalist demonstration in the Fenian period was twenty – and this was on the occasion of a local Fenian's funeral – while attendance on other occasions could be as low as between five and nine societies.[58] In spite of the apparent decline in its popularity, however, the political demonstration can still be regarded as a barometer for the Fenian sympathies of different trades. There were, it must be remembered, different reasons for the considerable fluctuations in the level of trade-society participation in such demonstrations. Those held on weekdays were, for obvious reasons, less well attended than those held on Sundays. Some societies objected to the extra expense involved in taking part in such events, and considering that by the early 1880s a big demonstration could collectively cost the city's trades over three hundred pounds, this was indeed a major consideration. Moreover, some trades tried to preserve harmony in their ranks by the avoidance of all contentious political issues. This was particularly evident in the case of the printers' society, several of whose members were prominent Fenians, but which avoided political demonstrations because many other members were unionist in politics or English by birth.[59] At the other extreme of the political spectrum was the situation where trade societies refused to participate in a Fenian demonstration because they felt thorough-going nationalist principles were being diluted by the introduction of other issues. Such a scenario emerged in 1873 on the occasion of a local demonstration for Home Rule and Amnesty. This demonstration was unwisely arranged without prior consultation with the city's Fenian element, who promptly denounced the introduction of Home Rule as a betrayal of 'pure' nationalist demands. Scenes of confusion ensued at a public meeting, and three trade societies – the boiler makers, farriers and coopers – refused to participate because of what they saw as unjustified diversion from the Fenian and Amnesty issue. Thus, bearing all these variables in mind, and taking into account the imperfect nature of the statistics available in both contemporary newspapers and in official files, it would appear that the local bakers, carpenters and tailors were the most consistent supporters of Fenian demonstrations, and that the greatest turn-out (as a percentage of all union members) was by the tailors, carpenters and coopers.[60] The survival of militant nationalist sympathies among the artisans was, moreover, facilitated by the tenacity with which Fenianism and its related cover-groups continued to operate from the late 1860s onwards. The Fair Trial Committee, established to defend the Fenian prisoners after the abortive rising of March 1867, was one such body, as was the similarly motivated and more long-lived Amnesty Association, both organisations having branches in Cork. Equally important were the local National Reading Room, which began as a branch of James Stephens' National Brotherhood of St. Patrick but in 1864 broke away to become an independent local Fenian body, and the Cork Working Men's Association which combined its role as a genuine friendly and benefit society with its less publicised (but no less widely recognised) role as a Fenian front group.[61] Although these bodies were subscribed to by artisans as individuals, and not by trade unions as collective entities, it had become evident by the late 1860s that the unions had become, if not directly involved, then inextricably identified with militant nationalism. In 1867 the local trades council's best efforts proved powerless to prevent seven of its constituent trade societies from participating in a demonstration to honour the Manchester Martyrs, while three years later a new trades council based in the Mechanics' Hall actually won popularity among the trades not by eschewing politics but by identifying closely with the underground republican movement.[62] This 'republicanisation'[63] of the artisans had progressed so far by 1872 that the Mechanics' Hall spokesmen helped to outlaw the infant local branch of the First International by arguing that international socialism was incompatible with militant separatism. In the same year, the militants in the Mechanics' Hall, in an obscure struggle which briefly raised its head in the parliamentary election, succeeded in ousting the moderate nationalists, ensuring that within two years of its establishment, the Mechanics' Hall had become almost totally identified with Fenianism.[64]

As the militant nationalist movement went to ground in the decades after 1870, it becomes progressively difficult to assess its appeal for local artisans. Some individuals certainly remained active in the shadowy republican underground, but even among the uninvolved generality of artisans, a residual, if largely rhetorical, sympathy remained.[65] This was revealed almost by chance in the occasional representations of republican heroes and slogans on trade-union banners, as in the case of the painters' banner, which in the mid-1870s included the slogan 'Remember Brian Dillon', or that of the farriers which in 1890 bore medallions of Flood, Emmet, Mitchel and Parnell. Most of all, it came out in that throwaway but telling phrase 'God Save Ireland' appearing on the painters' society banner in 1873 and 1875, that of the coopers in 1880, and on anti-importation notices posted throughout the city in 1881.[66]

By the early 1880s the political situation in Cork City had become quite complex. Besides the unionist section of the population, itself held together only by its common antipathy towards Home Rule, the local nationalist ranks presented a far from homogeneous picture, consisting of several different groupings whose only common denominator was opposition to the Act of Union of 1800. The first three of these groupings, the Home Rule members of the town council, the Cork branch of the Land League, and the trades, supported Charles Stuart Parnell who, in a hard-fought election of 1880, had been returned as one of the parliamentary representatives of the city. The fourth group, the Fenian element, commonly known as the Nationalists, was itself a divided body, the majority regarding Parnell and all constitutionalists as traitors to the cause of militant separatism. The four groups were not, however, mutually exclusive, and the frequent overlapping of membership confused the situation further.

The local trades and the Land League were on the worst possible terms since soon after the latter's inception in 1879, and the League's dissolution and reconstitution as the National League (largely a paper exercise) did nothing to change the situation. To a considerable extent, this antipathy was due to the trades' jealousy regarding the League's attempted monopolisation of a number of local public demonstrations in the early 1880s, but the major reasons were practical, and were the product less of political than of socio-economic tensions. The leadership of the League, country-wide, like that of other constitutional movements, was dominated less by farmers than by 'a discontented segment of the town population' from outside the ranks of the artisans.[67] In Cork, too, while farmers from the outskirts of the city played a prominent part, the most important spokesmen were merchants, master tradesmen, shopkeepers and vintners, and at least twenty per cent of the identified leadership had sufficient property qualifications to hold office as Poor Law Guardians, town councillors and positions on other public boards.[68] Such prominent Leaguers, involved in the cause of the tenant farmers, were largely indifferent to the problems of the city trades, paying lip-service to their interests but otherwise ignoring them. In the mid-1880s, for instance, trade requests that the League support local shipbuilding workers' demands for higher wages got no hearing, and the League broke its promise to campaign for more public building works in the city and to help the working millers by enforcing a boycott on bakers using imported flour.[69] Moreover, the fact that some Leaguers, in their capacity as employers of labour, came into conflict with the organised trades, certainly embittered relations between the two groups. The most prominent example of this involved a dispute between the Corkcutters' Society and the partners in a local bottling firm. The partners, John O'Connor and Robert Walsh, leading city Land Leaguers, were accused by the corkcutters and the trades council of trying to force a wage cut, and of replacing the non-compliant corkcutters by unskilled labour. The details of the dispute were clouded by conflicting evidence, but the effect was the worsening of relations not alone between the trades and the firm involved, but also between the organised trades and the National League.[70]

At a wider level, too, the interests of the trades and the League diverged. Trades' resentment against farmers, a normal aspect of town-country rivalry, was strengthened by the farming community's perceived failure to patronise locally-manufactured goods and establishments employing fair labour. The coopers complained of the farmers' preference for imported glass and zinc milkpans instead of the locally-made coopered items, and the coachmakers claimed to have

> suffered terribly and uncomplainingly for a few years past from the effects of the land agitation, and it is much to be regretted that the farmers, so far from recognising the great sacrifices they have made, give their patronage, in most cases, to those establishments where members of the association are not employed.[71]

The main issue, from the trades' viewpoint, was the League's ban on foxhunting. This widely effective ban, first enforced in 1882, and stepped up again in 1887 as a protest against the arrest of the League leader and journalist, William O'Brien, was intended as a harassment of the landlords and gentry, but its more immediate effect was to deprive the city trades of their usual seasonal employment in providing the gentry with the requirements of the hunting-season. The farriers, tailors and bootmakers of the city were the most severely affected, the tailors' fortunes being particularly shaken when, in early 1882, some fifty members of the local union were either on short time or unemployed because of the fall-off in demand occasioned by the ban. Later in the same year the union calculated that its members' average weekly hunting-season earnings had fallen from thirty to twelve shillings, while in 1887 the severity of the problem was underlined when one city establishment let go twenty-five men – one third of its staff. Trade complaints to the League proved unavailing, even a deputation to Michael Davitt in 1887 having no result.[72]

It was hardly surprising, then, that for the Cork trades, severely affected by the depression of the 1880s, the land agitation was an unwelcome clog in the progress of manufacture and industry. While local Leaguers indulged in theatrical invective against 'the evicting and cruel-hearted landlord', the trades made it clear that they had no ill-feeling towards landlords *qua* landlords, and denounced the League's campaign as 'an unfortunate war of classes' which robbed the trades of their best customers, the gentry. Thus, while in the early 1880s the occasional local trade-union banner took up the rhetoric of the land agitation with such slogans as

'The Land for the People', in general the League's promises of liberty and prosperity following on the reform of the land system met with a cold reception from the city's artisans, who claimed that 'the trades of Cork had suffered more, and lost more money by [the land agitation] than all the farmers in Ireland'.[73] Indeed, it seemed for a short while that the animosity of the Cork trades towards the League might also affect their relationship with Parnell, for when repeated letters to the latter, calling for the discontinuance of the hunting ban, failed to elicit a single reply, there were some murmurs of discontent within the trades council. However, these were quickly hushed up, and the blame transferred from Parnell to the unpopular local officers of the League branch.[74]

Whatever their hidden resentment towards Parnell in his role as League leader, the Cork trades warmly supported him in his capacity as leader and embodiment of the Home Rule Movement. Reorganised in 1881, and claiming by 1886 to represent between two and three thousand artisans, the local trades council saw itself, in fact, as the bastion of Home Rule in the city. With such a large membership, which included men of both nationalist and unionist sympathies, the trades council could not, of course, speak with a totally unified political voice, and any political pronouncements by the council executive tended to cause mutterings of dissension in the ranks. But because the number of Protestant artisans in the city appears to have fallen considerably since the 1840s, the unionists were never more than a small minority within the council.[75] Moreover, because the council reorganisation coincided with the beginnings of the land and Home Rule agitations, the trades council and its constituent trade societies were, in spite of the squabbles with the League, swept along on the wave of popular excitement until it proved almost impossible to detach it from the nationalist side in politics. Even ecomomic issues were increasingly expressed in the language of Home Rule and the land agitation. During 1887 when the Plan of Campaign was at its height, and a wave of agrarian violence was directed against process servers and caretakers of evicted farms, a purely economic quarrel between the city's long-established carpenters' society and the local branch of the

British-based Amalgamated Society of Carpenters and Joiners was couched in contemporary political rhetoric. Each group accused the other of betraying the nationalist cause by working at their trade on farms held by caretakers, while the local society, dismissing the others as 'English dupes', described its own autonomy in the political terminology of the day:

> With an unsullied record of two hundred years, we decline to sell our birthright, and on the principle of Home Rule, prefer to govern ourselves.[76]

The methods of the land agitation also became part of the urban labour scene. In 1881 a trades council protest against the importation from England of building materials for a new hall of residence attached to the Queen's College was accompanied by the boycotting techniques becoming so common in the land agitation, while in 1890 a dockers' and seamen's strike was immeasurably complicated by the local union branches' refusal to handle boycotted cattle which were being exported from the port of Cork.[77] Already in 1881 the nationalist tendencies of the council had been made clear when the city's two Home Rule representatives, Charles Stewart Parnell and John Daly, were conferred respectively with the council's honorary presidency and vice-presidency, while in the Home Rule and pro-Parnell public demonstrations of the 1880s (as had been the case in the Fenian processions of the previous two decades), the trades spared no expense.[78] It was calculated that a big demonstration could cost the trades council over three hundred pounds at a time when the average earnings of a skilled man in full employment was between four and five shillings and two such demonstrations with one on a more modest scale took place between October 1881 and December 1882. Though the colourful pageantry and sense of excitement of these events probably accounted as much as political commitment for the individual artisan's participation, the fact that between fifty and eighty per cent of the trade council's membership took part must surely suggest a high level of support for Parnell and Home Rule.[79]

The problems of such politicisation came to light very soon.

In 1882 one of the printers' delegates, John Henry Jolley, a Protestant in religion and a unionist in politics, was elected president of the council. On his election, he committed himself to keep separate his politics and his presidency, and thereafter scrupulously honoured his promise. The growing tendency of the trade societies to look at everything through nationalist glasses, however, was evident when Jolley was accused by more paranoid nationalists in the trades council of 'detach[ing] the tradesmen from their traditionally nationalist principles' – a suspicion which was sharpened when he predictably refused an invitation to sit on the local council of the National League. Though the invitation had been refused largely because of the animosity between the trades and the League, and because the latter had not consulted the executive committee of the trades council before extending their invitation, the resulting mud-slinging threatened to tear the council ranks asunder. Yet, for all this, though the acrimonious squabble convinced some members that all political discussion should be outlawed from the trade council, it proved impossible to enforce such a ruling in the political atmosphere created by the escalating land agitation, the Parnellite election victory of 1885, and the introduction of Gladstone's Home Rule Bill in 1886. Indeed, when a political ban was finally proposed in 1887 'with a view to strengthen the position of, and promote a better feeling of goodwill and confidence among all classes of our fellow-citizens', not a single delegate could be found to second the motion, one individual speaking for all when he declared that 'they were not going to shut their mouths on politics when they had occasion for it.'[80]

This was the keynote for the remainder of the decade, and just as in Dublin nationalist sympathy was 'the most important part of the workers' relationship with politics', so, too, by the time of the Parnellite split in late 1890 the Cork trades were so closely identified with the Home Rule side that the controversy threatened to put an end to the fragile unity of the trades council.[81] The trades council was, in fact, so evenly divided between Parnellites and anti-Parnellites that neither side dared to propose a vote on the issue lest the organisation be torn apart. But the Parnellites apparently had the upper hand, and in 1891 succeeded in ousting from the presidency and secretaryship the anti-Parnellites, Eugene Crean and Michael Austen, replacing them by the Parnellites Robert S. McNamara and Charles Cogan.[82] During the following months council meetings were marked by constant political bickering and occasional flare-ups: late in January 1891 trouble erupted when a minority of five anti-Parnellites failed to reverse the council's decision to make their meeting hall available for a meeting of the Parnellite members of the National League; a week later, an attempt to force through a vote of confidence in Parnell was defeated amid scenes of chaos; at the following meeting, when some delegates varied the theme by proposing a vote of censure on Parnell, the meeting dissolved in mayhem; three weeks later similar scenes occurred when the Parnellites tried again to pass another vote of confidence in their hero; and when the St Patrick's Day public parade of 1891 was monopolised by the Parnellites, who turned it into a demonstration in favour of 'the Chief', the participation therein of the trade council officers and twelve of the nineteen affiliated societies caused a further furore in council ranks.[83]

By late 1890 the bitter divisions in local politics had been formalised as the anti-Parnellites established the Cork National Committee and the Parnellites revived the National League and elected Parnell as its president. Members of the trades council were prominent in each of the rival bodies, while the divisions extended into the ranks of the individual trade societies. Though some societies, like the engineers and farriers, were evenly split, it seems that certain trades were more strongly Parnellite than others. The carpenters, for example, asserted their loyalty to Parnell by refusing to re-elect Eugene Crean as the trades council delegate when he took the anti-Parnellite side, and their society's band, along with that of the tailors, nailed their colours to the mast by playing in honour of Parnell when he visited Cork in the early weeks of the split.[84] Participation by a trade society in such pro-Parnell demonstrations was, as in previous decades, the main barometer of a trade's political sympathies, and successive demonstrations of this type in the early 1890s pinpointed the main bastions of Parnellism among the trades as the societies of coopers, carpenters, cabinet makers, plasterers, pork butchers, builders' labourers, brewery workmen and the dock labourers of Passage West. The ban on party political allignments within the trades council from 1892 onwards, together with the expense of participation in demonstrations, deterred many societies thereafter from further public manifestations of Parnellism, but some old faithfuls remained. For example, the coopers and plasterers marched in 1895 in honour of Parnell's successor, John Redmond, while the coopers' Parnellite loyalties extended to lending their scarves to a local band playing at the Dublin Ivy Day demonstration of 1893, and sending seventy of their own society men to a similar Dublin demonstration in 1895. Likewise, the Cork stonecutters' society sent a delegation and wreath to the Dublin Ivy Day demonstration for at least three years in succession.[85]

It was at this stage that the shady links between Parnellism and Fenianism among the trades surfaced in all their complexity. By the late 1880s the underground republican movement was to all appearances extinct, but was being revived again by the early 1890s when the various extremist factions reunited, revealing their presence through the continued staging of public republican funerals and the erection of memorials in honour of dead Fenians.[86] After 1891, as noted by Leon Ó Broin, there were close connections country-wide between Parnellism and militant nationalism. This link is evident in microcosm in Cork City, where many of those supporting the discredited leader were also involved in the Fenian underground. Besides, while the degree of overlap between membership of the trades council and of the IRB remains most unclear, there is a tangible continuity between those trades which in the 1860s had been strongly Fenian, and those which in the 1890s were predominantly Parnellite − i.e. the coopers, carpenters and tailors.[87]

Parnell had represented Cork City in parliament since 1880 and his death in October 1891 precipitated a hard-fought contest between the Parnellite John Redmond and the anti-Parnellite (now described as Nationalist) Martin Flavin. The election proved a comfortable victory for the Nationalists, but what was significant from the trades' perspective was that this was the first election since the 1840s in which artisans took a distinct and assertive part. Most of this electoral participation was by individual artisans rather than by trade societies, but the contest also extended into the ranks of the divided trades council, the opposing factions being represented on the opposing election committees, and sending deputations ostensibly to quiz the rival candidates on their attitudes to labour-related issues but really to demonstrate publicly the rival trade factions' party-political loyalties.[88]

This was, however, the last open manifestation in the trades council of the politics of 'the Split', for two months later, the election of a new council president began the process of healing political divisions in that body. It is not now clear whether this resulted from a general weariness with internecine feuding in the council, but in a poll which dramatically crossed party lines, the presidency was given to the masons' delegate, Timothy Harrington, an anti-Parnellite who was determined to ban all party-political discussion from council ranks. This determination, together with the passage of time, ultimately rendered the ban completely effective so that during the next parliamentary election in 1895 the trades council, despite its individual members' political loyalties, acted as a unified body.[89]

But for all that, the trades had not really cleared their ranks of divisive party politics. If some had hoped that the 'political ban' would accommodate unionist artisans by diluting the council's basic nationalism, they were to be sorely disappointed. Put simply, the purpose of the ban was to strengthen the nationalist ethos of the council by erasing from its ranks the divisive classifications of Parnellite and anti-Parnellite. In effect, for the remainder of the century, the ban succeeded not in cutting the council off from politics but in restoring it to the position it had held in the 1880s – a body strongly Home Rule in ethos, and emotionally if not actively supportive of the underground militant movement. Even the trades' growing interest, towards the end of the century, in the concept of direct labour representation in local government did little to dilute existing political loyalties, as evidenced by the stance of that labour candidate in the city's north-east ward who addressed his audience from the house of the dead Fenian, Brian Dillon, while a green flag floated above him on a 'Ninety-Eight pike.[90] Such a Janus-faced stance was totally in keeping with previous trends. The trade council's participation in 1893 in an attempted local project to erect a Manchester Martyrs' memorial, and its role later in the decade in the local committee organising the centenary of the 1798 rebellion, clearly showed where the collective sympathy of the trades lay. Though there were many squabbles between the trades council and the local IRB during this period, these were less about fundamental principles than about trades and underground republicans contending for the honour of representing popular nationalism.

The progressive politicisation of the Cork artisans in a nationalist direction probably reached its apogee in the 'Ninety-Eight celebrations. In the euphoria of that centenary year, both the individual artisan and the collectivity of the trade were particularly susceptible to the romanticised presentation of the militant nationalist tradition. The trade and labourers' societies participated in time-honoured fashion in the commemorative demonstration in May of that year, decking their persons and their meeting rooms out with the symbols and colours of revolutionary nationalism. The builders' labourers presented their militant credentials by means of a provocative banner on which the words 'Rebel Cork' were divided by Irish pikes, and which, despite the constabulary's best efforts to force its removal, was hung flauntingly from a building in one of the city's main thoroughfares.[91] In similar fashion, the entry in the Coopers' Society minute book for 24 May 1898 revealed that touching mixture of pride and *naïveté* which by the end of the nineteenth century characterised the nationalistic politicisation of the average Cork artisan:

> Last night, May 23rd, being the Centenary anniversary of the rising in Ireland, was celebrated in Cork by all nationalists illuminating their houses, [and this] was splendidly carried out. Bands and tar barrels through the streets. We had our rooms got up on the outside, illuminated with fairy lamps, chinese lanterns, with a beautiful banneret, pictures of the United Irishmen of '98, etc., all of which was much admired so that the Cork Coopers' Society were not behind in paying a tribute of respect to the glorious Heroes of '98.[92]

NOTES

1 Jim Smyth, *The Men of No Property: Irish Radicals and Popular Politics in the Late Eighteenth Century* (Dublin, 1992), pp. 23-32, 232-82; Thomas Bartlett, *The Fall and Rise of the Irish Nation: The Catholic Question 1690-1830* (Dublin, 1992), especially pp. 294-9, 311-25; Samuel Clark and James S. Donnelly, Jr. (eds.), *Irish Peasants: Violence and Political Unrest 1780-1914* (Dublin, 1983), pp. 12-16.

2 Jim Smyth, *The Men of No Property*, pp. 31, 35-6, 172; Seán Ó Coindealbháin, 'The United Irishmen in County Cork', *JCHAS*, lvi, 1951, p. 23; *Freeman's Journal* (cited hereafter as *FJ*), 23 June, 3 July, 7 Aug. 1798.

3 Jim Smyth, *The Men of No Property*, pp. 94, 158-62, 171-2; Seán Ó Coindealbháin, 'The United Irishmen in Cork County', *JCHAS*, liii, 1948, p. 77; SOC, 1805: 1031/5, 10 (20 Mar. 1805).

4 Thomas Bartlett, *The Fall and Rise of the Irish Nation*, pp. 281-5; Ian D'Alton, *Protestant Society and Politics in Cork 1812-1844* (Cork, 1980), pp. 135-7; Daniel Owen Maddyn, *Revelations of Ireland in the Past Generation* (Dublin, 1848), pp. 184-202.

5 Thomas Bartlett, *The Fall and Rise of the Irish Nation*, pp. 281, 295, 320-35; Anon., *A Full and Accurate Report of the Proceedings at the Election for the City of Cork, 1820* (Cork, 1820); Anon., *The Entire Proceedings of the Election for the City of Cork, which commenced on Saturday 13th and terminated on Monday 19th March 1830* (Cork, 1830).

6 Thomas Bartlett, *The Fall and Rise of the Irish Nation*, p. 297; Day Papers, Cork Archives Council, 81.14; Thomas Sheahan, *Articles of Irish Manufacture*, p. 42.

7 Thomas Bartlett, *The Fall and Rise of the Irish Nation*, pp. 291-5; 307-8, 327-8; William Fagan, *The Life and Times of Daniel O'Connell* (Cork, 1848), Vol. I, pp. 109-14.

8 Song entitled 'Paddy Bull's Remarks on the County Election', (October 1812), National Library of Ireland, Broadside Collection.

9 Fergus O'Ferrall, *Catholic Emancipation: Daniel O'Connell and the Birth of Irish Democracy 1820-1830* (Dublin, 1985), pp. 68, 171, 223-337.

10 *CC*, 16 Oct. 1830.

11 Jim Smyth, *The Men of No Property*, pp. 146-156.

12 SOC, 1805: 1031/5, 10; Anon., *Report of the Proceedings at the Cork Election 1820*; Anon., *Proceedings of the Cork Election 1830*. In particular, a very large number of coopers figured in the city's freeman electorate.

13 Ian D'Alton, *Protestant Society*, pp. 138-9.

14 *CMI*, 21 July 1821.

15 Norman Gash, *Reaction and Reconstruction in English Politics* (Oxford, 1965).

16 Ian D'Alton, *Protestant Society*, pp. 123-200.

17 Fergus D'Arcy, 'Dublin artisan activity', pp. 37-8; Thomas Sheahan, *Articles of Irish Manufacture*, pp. 184-9; *CC*, 30 Nov. 1830.

18 *CC*, 12, 16, 19 Mar. 1832; Diary of Otto Travers, Mar. 1832 (National Library of Ireland, microfilm).

19   *CC*, 19 Apr., 15 June, 1 Sept. 1832; *CMC*, 9, 13, 20 June, 13 July, 19 Nov. 1832; *Waterford Chronicle*, 2, 14, 16, 23, 30 June, 21 July 1832. Waterford had been the first to initiate such a movement early in June 1832, followed within a few weeks by Cork, Clonmel, Tipperary, Kilkenny, Limerick and Dublin.

20   John Foster, *Class Struggle and the Industrial Revolution*, pp. 132–3.

21   *CMC*, 27 June, 18 Oct. 1832. Membership was initially open to subscribers of a minimum of one penny per month, but this was soon raised to one penny per week to meet expenses.

22   The *Cork Mercantile Chronicle* was edited by the radical Thomas Sheahan, a selection of whose writings, accompanied by some personal comment, can be found in his *Articles of Irish Manufacture: Or Portions of Cork History* (Cork, 1833).

23   *CMC*, 12 Dec. 1832; *People's Press*, 2 May 1835. The People's Hall was more restrictive in its membership than was the Cork Trades Association, the trusteeship being limited to those paying subscriptions of over a shilling.

24   *CMC*, 12 Dec. 1832; *People's Press*, 2 May 1835; *CC*, 17 Nov. 1835; *SR*, 20, 22 July 1837.

25   *SR*, 13 Feb., 27 May 1841; *CE*, 8, 17, 20 Dec. 1841, 11 Apr., 30 May 1842. Mallow Lane was the former name for Shandon Street.

26   *CMC*, 17 Aug., 19, 20 Oct. 1832; Daniel Owen Maddyn, *Ireland and its Rulers*, vol. 1, pp. 197–8.

27   *CMC*, 12, 14 June 1833, 3, 12 Mar. 1834.

28   Daniel Callaghan, in particular, who was noted for his low attendance rate in the House of Commons, did not appear in a single parliamentary division between January 1833 and April 1834. The victorious Tory candidates in the 1835 election were Joseph Leycester and William Chatterton, who were subsequently unseated when a parliamentary enquiry found them guilty of 'running bucks' – i.e. polling voters in respect of houses which they no longer occupied. *CC*, 17 Jan. 1835; *First and Second Reports of the Select Committee on Fictitious Votes (Ireland)*, HC 1837–38, xiii, I, Qs. 2832–37, 3783–85; *Hansard* 3, 1833–34, xv–xxiii.

29   See below, p. 142–4.

30   Ian D'Alton, *Protestant Politics*, pp. 165, 212–14.

31   F. S. L. Lyons, *Ireland since the Famine* (Glasgow, 1971), pp. 105–8, Kevin B. Nowlan, *The Politics of Repeal* (London, 1965), pp. 80–93; D. George Boyce, *Nineteenth Century Ireland: The Search for Stability* (Dublin, 1990), pp. 84, 95.

32   *CE*, 15 June, 22 Sept. 1847; *SR*, 14 Mar. 1848; Fergus D'Arcy, 'Dublin artisan activity', p. 73.

33   *CE*, 20 Dec. 1847; *SR*, 15 Feb., 7, 30 Mar. 1848. Maura Murphy, 'Repeal and Young Ireland in Cork politics 1830–50', (Unpublished MA dissertation, National University of Ireland, 1975), pp. 114–16.

34   For an analysis of the issues in dispute within the Irish Confederation in early 1848, see D. George Boyce, *Nineteenth Century Ireland*, pp. 115–18.

35 For parallel events elsewhere, see Emmet O'Connor, *A Labour History of Waterford*, pp. 54–7; Fergus D'Arcy, 'Dublin artisan activity', pp. 65–78.

36 *SR*, 14, 30 Mar., 20 Apr. 1848. It was claimed that the meeting held to establish the Citizens' Club was 'for the most part a trades' meeting' and that the first eight hundred members of the club were drawn mainly from the ranks of the trades.

37 *SR*, 2, 20, 23, 30 May, 1 June 1848.

38 *CC*, 4, 11, 13, 18, 20 Apr. 1848; CSORP.OR, 1848: 6/397, 405, 424, 447, 464, 489, 505, 574.

39 *SR*, 2, 30 May 1848; *CC*, 3 Apr., 3, 6 June 1848. The trades marching in the Meagher demonstration were the bakers, bootmakers, broguemakers, carpenters, hatters, masons, nailors, paperstainers, plasterers, sawyers, shipwrights, smiths, tailors, and 'many others'.

40 *CC*, 6, 20, 25, 27 July, 5 Aug. 1848; *SR*, 18 July 1848; CSORP.OR, 1848: 6/866, 1025, 1026, 1256.

41 D'Arcy, 'Dublin artisan activity', p. 77; *Irishman*, 16 Nov. 1849, 2, 16 Mar., 6 Apr. 1850.

42 *Report from the Select Committee on the Cork City Election Petition*, HC 1852–53 (528), xi, I; K. T. Hoppen, *Elections, Politics and Society in Ireland 1832–1885* (Oxford, 1984), pp. 442–3.

43 *CE*, 22 Aug. 1853.

44 *CE*, 23 Apr. 1851, 23 Mar. 1857, 9 May, 20, 29 June 1859; John Boyle, *The Irish Labour Movement*, pp. 54–5.

45 *CC*, 16 Jan. 1858; *CE*, 5 Nov., 1, 10 Dec. 1858; CSORP, 1858: 17986, 20370; E. R. R. Green, 'The beginnings of Fenianism', T. W. Moody (ed.), *The Fenian Movement* (Cork, 1968), pp. 16–18.

46 *CC*, 6, 15, 25 July 1848; CSORP.OR, 6:872, 973, 990, 998.

47 *CE*, 12, 13 Dec. 1861, 11 Mar. 1863, 18 Aug. 1864.

48 Fenian Papers, 1866: F–2091 (filed with F–2112).

49 Tom Garvin, *Nationalist Revolutionaries in Ireland 1858–1928* (Oxford, 1987), p. 38.

50 John Boyle, *The Irish Labour Movement*, p. 62; Desmond Ryan, *The Fenian Chief* (Dublin, 1967), p. 327; Shin-ichi Takagami, 'The Dublin Fenians 1858–1879' (Unpublished Ph.D. thesis, Trinity College, Dublin, 1990), pp. 80–1, calculated that fifty-nine per cent of identified Dublin Fenians between 1865 and 1871 were artisans; 11·4 per cent were unskilled workers and 13·7 per cent were shop assistants and clerks. The same pattern was evident in Waterford: see Emmet O'Connor, *A Labour History of Waterford*, pp. 78–9.

51 Irish Crimes Records, 1865–70, vol. i, Fenianism: Index of Names; Fenian Papers, 1865: F–233 (1 and 2); CSORP, 1867:22537; Maura Murphy, 'The role of organised labour in the political and economic life of Cork City 1820–1899 (Unpublished Ph.D. thesis, University of Leicester, 1980), pp. 215–19; Tom Garvin, *Nationalist Revolutionaries in Ireland 1858–1928* (Oxford, 1987), pp. 23–40.

52 Fenian Papers, 1869, 5354–R.

53 *CE*, 4 Feb., 7 Nov. 1859, 22 June 1860, 14 Sept., 9, 31 Oct., 4 Nov. 1861;
    CDH, 11 Jan. 1861; CSORP, 1861: 8418 (filed with 1877: 3591); Takagami,
    'The Dublin Fenians', p. 20; Leon Ó Broin, *Fenian Fever: An Anglo-American
    Dilemma* (London, 1971), pp. 3–4; E.R. Norman, *The Catholic Church and
    Ireland in the Age of Rebellion 1859–1873* (London, 1965), pp. 96–8.

54 *CE*, 4 Nov. 1861, 9 Aug. 1864, 2 Dec. 1867, 22 Aug. 1871, 25 Aug. 1872,
    9 Oct. 1873, 31 Jan., 22 Nov. 1875, 21 Dec. 1876, 24 Feb. 1877.

55 Emmet O'Connor, *A Labour History of Ireland 1824–1960*, pp. 42–3; Takagami,
    'The Dublin Fenians', pp. 358–9.

56 *CE*, 11 Oct. 1880; Fenian Papers 1871: 7325-R; Irish Crimes Records 1865–
    70, vol. i, Fenianism: Index of Names.

57 Leon Ó Broin, *Revolutionary Underground* (Dublin, 1976), pp. 13–14; *CE*, 14
    Sept., 7, 19, 11 Oct. 1864; Larcom Papers, MS. 7587, National Library
    of Ireland, 2 Oct. 1864.

58 *CMC*, 12, 16, 19 Mar., 25 June 1832; *CE*, 9 June 1845, 4 Nov. 1861, 9
    Aug. 1864, 2 Dec. 1867, 22 Aug. 1871, 25 Aug. 1872, 9 Oct. 1873, 31 Jan.,
    22 Nov. 1875, 21 Dec. 1876, 24 Feb. 1877. Trades attendance at successive
    Fenian demonstrations in Cork City and elsewhere were as follows:
    McManus Funeral 1861 – 12; Mathew Monument Unveiling 1864 – 18;
    Manchester Martyrs' Demonstration 1867 – 7; Pro-France Demonstra-
    tion (during the Franco-Prussian War) 1871 – 11; Brian Dillon Funeral
    1872 – 9; Home Rule and Amnesty Demonstration 1873 – 15; Amnesty
    Demonstration 1875 – 5; O'Connell Centenary (Dublin) 1875 – 8; Michael
    F. Murphy Funeral 1876 – 20; John O'Mahony Funeral 1877 – 7. It must
    also be borne in mind that the number of trade societies was lower in
    the 1870s than had been the case in the 1830s, since several trades had
    collapsed in the intervening forty years.

59 *CE*, 2 Dec. 1867, 4 Oct. 1880, 4 Sept. 1888; Cork Typographical Society
    Minute Books, 12 Feb. 1898.

60 The total number of Fenian demonstrations in which each Cork trade society
    participated, out of a total of ten, between 1861 and 1877 was as follows:
    bakers, carpenters, tailors – 9 each; slaters, plasterers, painters, shipwrights
    – 8 each; bootmakers, coopers, masons – 7 each; stonecutters – 5; cabinet
    makers, coachmakers – 4 each; corkcutters, curriers, plumbers, victuallers
    – 3 each; farriers, smiths – 2 each; bootrivetters, hatters, millers,
    paperhangers, paperstainers, sawyers, ropemakers – 1 each. The consistently
    greatest turn-out as a percentage of total union membership was by the
    tailors (*c.* 100 per cent), carpenters (*c.* 75–100 per cent), and coopers (*c.* 70–
    100 per cent). There is some correlation here with the Dublin scene where,
    as Takagami has shown, the most 'Fenian' trades were carpenters,
    shoemakers, tailors, bricklayers, painters, blacksmiths, bootmakers, cork-
    cutters, bakers and coopers. Takagami, 'The Dublin Fenians', pp. 82–3.

61 *CE*, 22 June 1860, 14 Sept. 1861, 12 Mar. 1864, 25 Mar. 1867, 2 Mar.
    1872; E. R. Norman, *The Catholic Church and Ireland in the Age of Rebellion*,
    p. 127; Fenian Papers 1869: 4666-R, 5335-R.

62 Fenian Papers, 1867: F–4994; *CE*, 28 Nov. 1864; Arthur Mitchell, *Labour in Irish Politics*, p. 14.

63 Marianne Eliott, 'Origins and transfer of early Irish Republicanism', *International Review of Social History*, vol. xxiii, 1978.

64 CE, 2 Jan., 21, 25, 27, 29, 30 Mar., 11, 21 Nov. 1872; Fenian Papers, 1872: 8105–R; Webb Trade Union Collection, sect. A, vol. iii, f. 45.

65 For names of Cork members of the IRB, see Crime Branch Special Reports (cited hereafter as CBSR) 1890: 2792/S, 1892: 5483/S, 1894: 9001/S, 1897: 1452/S.

66 Fenianism: Index of Names; CSORP, 1872: 12974; *CE*, 26 Aug. 1872, 13 Oct. 1873, 20 Mar. 1874, 22 Nov. 1875, 11 Oct. 1880, 7 Sept. 1881. Brian Dillon, an attorney's clerk and later a publican, was Head Centre for Cork in 1865. Convicted of treason felony in 1865, he was sentenced to ten years' penal servitude, but conditionally released in 1871 due to ill-health. He died in August 1872 and was buried in Rathcooney Cemetery in the northern liberties, where a monument was erected over his grave in 1874. 'God Save Ireland' was the call from the dock by Allen, Larkin and O'Brien, the Manchester Martyrs of 1867. The slogan was immortalised in the title and refrain of a song written by T. D. Sullivan.

67 Sam Clarke, 'The social composition of the Land League' *Irish Historical Studies*, vol. xvii, no. 68, 1971, pp. 447, 468–9: 'Shopkeepers . . . were the leaders of the movement. Without them there would not have been a Land League, since no other urban social group could so easily have identified its interests with those of the farmers. They played a crucial role: farmers became politicized as a result of the Land League, but townsmen, above all, shopkeepers, initiated the movement and provided it with badly needed leadership.'.

68 *CDH*, 19, 26 Apr., 10, 17, 31 May 1880, 19 Dec. 1882. Of the forty-five principal Leaguers in the city, there were six merchants, four vintners or shopkeepers, three manufacturers, two medical men, and one commercial traveller.

69 *CE*, 13 May 1881, 21, 22, 29 Oct., 9 Nov. 1886, 13 Jan. 1887.

70 *CE*, 26, 30 Oct., 2, 3, 6, 7 Nov. 1883.

71 *CE*, 13 May, 7 Oct. 1881, 21 Oct. 1886; *CDH*, 13 May 1881.

72 L. P. Curtis, 'Stopping the hunt, 1881–1882: an aspect of the Irish Land War', C. H. E. Philpin (ed.), *Nationalism and Popular Protest in Ireland* (London, 1987), pp. 349–402; *CE*, 10 Nov. 1882, 3 Feb., 23 Nov. 1887.

73 *CE*, 7 Oct. 1880, 11 Dec. 1882.

74 *CE*, 1 Nov., 11 Dec. 1882.

75 The dearth of census detail on religious affiliation until 1871 precludes any real analysis of the changing patterns of denominational allignment in Cork working-class life. As pointed out by Ian D'Alton, 'Keeping faith: an evocation of the Cork Protestant character, 1820–1920', O'Flanagan and Buttimer (eds.), *Cork: History and Society*, p. 781, two thirds of Protestant males could be described as being in skilled occupations, but the poorer

classes of Protestants noted in the 1840s had disappeared. An analysis of the census figures between 1871 and 1901 suggests that religious denominations other than Roman Catholic accounted for between 83·5 and 84·25 per cent of the total city population, and for 70·7 and 100 per cent of the major skilled occupations. *Census of Ireland* 1871–1901; Maura Murphy, 'Social and economic structure of nineteenth century Cork', pp. 148–51.

76 *CE*, 15, 16, 21, 22, 24, 26, 28 Mar. 1887.

77 *CE*, 19, 20 July 1881, 31 Oct., 1, 3, 4, 5, 6, 8, 10, 12, 13, 15, 18 Nov. 1890.

78 *CE*, 11 Apr. 1881.

79 *CE*, 4 Oct. 1880, 11 Apr., 30 July, 4 Oct. 1881, 11 Dec. 1882, 24 Sept. 1885, 14 Oct. 1886. There was an average participation of 1,600 men in each of the big Parnellite demonstrations of the early 1880s when the total membership of the trades council was between two and three thousand.

80 *CE*, 30 July, 26 Oct., 23 Nov. 1883; *United Ireland*, 21, 28 July 1883, 21, 28 Apr. 1887.

81 Brendan McDonnell, 'The Dublin labour movement', p. xxiii; *CE*, 29 Nov., 3, 10, 17 Dec. 1890; F. S. Lyons, *Ireland since the Famine*, pp. 197–200. In Cork, Parnell's 'Manifesto to the Irish People' in November 1890 precipitated a split in the municipal council where the majority of nationalist members sided with Parnell while twenty members opposed him. The anti-Parnellites in the town council were led by Eugene Crean, who was also president of the trades council. The vice-president of the trades council, Robert S. McNamara, took a prominent role on the Parnellite side.

82 *CE*, 10 Dec. 1890, 16 Jan., 10 Apr. 1891, *Labour World*, 3 Jan. 1891. Crean was actually removed from his position of trades council delegate by his own trade society, the predominantly Parnellite Ancient Corporation of Carpenters. Austen, a printer, was already unpopular with many of the trades because of his deep involvement in the organisation of the city's unskilled workers.

83 *CE*, 30 Jan., 20, 26, 28 Feb., 9, 14, 16, 18 Mar. 1891.

84 *CE*, 10, 12, 19 Dec. 1890, 16 Jan., 7, 12 May 1891; *CDH*, 13, 19 Dec. 1890. Eugene Crean, former president of the trades council, was prominent in the National Committee, while the sitting president, Robert S. McNamara was active in the National League.

85 *CE*, 18 Mar. 1891, 8 Oct. 1894, 18 Mar., 7 Oct. 1895, 12 Oct. 1896; Cork Cooper's Society Minute Books, 5 Oct. 1893; *Reports on Trade Unions*, [C-8644] HC 1897, xcix, 275, 2–3; [C-9013] HC 1898, xiii, 127, 2–3. The first Parnellite demonstration held in Cork after the split was that on St Patrick's Day 1891; a similar demonstration in honour of John Redmond took place in 1895, while every year the anniversary of Parnell's death, Ivy Day, was marked by a big demonstration in Dublin. The plasterers who marched in the 1895 demonstration were those who remained with the local Cork society when a number of members joined the National Association of Operative Plasterers in 1894. The Cork Stonecutters' Society was a local

society which remained independent when the majority of local stone-cutters joined the Operative Stonecutters of Ireland, an Irish amalgamated union set up in the early 1890s.

86 CBSR, 1890: 94/S; *CE*, 17 Aug. 1888, 9, 12 Dec. 1890, 11 Sept. 1891, 14 Aug. 1893.

87 Patrick H. Meade, a confidant of leading Fenians and a leading light in the Young Ireland Society (a Fenian front-group) took a leading part on the Parnellite side in Cork City. Moreover, when Michael Austen, a printer and erstwhile secretary of the trades council, and himself an IRB member, took the anti-Parnellite side, his greatest execrators were to be found among the local ranks of the IRB. CBSR 1891: 9001/S, 2792/S; *CE*, 4 Oct. 1883, 16, 17 Dec. 1890.

88 *CE*, 30 Jan., 20 Feb., 14, 16, 18 Mar., 20, 21, 24, 27, 30 Oct., 4 Nov. 1891. In the 1891 election the Conservative candidate, Captain Sarsfield, though he received a sizeable vote, was really out of the running. The final poll was 3,669 for the Nationalists, and 2,159 for the Parnellites.

89 *CE*, 12 July 1895; *CDH*, 10 July 1895.

90 *CE*, 1, 5, 12 Dec. 1898.

91 *CE*, 18 July 1898.

92 Cork Coopers' Society Minute Books, 24 May 1898.

4

Instruments of Politicisation

To what factors can we attribute the progressive politicisation of the Cork artisans in the course of the nineteenth century? There is no doubt that the personal charisma and organisational drive of Daniel O'Connell in the 1830s and 1840s accelerated what one historian has termed 'the emergence of the habit of democratic politics, and the gradual, uneven and complex transformation of Catholic peasants into citizens and Irishmen'.[1] In Cork, as elsewhere, the personal reputation of O'Connell among the populace had been enhanced by his victory in the Clare election of 1828 and the ensuing measure of Catholic Emancipation, and the popular ballads bawled about the streets proclaimed him to be

> . . . the patron of our isle,
> And the pride of all our nation,
> May heaven propitious on him smile,
> And crown him with salvation.[2]

In the context of Cork City and County, moreover, O'Connell's fame, among the lower classes in particular, was further burnished by his recent activities as counsel for the defence in the so-called Doneraile Conspiracy case.[3] The last-minute arrival of O'Connell at the courthouse, his eloquent defence of the accused, and his ultimate role in their acquittal, formed the stuff of which ballads were made. From that point onwards, not only was the 'counsellor's' reputation enforced as 'the Irishman's shield', but his hero image was now fitted firmly into a local context with which the common people could identify.[4] Thus, when he launched the Repeal campaign in autumn 1830, the Cork artisans responded enthusiastically. O'Connell's obvious political opportunism apparently failed to shake their faith in him, for although he soon ditched Repeal in favour of parliamentary reform, his resurrection of the campaign in late 1832 was greeted by the artisans with as much enthusiasm as if he had never deviated from it. Similarly, when after six years of the Whig Alliance he again resuscitated Repeal in 1841, the Cork trades like their Dublin equivalents immediately rallied round their hero. The hostile Tory press was not slow to point out the apparent political gullibility of the trades, as on the occasion of the visit to Cork in 1835 of the Liberal Lord-Lieutenant Mulgrave:

> The trades marched out full fig to greet
> King Daniel's nominee,
> With symbols, flags, and all things meet
> To welcome such as he . . .
> . . . Stout of limb they all trudged out,
> To meet the favoured man;
> And waved their hats with scream and shout,
> As they were bid by Dan . . .[5]

But, despite appearances, the artisans were not mere puppets controlled by the whim of O'Connell, and his exhortations were an accelerator, not a creator, of Repeal enthusiasm. Ever since the first calls for Repeal in 1830 it was clear that the trades' pro-Repeal motivation was largely materialist and that the experience of economic distress was probably the greatest incentive of all towards political involvement. In his monumental study of the early nineteenth-century English working class, E. P. Thompson summed up the reasons for politicisation thus:

What we can say with confidence is that the artisan *felt* that his status and standard-of-living were under threat or were deteriorating between 1815 and 1840. Technical innovation and the superabundance of cheap labour weakened his position. He had no political rights and the power of the State was used, if only fitfully, to destroy his trade unions . . .Not only did under-pay . . . make for overwork; it also made for *less* work all round. It was this experience which underlay the political radicalization of the artisans . . .[6]

In some ways, this assessment provides a blueprint for explaining the politicisation of the Cork artisans, who shared the belief of many of their contemporaries that Irish economic problems had political roots. They traced these roots directly to 'the accursed . . . the infernal . . . the horrible Union' and were convinced that such economic ills could be remedied only by political solutions. More recent research in British social history would rightly question many of Thompson's conclusions, suggesting that economically-spurred worker politicisation was not so much constant as concentrated in those times when 'the whole social and economic order of the worker was under threat'.[7] In the Irish context, too, the clearest expression of artisan political discontent was heard in times of depression and displacement of traditional skills. This is particularly true of the 1830s and 1840s when the impetus towards political participation by the artisans of Cork was almost entirely economic. Those local trade societies which responded so eagerly in 1830 to the launching of the Repeal campaign were, since the mid-1820s, experiencing a period of severe depression and unemployment.[8] They consequently saw in Repeal the ultimate economic panacea which would 'obtain for Ireland a legislature capable of appreciating her interests and relieving her wants'. This osmosis of the economic with the political partly explains why the artisans so readily accepted O'Connell's frequent U-turns from Repeal to reform and vice versa. For many artisans, indeed, there was no fundamental difference between Repeal, reform and patronage of local manufacture, for they were all aspects of the same long-term objective of economic revival. This overlapping of different means towards the same end was admirably illustrated by the local tailors' society which, in a political demonstration in March 1832, carried 'a large green silk flag on which was seen a bust of William IV and two angels sounding through trumpets into his ears – 'Reform – Repeal'.[9]

Such interweaving of the skilled artisan's political and economic aspirations reached its apogee in the rhetoric surrounding the local manufacture revival campaign of the early 1830s. Determinedly non-political at its inception, this movement could not deflect the artisans from their recourse to the Repeal panacea. At the first public meeting of the revival, nine of the ten platform speakers took pains to avoid any contentious references to the Act of Union. The tenth man, a cotton weaver and representative of a dying trade, spoke of little else. Just as contemporary English weavers were 'haunted by the legend of better days',[10] so, on this occasion, the Corkman's speech exuded a parallel nostalgia, chronicling the decline of the Cork textile industry, the flooding of the local market by English cloth, the cutting of weavers' wages and the destruction of communities. To roars of approval from his audience he spelt out the solution:

> We seek for justice, common justice, and, with the blessing of God we will obtain it. There is but one measure that can give real relief to the country – the Repeal of the Union.[11]

No arguments could dilute this economically-based patriotism. In a pro-revival procession some days later, thirty-nine trades reputedly amounting to five thousand men marched in formation, bearing banners whose imagery reflected the artisan's concepts of patriotism, local pride, trade loyalty and hard-headed economics. The grand banner of the procession epitomised this interweaving of identity, hope and, indeed, political *naïveté*:

> It was an immense sheet on which were beautifully painted the genius of Ireland, standing beside the harp in a finely diversified country. On her right was a poor, gaunt-looking, ragged and famished artisan, to whom she was represented as stretching forth the hand of relief. On her left, considerably above her level, was the genius of plenty, pouring out her cornucopia, the abundance of the earth, for which fertile Ireland is celebrated. This figure pointed with the finger of the right hand to a scroll, which was unfolded over the head of the genius of Ireland, and which contained the words – 'The Revival of Irish Manufacture'.[12]

In the early days of the manufacture revival, such economic patriotism coexisted happily with a determined spirit of loyalty to the crown. The trade-union banners of the period, while devoting most of their political imagery to the support of O'Connell and Repeal, were also intensely proud of their position as loyal subjects of the crown, bearing pictures of William IV and the motto 'God Save the King', while in some cases adding the soubriquet *loyal* to the title of their society. This dual sense of loyal and patriotic identity was further enforced through a variety of twin symbolisms – harp and crown; harp surrounded by a wreath of rose, thistle and shamrock; allegorical figures of England, Ireland and Scotland bearing the Irish ensign and Union Jack; or Erin petitioning Victoria in a gesture redolent of sisterly supplication.[13] Yet, these 'marginal Britons' were soon to move in a more exclusively nationalist direction as manufacture revival euphoria gave way to disillusionment.[14] Scarcely five months after the revival's inception, as it quite clearly failed to achieve its original objectives, artisans' speeches became increasingly anti-English. Even more detached observers shared the trades' growing cynicism, complaining that 'no particular branch of manufacture was revived, nothing substantial done, though a great deal of noise was made'.[15] Thus, manufacture revivalists of all classes, embittered by failure, were drawn almost inevitably to contrast the real or supposed merits of locally produced goods with what they testily described as 'slop English shoes' and English hats which were 'the merest rags and not worth ten shillings'. But there was more to it than that. Even from the beginning of the movement, the speeches of artisan revivalists, in particular, had revealed a latent anti-Englishness which obviously derived from either hearing or reading partisan nationalist accounts of historical events. One such speech, delivered by the typical token artisan at the first manufacture revival meeting in the city in 1832 perfectly epitomised this contradictory combination of historical knowledge and misinterpretation, ending significantly with what appeared to be a direct echo of Emmet's famous speech from the dock:

> No people have ever been so cruelly treated as we have been. Gengis Khan and Temerlane, the great destroyers of the human race, finished their victims at once, and put them out of pain: they did not destroy the industry of unborn generations by

perfidious laws. Witness William III's acts against our woollen
trade, that we so severely feel at this day. British tyranny is worse
than Egyptian bondage. Pharoah ordered the Israelites to make
brick without straw – our taskmasters want taxes without trade
. . . Let our country be ranked once more among the nations
of the earth, and be what nature and nature's God intended it
should be – free and independent.[16]

The press comment that this speaker 'was repeatedly cheered during the delivery of his speech and withdrew amidst long-continued
applause' suggests that his sentiments fell on receptive ears and
that anti-English feeling was not at all difficult to arouse.

Such an anglophobic gut-reaction by a Cork working-class
audience in the early 1830s certainly supports the recent con-
tention of Smyth and Bartlett that popular politicisation was
already well under way, fuelled by a combination of economic
distress and inherited historical myths.[17] Even in this period of
self-conscious loyalty, the trade-union banners hinted at a more
assertive frame of mind, shaped by the belief that Repeal would
expedite the political reincarnation of Grattan's parliament of
1782. In 1832 the painters' banner bore the slogan 'Ireland no
province', the weavers' and woolcombers' banners carried the
promise 'Resurgas – '82', while in 1845 the shipwrights mar-
ried words and symbols to express the same resolve – the Irish
harp surmounted by the imperial crown with the assertion: 'It
was and shall be'.[18] Thus, the ground was already prepared for
the growth of a more clearly articulated militant separatism
among the artisans of the late 1840s. This too, like previous surges
of politicisation since the 1820s, was partly a response to economic
distress. The influx of starving famine refugees from the country areas, the increase in food prices, and the ongoing problem
of unemployment among the trades combined to produce an atmosphere of despair intermingled with anger. Apart from the
testimony of the trades themselves, contemporaries in the late
1840s frequently noted the degree to which, among more distressed craftsmen, customary artisan pride had been suffocated
by on-going hunger. One reporter making his way in early 1847
through the north-side area of Mallow Lane, Clarence Street and
Peacock Lane, noted:

> At every tenth step I took I was met by cravers for bread – men, women and children – tradesmen, in whose breasts the last spark of pride was forever extinguished . . .

while another individual commented on how

> numbers of the poorer classes of tradesmen, from whom he least of all expected applications for relief, had come to him in the last week and told him their families were starving.[19]

While all artisans were not reduced to this level of distress, the rate of unemployment was certainly very high, compounding the problem of spiralling food prices already discussed in chapter 1. Did this experience of extreme distress further the politicisation of the artisans? The only honest answer is that we do not know, handicapped as we are by the dearth of artisan autobiographies, the limitations of newspaper coverage of trade-union activities, and the episodic nature of Dublin Castle's records of the emerging revolutionary movement in the late 1840s. The most that can be said is that economic distress seems to have sharpened political discontent, since it is from the mid-1840s onwards that one meets the increasingly frequent occurrence of seditious utterances like 'To Hell with the Queen' while records suggest a strikingly direct correlation between a trade's unemployment rate and its support for the rising nationalist-democratic movement.[20] The revolutionary Citizens' Club of 1848 was joined by thirty of the forty unionised painters, whose unemployment rate was claimed to be ninety per cent, while the severely distressed paperstainers (only three of whose eighteen members were fully employed in 1846) had twelve representatives in the club.[21]

Similarly, the enthusiasm for Fenianism among the skilled artisans twenty years later reflected, to some extent, the severity of the prevailing economic depression. Pending more detailed research on Cork Fenianism, one must avoid any unqualified attribution of Fenianism to economic downturns. As Takagami has demonstrated for Dublin, the first wave of Fenian expansion in the early 1860s and the third in 1866–67 coincided with a deteriorating economic situation, while the second phase in

1864–65 took place when conditions were improving.[22] Similarly, Comerford sees Fenianism as taking root in a period of economic improvement. His assessment of the movement as embracing many 'smart young wage-earners' of the emerging white-collar sector certainly holds true for Cork City where almost twelve per cent of the brotherhood's membership was drawn from among clerks and shop assistants. But there was also a distinct correlation between strongly pro-Fenian trades and those in which unemployment and low earnings were most common. Coopers and carpenters, well represented in local Fenian ranks, were in considerable distress. The average journeyman cooper's earnings in 1862 were reputedly less than those of many unskilled labourers, while fewer than half the unionised carpenters were at work, both unions emigrating their members to ease the pressure on the employment market. As for the shoemakers who, of all trades, had the highest identified representation in the local Fenian movement, their wretchedness was proverbial: they headed the list of artisans entering the workhouse each year in the mid century, while by the late 1860s the Cork Indigent Roomkeepers' Society, which aided 'respectable mechanics and their families in temporary distress', gave relief to more shoemakers than to any other class of skilled worker.[23]

Such economic distress proved a catalyst for the spread of nationalist politics well into the latter half of the nineteenth century. In 1886 a section of the operative tailors joined the National League *en masse*, declaring in tones reminiscent of the artisan Repealers of the 1830s

> that the consummation of Home Rule, by opening up trade and manufacturing industry, [would] once more and forever restore peace and prosperity to our dear old land.[24]

Yet, as a politiciser, economic distress was a double-edged sword. As Geary concluded in his study of European labour protest, the 'poverty explanation' of protest is not totally satisfactory. While downwardly mobile workers certainly tended to become politically involved in both the British and continental contexts in the 1830s and 1840s, the total destruction of a craft resulted in complete political inertia.[25] Similarly, the Cork experience suggested that while temporary or cyclical distress sharpened the political instincts of the artisan, prolongued or terminal depression completely sapped the political energies of the members of a trade. It was significant that, whereas the city's weavers had responded enthusiastically to the Irish Manufacture campaign of the early 1830s when there still seemed hope of revival, they gave but feeble support to the similar movement of the early 1850s when all hope had disappeared. In the same way, the economic downturn of the early 1880s seriously impeded artisan political involvement, as suggested by the number of local trade societies pleading depression and lack of funds as an excuse for not contributing to the Parnell Defence Fund or joining in pro-Parnell demonstrations.[26] Moreover, there is some evidence to suggest that by the 1880s the political panacea for economic ills was losing its general appeal, and that political solutions to economic ills were seen as last resorts rather than infallible cures. It was significant, for instance, that in 1886 the local tailors were the only trade to collectively join the National League, and that even their naïve hopes of Home Rule were not expressed with the heady excitement of half a century previously, but with the disappointment consequent upon yet another failed manufacture revival movement.[27] The truth was that while artisans might still maintain the façade of unquestioning trust in nationalist solutions to economic ills, behind the scenes they were becoming more hardheaded. Thus, while in 1895 the prominent part taken by the coopers in a local pro-Redmond demonstration apparently confirmed their continuing commitment to nationalism, the entry in their society's minute book reveals a more pragmatic motivation – 'to show up the injustice of the Government in putting on an increased tax on beer and spirits'.[28] A year later, the same disarming pragmatism appeared in the form of a rhyming address presented by local dockyard workers to the Lord of the Admiralty on his visit to the city:

> We care not whether your colours be orange or green,
> We only want work in the name of the Queen.[29]

If artisan nationalism was materially based, so, too, the slow progress of the skilled trades towards the concept of labour

representation on the municipal corporation was equally fuelled
by economic grievance, particularly by the issues of unfair labour
and importation, which caused considerable friction between
trades and local authorities in the last two decades of the century. From as early as 1840, when the Municipal Corporations
Act threw open the hitherto closed corporation to Catholic
middle-class representation, it was clear that collectively, the
trades had considerable reservations regarding the capacity and
will of the reformed corporation to protect the interests of the
skilled artisan.[30] But the suspicions were articulated most clearly during the 1880s when the trades headed their complaints
against the corporation with three major issues: the employment
of non-union or 'unfair' labour in corporation contracts; the use
of imported goods in such contracts; and the corporation's failure
to set up public construction works which would provide employment for tradesmen and labourers in times of depression. All
these issues came together in the debate of 1882 concerning the
provision of municipal buildings for the city. Since the closure
of the Mansion House in the early 1840s Cork had no official
civic centre except the so-called Municipal Buildings on the South
Mall whose unimpressive appearance was seen as undermining
civic pride. The municipal corporation itself was divided on the
matter for some members backed by the local Ratepayers'
Association opposed any expenditure on a new city hall as an
inexcusable extra burden on the city rates, while others insisted
that such a building was a necessity for a city of Cork's size,
and argued that the additional rate load would be justified by
the amount of extra employment provided by the building of
a city hall.[31] The trades, especially those within the depressed
building sector, predictably backed the project, and when it was
defeated in the corporation their resentment mounted. Trades
discontent with the municipal authorities was further fuelled by
the lack of interest shown by many corporation members in the
contemporary manufacture revival movement. To combat this
disinterest, the trades council began a concerted canvas of town
councillors and members of the local harbour board, seeking the
establishment of public works, the demolition of old buildings,
painting of bridges, flagging of streets and building of housing

schemes under the provisions of the Labourers' Act of 1883.[32] The outcome led to even more acrimony between trades and corporation, for although the latter body took sufficient notice of the trades' demands to appoint a special committee to investigate unemployment in the building trade, action went little further. A few paving and painting contracts were given to local employers but this gesture was to a large extent self-defeating since some of the new contractors were employers of unfair labour while others were reputedly given the work solely because of their friendship with members of the city's public boards.[33] Furious at the half-hearted response to their demands, the trades council made its first recorded open outburst against the municipal corporation which it described as

> driv[ing] the trades of Cork into secret societies and organisations if they were not fairly dealt with, and it would ultimately come to that if they did not get fair play . . .[34]

From 1888 to 1896 a veritable stream of complaints went forth from the trades council against importation by the local public boards: imported timber and bricks were used in corporation building works; the plastering contract for the Lunatic Asylum was given to Dublin and London firms; the building of jetties was promised to an English firm; the furniture for the new Court House was imported.[35] The case of the Court House furniture caused the greatest furore. In response to trades' pressure the town council had included in the furnishing and plumbing contracts a clause guaranteeing the use of only locally made work. When it was discovered that the plumbing contract had been given to a Scottish firm, and that many of the large city establishments supplying the furniture had evaded the local manufacture clause, the trades council, plumbers' society and cabinet makers' society were up in arms. The plumbers failed to gain any satisfaction but the cabinet makers went so far as to place pickets on the Court House to watch all furniture deliveries. Indeed, they pressed the corporation so hard that they secured the removal of all imported furniture from the building, and the substitution of locally made items.[36]

In Cork, as in contemporary Dublin, the parallel issue

concerning employment of unfair labour, both in private firms and on public board contracts, further embittered trades–corporation relations. From the mid-1880s onwards, as the trades' tendency to canvas for and against individual town councillors became more frequent, the main criterion upon which candidates were judged was their record, as employers, on the question of fair labour. Since the bakers and tailors were the trades traditionally most affected by the incursions of non-union labour, they were the ones who were most active in pressing the trades council as a body to intervene in the municipal elections and they were strongly backed by those in the building trades who were directly affected by the awarding of public board contracts.[37] From the early 1890s onwards the trades council pushed for a fair labour clause in such contracts but these efforts were no more successful than the drive against importation, for although some successes were recorded, many contracts continued to go, as late as 1898, to contractors who avoided the fair labour clause.[38]

Though economic depression's effectiveness in fuelling artisan nationalism, then, declined with the passage of time, it was still a powerful shaper of trade attitudes at municipal level. Moreover, it remains the background against which one must examine other political catalysts, especially the role of those individuals and social groups whose contact with the artisan classes pushed the latter in the direction of nationalist politics. Just as elsewhere in Europe a well-established middle class was always a prerequisite to drawing the artisanate into the prevailing cultural and political system, so in Cork the greatest political influence came from those above the artisan on the social scale – the substantial middle class and petty bourgeoisie – though as the century passed there was evidence of increased political pressure from white-collar workers and labourers.[39]

The precise influence of the more prosperous mercantile and manufacturing middle class on the artisans is difficult to define. There is no doubt that up to the 1840s city politics in Cork were dominated by this élite or, as John B. O'Brien has more accurately demonstrated, by a dual élite – the Catholic merchant élite determined by wealth, the Protestant one by 'religion, consanguinity and, to a lesser extent, money'.[40] The Municipal

Reform Act of 1840 displaced the Protestant élite's control of local government almost overnight, replacing them by a largely Catholic merchant and retailer-dominated body which remained virtually unchanged until the early twentieth century.[41] Similarly, in the city's parliamentary representation Catholic merchant domination had been ensured since the election of 1832 when the Catholic Daniel Callaghan took over the parliamentary seat previously held by his Protestant brother, Gerard. From that date onwards, although Protestants and non-businessmen periodically represented the city in parliament, the generality of MPs were Catholic merchants and manufacturers.[42] But while merchants and large manufacturers thus dominated the Cork political scene in the course of the nineteenth century, their direct influence on the artisans is difficult to assess, since there was relatively little immediate contact between them. This was true on both sides of the religious divide. Among Protestants there was little connection between the merchants and businessmen of the Masonic Lodges on the one hand and the largely lower-middle-class Orange Lodges and lower-class Protestant Operative Association on the other.[43] On the Catholic side there was just as little, or perhaps even less, contact between the merchant élite of the Chamber of Commerce and their humbler co-religionists, since their majority status precluded even that limited solidarity manifested by Protestants as an increasingly beleaguered minority. Residential segregation, while not absolute, increased progressively from the late eighteenth century onwards. Indeed, as Ian d'Alton has suggested, although the city was becoming ever more politically divided along religious lines, any ghettoisation was economically based. Poor Catholics and poor Protestants lived crowded together in the low-lying central areas, ensuring that the suburbanised merchants had little routine contact with the artisan who lived in the city centre or peripheral working-class areas.[44]

On the other hand, as in the case of many urban centres in the British Isles, there was at political level a degree of intimacy (not always harmonious) between economic and political élite on the one hand and the lower class on the other. Such intimacy was possible where population increase had not yet conferred

anonymity on the individual and where the mutualities of a traditional production system had not yet been eliminated by the
development of large-scale business enterprises.[45] In such urban
centres, where there existed 'a frame of reference of shared gossip
and of intimate knowledge of the manners and foibles of even
minor participants in public affairs', private matters soon became
common knowledge.[46] Cork was no exception: its population
was relatively small, its politics local and inward-looking, and
its populace noted for their cutting wit. One visitor to the city
in 1843 described Corkmen as

> Rather sharp. They like to make themselves merry at other peo-
> ple's expense, and are distinguished from all the other Irish by
> a peculiar, keen, ironical humour. They soon discover anyone's
> weak side, and are merciless in the use of their keen but cutting
> sarcasms.[47]

This characteristic came across clearly in the cross-chat when
élite and plebeians were thrown together at election time,
nameless members of the mob exchanging witticisms with candidates and their genteel backers, and, in the process whimsically
described by Hoppen as 'digging out the dirt', the foibles of the
platform speakers being ruthlessly exposed by the cat-calls of
smart alecs in the gallery.[48]

Moreover, platform speakers from the upper middle class,
despite their vulnerability to the wits in the crowd, had considerable
political influence. The artisans and working men who attended
public meetings took away with them some of the sentiments ut-
tered from the platform, and modelled their own occasional public
speeches directly on those of their social superiors. A literate and
newspaper-reading public, considered by Weber as an essential
catalyst to politicisation in nineteenth-century France, was no less
vital in popular politicisation in Cork, but before the 1850s the
newspaper was outside the purchasing capacity of the average artisan. This is why public meetings were such a vital instrument
of politicisation, regarded as they were by contemporaries as the
poor man's substitute for newspapers.[49] It was precisely on these
grounds that in 1832 the local radical, Thomas Sheahan, defended
the holding of large-scale public meetings:

Newspapers are too high-priced for the great mass of our people
to read them – it is therefore, only through the instrumentality
of such meetings . . . that they can be taught what is beneficial
to them, and instructed how to attain it.[50]

It was, however, the combination of press and public meeting
which proved the most effective politiciser, the speeches delivered
at one day's meeting being reported *ad nauseam* and practically
verbatim in the local press of the following day. It is even more
difficult to determine who read the press reports than to discover
who attended the public meetings, but although high newspaper
prices and widespread illiteracy might dilute the political influence
of the pre-famine newspaper, the politically interested working
man found in the numerous reading rooms of the city at least
some opportunity to follow the proceedings of the previous day's
meeting at second hand.[51] The increasing capacity of the public
to widen its horizons through reading, and the response of
authorities, entrepreneurs and press to this phenomenon, was
reflected in a number of ways. The number of newsagents' shops
appearing in local trade directories quadrupled over the last three
decades of the century, while in the early 1890s a free public lending library and newsroom opened and a new evening newspaper,
the *Evening Echo*, was launched, soon being recognised as the
'working-man's paper'.[52] As the century passed, moreover,
newspaper prices fell, while literacy rates in the city rose from
just under sixty-five per cent in the 1850s to over eighty-four
per cent by the late 1890s.[53] Consequently, press reports of
political speeches made at public meetings became even more
accessible to a constantly widening reading public. Although this
in itself detracted from the public meeting's role as sole politiciser
of working people, it also increased the capacity of platform
speaker's ideas to reach a wider social spectrum through the
medium of a cheap press. Certainly, right through the century
and beyond, artisans and working men continued to pour into
public meetings which, like that in support of an amnesty for
Fenian prisoners in October 1873, could muster an attendance
of up to ten thousand. Though this level of attendance was not
always reached, it was indicative of the popular attraction of
public meetings that when meeting organisers wanted to ensure

peaceful proceedings, they limited admission to ticket-holders only.[54]

If the political impact of the public meeting was considerable, the most immediate political influence on the artisan was exercised by those only marginally above him on the social scale – master craftsmen, shopkeepers, pawnbrokers and publicans – that 'class above the masses' which, as Foster expressed it, 'had (or might think it had) some stake in the system', and saw itself as epitomising that most Victorian of qualities, respectability.[55] The average journeyman had a close and constant relationship with these 'men in the middle', among whom he numbered not just his employer, but also his immediate landlord, his local publican, the shopkeeper with whom he often operated on a credit basis, and the pawnbroker on whom in hard times he depended for survival.[56] Hoppen has noted the country-wide political power of these pawnbrokers, many themselves voters, whose economic interaction with the lower classes enabled them to control votes and organise the mobs which proved such a vital force in elections. In Cork City the pawnbrokers were prominent in politics, backing the radical People's Hall in the 1830s, forming the backbone of the Anti-Ministers' Money campaign of the late 1840s, and providing much of the impetus for successive burgess associations in the city from the mid century onwards.[57]

The relationship between urban landlord and tenant, too, had considerable implications for the political harnessing of artisans and working men. This relationship between landlord and enfranchised or politically conscious tenant was the source of much controversy in nineteenth-century Ireland. In the 1840s the rural landlord was, of course, given a very bad image by the O'Connellite press and popular orators. Not alone was he branded as a tyrant who made leases dependent on political conformity at election time, but even his subsidised emigration schemes earned him the description of 'an exterminator . . . freighting his ships and sending off the people to America.'[58] By the 1880s the rhetoric had hardly changed, as local Land Leaguers thundered against 'the evicting and cruel-hearted landlord' and made considerable political capital from landlord pressure on rural electors.[59] Yet, it was significant, particularly in the earlier decades, that while popular politicians in the city roundly condemned such political pressure when exerted by Tory landlords on rural tenants, they were quite willing to accept it as the natural order of things when exercised on behalf of the popular side in the urban context. The fact of the matter was that urban landlords, too, just as in British centres, had considerable clout, particularly before the rise of mass politics and the passing of the Ballot Act of 1872 conferred a certain degree of protective anonymity on the individual voter. Thus in the Cork City election of 1832 two minor distillers on the popular side claimed, with no apparent sense of embarassment, to have secured a Repeal pledge from sixty-eight of their city tenants, while in 1848 a pawnbroker-landlord on the city's north side apparently recruited his tenants into the Confederate Club of which he was president.[60]

From the mid nineteenth century onwards, as Garvin points out, many political movements in Europe were dominated by 'relatively well-educated men from the middle reaches of society, and mainly from the lower middle class.'[61] This, hardly surprisingly, is equally applicable in the case of nineteenth-century Cork where, apart from the political control they incidentally exercised in their capacity as employers and landlords, the petty bourgeois groups played a considerable role in shaping and managing those local political and socio-economic movements evolving from the 1830s onwards.[62] This was particularly evident in the successive manufacture revival movements between 1830 and 1850 in which small manufacturers, retailers and pawnbrokers took the most prominent part. In the same period, radical local political bodies – the Cork Trades' Association and its offshoot, the People's Hall – were dominated by the same groups.[63] Indeed, the political importance of these latter two bodies for the politicisation of the artisan must be stressed, for it was through contact with and manipulation by their disgruntled petty bourgeois leadership that local artisans, hitherto organised politically only under their respective trade-union banners, joined the political mainstream.[64] While these ostensibly radical associations really derived from a petty local power struggle between rival middle-class interest groups, their rhetoric was couched in terms of democratic principle, promising to 'bring the honest elector and the unrepresented thousands together' and to 'secure for every man . . . his rights as a citizen'. Although artisans joining these bodies were virtually dragooned into a conflict which did not really concern them, the diet of democratic ideas on which they were fed – no matter how indigestible – inadvertently sharpened their awareness of wider political issues.[65] Thus, through political leadership combined with an element of social control, the lower middle class accelerated the artisan's progress towards political involvement.

It was possibly within the workplace that the artisan was most susceptible to the political clout of his social betters. In a period when the employed artisan spent at least ten of the twenty-four hours of each day, and six-and-a-half days of each week at work, the employment milieu inevitably helped to shape political attitudes. Studies of individual industrial towns in contemporary Britain have revealed just how powerful was the political influence of the large employer, particularly in the factory setting.[66] In Ireland the political influence of employers must also be considered vital, as in the case of Limerick's James Spaight in the 1850s and Dublin's Sir A. E. Guinness in the 1870s. In the Cork context, too, there is some evidence of direct political pressure by the business élite, particularly in the first half of the nineteenth century, though whether in the form of influence or coercion is now difficult to decide. The conservative *Cork Constitution* in 1840 accused the larger O'Connellite firms of stopping money from employees' wages for the O'Connell Tribute, while in 1859 the same paper approvingly recorded the presence in the polling booths of the proprietors of many of the city's 'first establishments'.[67] That direct references to large employer influence in the political sphere are not more frequent in the Cork context may be due to the fact that merchants and larger manufacturers could often be quite remote from their workers. Firstly, the sheer size of a large workforce precluded frequent contact between employees and employer. Secondly, in the case of provision and butter merchants in particular, a large proportion of the workforce was employed on a subcontracting basis by carriers and master coopers, which meant erecting a buffer between merchant and workers. Thirdly, in some cases employer and workers were of different religious persuasions, eliminating a potentially vital link between them.[68] It seems, in fact, that employer influence in Cork may well have been exercised less by the really big businessmen than by those of the middle or lower grades, if only (as the introduction to this work has suggested) because the greater number of skilled artisans in the city worked in the small workshop milieu rather than in that of the large firm. Such a middle grade or small employer was likely to be a working master craftsman (or, in some cases, his widow) employing anything up to forty workers, but usually fewer than a dozen.[69] The close contact between employer and worker in such conditions certainly facilitated political control in various forms. During the Repeal campaign of the 1830s, for instance, the O'Connell Tribute was more frequently collected by the small master in the workplace than by the extensive employers, though to what extent such contributions were voluntary or forced is not now clear. The small employer could also exercise substantial control over the votes of those who worked for him. The paucity of references to this phenomenon is probably due less to its infrequency than to the fact that it was considered too usual to merit attention. The Select Committee on Fictitious Votes in 1837 was told of one voter who had always voted Conservative while employed by a local jeweller who supported the local Conservative side. The only reason this fact was noted was that in the election of 1837 he had transferred his allegiance to the popular side, consequently losing the annuity of eight pounds which his employer had allowed him on going out of business.[70] The early militant separatist movement showed the same syndrome of employer influence, some local Confederate Clubs in 1848 being led by the employers of those forming the rank and file, the Hegarty Brothers, extensive tanners, typically heading the Wolfe Tone Club in which the tanyard porters and clerks predominated.[71] Such paternalistic control of workers certainly survived into the 1850s when one of the biggest employers in the local cabinet making trade recruited fifty-two of his employees into the local manufacture revival movement and to further the cause committed each one (by what means we know not) to buying a winter coat of local manufacture.[72]

For the artisan, however, the politicisation process in the work context was ultimately less a matter of control by one's superiors than of contact with one's peers, the social contacts of the workplace playing a vital part in shaping political ideas. Just as in British cities, where factory workers pressurised each other politically and the social contacts and 'solidarities of craft and workshop' enforced a cohesive political consciousness among artisans, so in the Cork context strong political pressure was exerted by workers upon one another in their place of employment.[73] The widespread espousal of Fenianism by working men in the 1860s, for instance, was considerably influenced by the nature of the workplace. The factory or large workshop in which was concentrated a large workforce was considered by contemporaries to be the real breeding ground of Fenianism, and surviving lists of Fenian suspects in Cork City suggest that, just as Takagami found in the Dublin context, this was indeed the case. The tobacco twisters, shipwrights and engineering workers, who together accounted for sixty-seven of the 166 Cork Fenians identified by Dublin Castle, all worked in such large establishments. In the Ballincollig area, some five miles west of the city, at least thirteen of the twenty-six listed Fenian suspects worked in the gunpowder mills, while the degree of Fenian involvement of the brewery workers was evident when, on the morning following the abortive rising of March 1867, scarcely half the employees of Murphy's Brewery arrived at work, having secretly left the city on the previous night in order to initiate the rebellion in the countryside.[74]

Even more importantly, the nationalist identity of the individual artisan was both assumed and enforced through his membership of a craft. This was particularly true in the first stages of politicisation in the early 1830s when the craft was to all intents the only framework of organisation available to the artisan. Alternative channels of politicisation became available over the following two decades – the Protestant Operative Association for loyalists, the Repeal Association for O'Connellites, and (as will be discussed later) incidental politicisers such as temperance and mortality societies and musical bands. But in the early 1830s, because of the minimal opportunity available to working-class individuals to make their mark publicly, and because of the skilled man's close identity with his craft, the artisan tended to operate politically under the umbrella of the trade. The consequently vital role of the trade union as politiciser was obvious to artisans and public men alike. When in 1832 O'Connell sought to transform Cork's local manufacture revival movement into a pro-Repeal campaign, he did so by appealing first to the trade societies, and he repeated the performance in 1842. This was an eminently sensible move, since the trades saw themselves as having a distinctive collective role not only in the economic sphere but also increasingly in the political domain – a collective role which they jealously guarded from internal fragmentation. Just as the trade societies closed ranks to enforce the union code in the area of wages and working conditions, it attempted to enforce similar uniformity on the political activities of its members. Such attempted control was facilitated by the restricted nature of the contemporary franchise which put individual voters under extreme pressure from the group as a whole. Thus in the 1830s when it was calculated that scarcely one in ten of the city's artisans were enfranchised, the individual's vote was not his own but was, in contemporary radical terminology of public accountability, 'held in trust for the good of the people'.[75] In such a context, the trade society exerted immeasurable pressure on the voters in its ranks, closely monitoring individuals to prevent any breaking of ranks or, where it did occur, punishing it accordingly. Thus, in the election of 1832 society secretaries took it upon themselves to pledge individual members' votes in support of the popular side so that early in the election campaign twenty-five trades had pledged themselves in favour of the O'Connellite candidates, and some twenty-five other trades were to be persuaded to do likewise, while three nailors who refused to vote in conformity with society directives were ostracised by the rest of their society. Similar shaping and monitoring of individual members' political action by a trade society was obvious in 1845. In the case of half the trade societies marching in the Repeal procession of that year, political affiliation was apparently interwoven with union membership, each individual artisan either wearing the Repeal button or carrying the associate membership card of the Repeal Association. On this occasion, moreover, a section of the tinplate workers' society was condemned by the liberal press for refusing to march in the demonstration, the relevant information being almost certainly passed on to the newspaper from sources within the men's union.[76]

Such claustrophobic political control within the trade hardly outlived the 1840s. The reasons for this decline of trade political control are impossible to pinpoint, but they may be traced to the shaking of political certainties with the fragmentation of the popular side during the O'Connellite-Young Ireland controversy of the mid-1840s. The political unanimity of the trade had certainly broken down by the late 1840s, and it was only with difficulty that these differences were patched up. Yet, despite this fragmentation of the trade society's political identity, it still remained the only real contact point between artisans and public men. It was significant, therefore, that in 1848, the local Irish Confederates, in the absence of any trades council with whom they could parley, took trouble to make contact with the various trade societies via individual society members.[77] A similar link between occupation and political recruitment was evident in 1848 when some of the revolutionary Confederate Clubs in the city were apparently established within particular trades and occupations. Tanyard porters predominated in the north-side Wolfe Tone Club, the mercantile assistants had their own club, and there are some indications that the Glanmire-based Confederate Club recruited most of its members from among the local shipwrights.[78] The distinct political role and potential of the trade society was still a reality in the early 1860s, when the local Fenian organisers of the 1861 McManus funeral first publicly recruited working-class support by contacting the trade society representatives, and certain trades like the coopers and tailors became closely identified with the underground republican movement.[79]

Even more significant was the way in which politicisation was interwoven with working-class amusements. One can hardly stress too much the importance of such popular social activity as shaper of popular political identities since, even more than employer and workmate influence, it helped to forge a set of common political loyalties irrespective of class distinctions. As Joyce expressed it in his study of nineteenth-century Blackburn,

> when leisure life outside work is considered, what becomes apparent is not only that work-derived status differences operated within a broad shared culture, but also that these differences were very often muted, often completely unrecognised in the hours outside work.[80]

Similarly, in the context of mid-nineteenth century Ireland, that feature so aptly described by Comerford as 'patriotism as pastime' helped to spread nationalist ideas and sympathies throughout a large spectrum of working people from different localities and occupational backgrounds. So closely intermeshed did the social and political become that not alone was politicisation accelerated by popular social activities, but social life was itself politicised.[81] Paramount in this regard was the public house, the 'primary focus of a great deal of working-class institutional life' and the main indoor place of amusement for artisan and labourer, which in the 1860s was the principal venue for Fenian meetings and recruitment.[82] It was in the public house that two major forces for politicisation converged. The first was the influence of the individual publican who, together with master tradesmen and retailers, formed part of the petty bourgeois group already prominent in local politics. Publicans in Ireland, as Hoppen has demonstrated, were 'one of the most powerful and permanent pressure groups in the country'. Functioning not only as suppliers of liquid refreshment but, more vitally, as moneylenders to master tradesmen unable to pay their men, and as paymasters to the dockland workers, they had considerable economic influence which was easily translated into political clout. Predominantly Catholic and nationalist, they thus served at election time as moneyholders, brokers between voters and candidates, and commanders of votes.[83] Apart from their very strong nationalistic inclinations, the fact that publicans worked on their own premises gave them considerable opportunities for subversion. In 1865 three of the six Fenian 'centres' in the city were publicans whose premises were used for meetings of the brotherhood, and by 1870 they were recognised by the authorities as doing 'more to foster sedition and encourage disloyalty than any other section of the community'.[84]

In the context of nineteenth-century English artisan culture, the public house and workshop were mutually 'reflected images', together acting as 'twin streams feeding the same collective values and beliefs', generally shaping and reflecting the ethos of popular Toryism, but at times of political excitement providing a milieu for group reading of radical and seditious newspapers.[85] This role of the public house as breeding ground for collective politicisation was replicated in the Irish milieu. If the main pub-related politiciser was the individual publican, the second major politicising force was the spirit of camaraderie (easily channelled in a nationalist direction) fostered by the mellowing effects of alcohol and the singing of patriotic songs. In Dublin, Cork and centres in between, as Comerford concluded, 'public-house conviviality was part of the very fabric of Fenianism'. But there is evidence that the Fenians were not the first to mix porter and patriotism. The interweaving of sedition and convivial drinking long preceded the Fenian period, the singing of revolutionary songs in public houses in 1804 being reported from the northern town of Newry. In the 1820s and 1830s the singing of seditious ballads by the 'peasantry in their sheebeen haunts' was noted from places as far apart as Cork and Sligo, while in 1843 the authorities rightly saw the public house milieu as vital in fostering enthusiasm for the Repeal movement.[86] The importance of the public house was that, even more than the large factory, it acted as a melting pot where different grades of working men rubbed shoulders and where political ideas spread. It was, moreover, interwoven in working-class society with public leisure and outdoor Sunday pursuits. The blurring of demarcation lines between country and town ensured that many of the pastimes of the urban lower classes were rurally based. Just as in early nineteenth-century England, the industrial town 'did not so much displace the countryside as grow *over* it', 'and retained rather more of the village than it acquired of the city', so in contemporary Cork, whose centre was little over a mile from the open fields, and much of whose population had rural roots, a great deal of working mens' leisure time was spent in the countryside.[87] Such outdoor leisure, with devotees across the entire spectrum of the working and lower middle class, provided not only the opportunity for mixing socially with individuals other than one's immediate workmates and neighbours, but also the facility for political fraternisation. Throughout Leinster and Munster in the 1860s and after, coursing, horseracing, football and boxing served as blinds for Fenian activities. This is reflected in the immediate hinterland of Cork City, where walking, bowling, ballgames and following the harriers provided a perfect cover for surreptitious drilling and military manoeuvres. Most importantly, all these pursuits ended up at evening time in the public house where the process of politicisation through conviviality was renewed.[88]

Other social milieux which certainly provided opportunities for fraternisation between working men and others were the various mortality and temperance societies and the musical bands proliferating in the city from the 1840s onwards. The original purpose of the mortality societies was, of course, totally unconnected with politics. They provided, rather, as a recent study on the subject has shown, 'a way in which the poor and potentially poor could save themselves from destitution'. To this end, individual members subscribed between a penny and tenpence per week towards funeral expenses and sometimes sick benefit. While by the end of the century such societies included a wide social spectrum in their ranks, the earlier bodies, like their English counterparts, were established specifically for the poorest classes and for those workers who had no recourse to a trade-union mortality fund. Thus, as 'one of the more important focal points for popular and especially urban social life in the nineteenth and early twentieth centuries', they provided a contact point for labouring men and artisans who were either outside trade-union ranks or whose union funds could not stretch to the expense of a funeral.[89] In this way, they bolstered the ethos of collectivism and mutuality among their members in a manner which both crossed occupational divides and established a certain lower-class cohesion.[90] Temperance societies, three of which had already existed in the city in the 1830s, became increasingly common in the 1840s when Fr Theobald Mathew's Temperance Movement swept all before it in a dramatic if transient war on drink.[91] Even when this early movement ground to a halt, temperance societies continued to be established, primarily in working-class districts, but because their membership was representative of all social classes, they provided opportunities for regular fraternisation between working men of diverse backgrounds. In addition, while the temperance and mortality societies were totally non-political in their original objectives, in times of high political excitement they became inextricably identified with popular nationalism. Though Fr Mathew had demanded a strict political neutrality from temperance societies, he was powerless to prevent O'Connell from capturing the crusade as an adjunct to his Repeal campaign, and by the early 1840s there was a close connection between the two movements. Moreover, the considerable overlapping of membership and close social contact between the trade societies and the Temperance Movement ensured that the politicisation of the artisan was now reinforced from two directions. So prominent a part was taken by temperance societies in the Repeal demonstrations of the 1840s in Cork, as elsewhere, that they were seen by the authorities as rivalling the public house in their role of popular politicisers, while in the 'Fenian years' of the early 1860s, temperance societies country-wide held meetings which were apparently 'more political than temperance'.[92]

Directly linked with the Temperance Movement was that other incidental but potent source of politicisation through socialising – the working-class musical band. Most bands of this sort were direct offshoots of the temperance societies, while others were linked with certain trade societies or associated with a particular city locality or place of employment. These bands were, to some extent, the musical embodiment of inter-locality rivalry, which at times degenerated into physical confrontations in which instruments were broken, windows smashed, and supporters subsequently appeared before the police court on charges of disorderly behaviour.[93] But the musical bands were distinguished by more than localism rooted in a particular urban setting: they were also noted, from the 1840s onwards, for their close identification with popular nationalism, when they became an essential feature of all local nationalist demonstrations of both the constitutional and militant traditions. They took a prominent part in the O'Connell Anniversary demonstration of 1875, the campaign in support of Fenian Amnesty in the 1870s, in the inevitable Fenian funerals, in demonstrations supporting the National League, and in the annual November commemorations of the Manchester Martyrs, which were backed by the underground republican element in their efforts to perpetuate and enforce latent popular militant nationalism.[94] Moreover, when the bitter Parnellite split of 1890 occurred, its divisive effects were filtered down to working-class level not only through press and clerical pronouncements but also through these highly politicised musical bands.[95] First splitting internally, as did almost every public body, different bands then identified with one or other faction and, overlaying their traditional localism with party loyalties, they continued the quarrel into the new century when they frequently beat each other to a pulp over the merits of their respective heroes.[96]

As these disputes between the bands suggest, much of this process of politicisation through pastime tended to foster an unthinking commitment to popular causes within a very wide sector of the working-class population. Within narrower circles, however, a more ordered (if no less partisan) politicisation was cultivated by those avowedly political organisations periodically established in pursuit of various nationalist objectives. From the 1830s onwards such organisations, no matter how divergent their aims, had one feature in common: they helped to politicise the more 'respectable' working men by harnessing their penchant for self-education. This was attempted largely through the medium of the reading room where, either gratis or for a nominal membership fee, the motivated working man could have access to newspapers, periodicals, books and lectures tailored to steer him in the 'correct' political direction. Reading rooms in smaller towns tended to be cautiously liberal and to depend on the benevolence of local grandees.[97] Those in Cork City, on the other hand, while dependent to a considerable extent on the contributions and goodwill of sympathetic middle-class individuals, were strongly O'Connellite. In 1845, under the aegis of the Repeal Association, reading rooms were set up in each city ward, some in liberal club-houses, others in rented rooms and in private houses. The reading rooms were open to penny subscribers who could then have access to such suitable literature as the liberal *Cork Examiner*, the reports of the Repeal Association, *Memoirs of Grattan*, Daniel O'Connell's *Memoir of Ireland*, and Dr Robert Kane's *Industrial Resources of Ireland*.[98] Two years later, in the heady days of Young Ireland, the local Desmond Club sought to propagate the romantically nationalist teachings and philosophy of Thomas Davis and the *Nation* by the same means. Its reading room was well stocked with local, national and some London newspapers and periodicals, and was the venue for classes in the Irish language, readings from the speeches of contemporary and former political figures, and lectures on such appropriate subjects as manufacture revival, early Irish society, the life and character of Wolfe Tone, the ballad poetry of Ireland, and (most telling of all) 'Our present liberty as a result of 'Ninety-Eight'.[99] In view of such lecture content, it required only a minor transition when militancy increased and a rash of similar clubs appeared in the spring of 1848 for the lectures on Irish history and culture to give way to military discussions and rifle drilling.[100]

The same interweaving of working class self-education and politicisation – or perhaps in this case self-education as a cloak for subversion – was apparent in the separatist movement of the 1860s, when the Cork National Reading Room provided not just a meeting place and library but also the main focus of Fenian organisation in the city.[101] As in the case of the romantic nationalist movements of the 1840s, this partly educational role was probably less important in its own right than as the precursor of more militant nationalism. Thus, when, at some unknown date in the late 1860s, the National Reading Room ceased to operate, its place was filled by the Cork Working Men's Association. The different style of title was not simply coincidental, for while the later organisation naturally shared its predecessor's commitment to separatist nationalism, it showed no recorded interest in culture but directed its energies towards social amelioration. It thus operated as a legitimate friendly and benefit society (which, as suggested earlier, was in its own right a typical politicisation instrument), and was involved for a time in the attempted unionisation of dockside workers and agricultural labourers. More importantly from the political viewpoint, it was an open secret in the city that the association was also a Fenian front-group and that its rooms were used as an arms depot.[102] The Cork Working Men's leading members were all active Fenians. The association co-operated briefly in the early 1870s with the English Agricultural Labourers' Union, which was attempting to organise in Ireland.

These small political subversive associations, perhaps even more than the considerably larger organisations of the Repeal and Home Rule tradition, enabled working men to politicise one another. Firstly, they allowed the individual working man to interact with a small committed group of like-minded individuals representative of many strata of the lower-middle and working classes. In summer 1848 the city's seventeen Confederate Clubs, with an estimated total membership of over four thousand, had facilitated such social and political interaction between skilled artisans, clerks, shop assistants, labourers, dealers, and publicans,[103] while the National Reading Room and Cork Working Men's Association of two decades later had the same social profile, but with a larger contingent of unskilled workers in the latter body.[104]

It was not just the social mix of the membership, but also the changing nature of the leadership of political organisations which suggests that, as the century passed the politicisation of artisans was becoming less dependent on the middle class than on those lower on the social scale. The changing nature of leadership, however, applies more to organisations connected with the militant separatist movement than with those of the constitutional tradition.[105] In the latter case, just as middle-class individuals had led the Repeal Movement of the 1830s and 1840s, they continued into the latter half of the century to dominate not only local government, but also the Home Rule Movement and the urban branches of the Land League.[106] In the militant nationalist movement of the late 1850s onwards, however, the leadership of the upper middle classes was noticeable by its absence. In Cork, as in other towns, this trend had already begun during the Young Ireland period of the late 1840s when the solid merchant leadership associated with the Repeal Movement gave way to that of a small (and unrepresentative) group of younger middle-class men, some university educated and all intellectually committed to a romantic nationalist vision cultivated by the *Nation* newspaper and greatly influenced by contemporary revolutionary events in France. Their posturings as *déclassé* leaders of the discontented masses proved short-lived as, following the fiasco of 1848, they immediately retreated back into respectablity and moderation.[107] While this U-turn was of little concern to the vast majority of the population, it did give rise within a very narrow circle of more extreme nationalists to a deep distrust of middle-class leadership – a phenomenon equally apparent in the experience of French and German worker radicals after the mid century.[108] This distrust was clearly articulated by the little-known and short-lived Irish Democratic Association which, founded in 1849, sought to propogate its ideals through the *Irishman* newspaper. With branches in several Irish and English centres, its pathetically small membership composed mainly of artisans, labourers, clerks and shop assistants, denounced the middle-class leaders of 1848 as 'a cautious, dodging pack of wretches'.[109] The Cork branch, whose membership of scarcely one hundred contrasted starkly with the reputed four thousand strong Confederate Clubs of the previous years, was ignored equally by trade unions, respectable middle classes and local press, and passed into oblivion when the *Irishman* newspaper collapsed in 1850.[110] Yet, its long-term significance must not be underestimated. Just as studies of British working-class development have revealed the importance of individual local leaders in spreading radical ideas and labour consciousness, and writers on Irish nationalism have similarly stressed the role of influential individuals in perpetuating the militant Irish nationalist tradition – 'a few men faithful and a deathless dream' – so the Irish Democratic Association formed the bridge across which nationalist activists carried their legacy from the faltering revolutionary movement of 1848 to the more tenacious Irish Republican Brotherhood of later decades.[111] Among these individuals was William O'Carroll, a master baker who had been active in the Wolfe Tone Club of 1848, and who was a 'centre' in the Cork Fenian Movement until, becoming bankrupt, he emigrated to Australia in 1862. Another was James Mountaine, a shoemaker, who had been active in 1848. Arrested and later acquitted due to lack of evidence against him, he then joined the local branch of the Irish Democratic Association. By the 1860s he had risen to become proprietor of a boot-trimming shop, and though there was never sufficient evidence to secure his conviction, he was correctly regarded by the authorities as 'a dangerous man, well-informed on any Fenian subject'. Similarly, Brian Dillon, 'Head Centre' of the Cork Fenians in 1865, had also been a member of the Irish Democratic Association.[112] In like manner, a later generation of committed individuals provided the essential link between the men of 1867 and the resuscitated Irish Republican Brotherhood of the 1890s. The builder, C. G. Doran, who had joined the Dublin Fenians in 1865 and organised the movement in Tipperary and Kerry, came to the Cork area in the early 1870s as part of the party working on the Queenstown cathedral. From then until the end of the century he was closely involved in the underground movement, being described by Dublin Castle intelligence in 1890 as 'the most ardent Fenian in the south of Ireland'.[113] Similar links through time were provided by individuals whose Fenian links were never proven, but whose behaviour rouses the suspicion of today's historian no less than it did that of the contemporary Castle authorities. The most long-lived of these was Cornelius P. O'Sullivan, master cooper and publican, who appeared in every Fenian-linked operation from the 1860s to 1900. He took part in the Manchester Martyrs' demonstration of December 1867, in the Amnesty campaign of 1873, and in every Fenian funeral from the early 1870s onwards; he was an organiser of the Fenian-linked Cork Working Men's Association of the early 1870s when he and others helped foment considerable unrest among the city's unskilled workers, was active in the attempt to have John Mitchel elected for Cork in 1874, defended IRB arms raids in 1880, took the Parnellite side in the split of 1890, and, as a Labour candidate in the local government elections of 1899, staged a campaign in which much of the rhetoric was more republican than Labourist.[114]

These individuals not only provided an element of continuity in underground local republicanism, but also illustrated how the direction of militant nationalism had passed from the hands of the upper middle classes, who had been dominant in the late 1840s. Leadership now rested with petty bourgeois representatives like publicans and retailers who, as suggested earlier, had been pushing into local politics since the 1830s, and who had such close contact with artisans and working men in the course of the daily round. The underground republican movement of the 1860s and 1870s, did, it is true, shake this petty bourgeois mould of local politics, by facilitating within its ranks leadership by individuals from a fairly humble social stratum. The Castle's distinction between 'respectable' and 'low' Fenians in Cork revealed the social mix within a movement whose most notable feature was its levelling of class and occupational barriers among its active members. In this period, in fact, as Takagami has also found in Dublin, the structure of the Fenian organisation and of its small cover groups allowed men of lowly social status to hold authority over others who, outside the brotherhood, would have been considered their social superiors. Thus, two labourers held high positions among the Ballincollig Fenians and a grocers' porter had considerable influence among the Fenians of the city, while in the Cork Working Men's Association of the 1870s it was not only the rank and file who were described as 'mostly quay porters and unskilled working men' but the leadership, too, included a number of individuals of equally humble social status.[115] However, towards the end of the century, as Garvin has pointed out, the resuscitated IRB was largely taken over by the 'relatively well-educated men from the middle reaches of society'. Although it still preserved its former capacity to accommodate men of more humble social status in places of influence, these were really not, as is evident in the case of C. P. O'Sullivan and C. G. Doran, 'men of no property'. Equally typical of well-heeled local IRB leadership in the 1890s were John Slattery, influential president of the Cattle Buyers' Association, and P. H. Meade, originally the son of a working cooper but now owner of three pawnshops and other city property to the total value of five thousand pounds.[116]

Thus the evolution of republican leadership at local level fitted into the general trend of nineteenth-century local politics to accommodate 'the class above the masses'. There was a sense in which the artisans were pushed from centre stage as the local National Foresters and the 'Ninety-Eight committee were progressively infiltrated by the republican underground movement, but for this precise reason the politicisation network became more complex and, perhaps, more effective. The public sphere of the artisan became less exclusive as he came to rub shoulders politically and socially not only with the inevitable labourers, clerks, shop assistants and substantial retailers, but also with the teachers and civil servants, who were such an essential part of the new nationalism of the late nineteenth century.[117]

In the Cork context, then, the process of artisan politicisation was achieved through a complex interweaving of economic, social, emotional and personal influences. Most of this politicisation process was obviously in the direction of nationalism, either militant, constitutional, or – more frequently – an ill-defined amalgam of the two. The strength of this emotional attachment to nationalism was clearly articulated in 1890 by the Cork trades council representative, Michael Austen, at the first conference in Dublin of the Irish Democratic Trade and Labour Federation. Contributing to a heated exchange on the relative claims of class and nation, Austen came down strongly on the side of nationalism.

> One of the essential characteristics of every Irishman should be his nationality. While every man present was a working man, and was most desirous of forwarding the cause of the working classes, it was, beyond doubt, a fact that wherever a workman was to be found, the country which gave him birth stood foremost.[118]

Whatever the exaggeration in Austen's statement, there was no doubt about the powerfully emotive hold of nationalism on the artisan of late nineteenth-century Ireland. But what of that other highly charged sense of loyalty mentioned by Austen – i.e. class consciousness? If the politicisation processes of the previous seventy years had sharpened the artisan's consciousness of the perceived community of the nation, had it also aroused his awareness of that other wider community to which he belonged – the working class?

NOTES

1 Donal McCartney, *The Dawning of Democracy: Ireland 1800–1870* (Dublin, 1987), p. 130.

2 Cambridge University Library, Bradshaw Irish Collection, vol. v, (ed. Madden): Counsellor O'Connell's Return to Parliament', printed by J. & H. Baird, 20 Paul Street, Cork, *c.* 1829–30.

3 This case concerned a murder attempt on a magistrate near Doneraile in the north of the county. Four men were convicted and sentenced to death. O'Connell's defence of the remainder, following a dramatic night ride from Derrynane to Cork, procured a verdict of 'not guilty', while the death sentence on the first four was commuted to transportation. For an account of the case, see Denis Gwynn, *Daniel O'Connell* (Cork, 1947), pp. 187–90.

4 Bradshaw Irish Collection vol. v, pp. 299, 561: ballads entitled 'The Doneraile Conspiracy', by A Mallow Rake (no printer cited) and 'O'Connell and Morrogh and the Cork Special Commission, A New Song', printed by J. & H. Baird, 20 Paul Street, Cork; CSORP.OR, 1830: M. 40, ballad entitled 'The Doneraile Conspiracy' (no printer cited).

5 *CC*, 6 Aug. 1835.

6 E. P. Thompson, *The Making of the English Working Class*, p. 289.

7 Patrick Joyce, *Work, Society and Politics*, pp. 312–13; *CMC*, 13 June 1832.

8 D'Arcy, 'Dublin artisan activity', pp. 37–8; Thomas Sheahan, *Articles of Irish Manufacture*, pp. 184–9; *CC*, 30 Nov. 1830. The trades most severely affected by the depression were the printers and the clothing and footwear trades.

9 *SR*, 2 Dec 1830; *CMC*, 19 Mar. 1832.

10 E. P. Thompson, *The Making of the English Working Class*, p. 297.

11 *CMC*, 13 June 1832.

12 *CMC*, 25 June 1832.

13 *CMC*, 19, 21, Mar., 25 June 1832; *CE*, 9 June 1845.

14 D. G. Boyce, 'The "marginal Britons": the Irish', in Robert Colls and Philip Dodd (eds.), *Englishness: Politics and Culture* (London, 1984), pp. 230–53.

15 *CMC*, 19 Nov. 1832.

16 *CMC*, 13 June 1832.

17 Jim Smyth, *The Men of No Property, passim*; Thomas Bartlett, *The Fall and Rise of the Irish Nation*, pp. 291–7, 311–25.

18 *CMC*, 19, 21 Mar. 1832; *CE*, 9 June 1845.

19 *CE*, 25 Jan., 19 Mar. 1847.

20 CSORP.OR, 1848:6/506; *CE*, 25 Jan. 1847. It was claimed that over one thousand local artisans were idle in January 1847, without counting the rural immigrants lately come into the city.

21 Other trades strongly represented in the new movement were the coopers (200 members in the Citizens' Club), shipwrights (80), bootmakers (31), broguemakers (28) and hatters (13). All of these, with the possible

exception of the shipwrights, were experiencing severe trade depression and high unemployment. *CE,* 31 Dec. 1847; *SR,* 22, 25 May 1848.

22 Takagami, 'The Dublin Fenians', pp. 49–52.

23 R. V. Comerford, 'Patriotism as pastime: the appeal of Fenianism in the mid–1860s', *Irish Historical Studies,* vol. xxii, no. 85, 1981, pp. 242, 247; Takagami, 'The Dublin Fenians', p. 82; Irish Crimes Records, Fenianism: Index of Names; Cork Union Workhouse Registers 1850-1890; *CC,* 1 April, 1868. An analysis of the social background of Cork Fenian suspects in the period 1865-70 (with Takagami's Dublin figures in parentheses) suggests that of 362 (474) individuals, artisans accounted for 46 (59) per cent, unskilled workers – 20 (11·4) per cent, shop assistants and clerks – 11·6 (13·7) per cent, publicans and retailers – 3 (7) per cent, merchants and 'dealers' – 3 (3·8) per cent, other identified categories – 5·5 (8·9) per cent, and unidentified – 11 (2·1) per cent.

24 *CE,* 29 Oct. 1885, 6, 11 Feb. 1886; *CDH,* 23 Nov. 1887.

25 Dick Geary, *European Labour Protest,* p. 16.

26 *CMC,* 25 June 1832; *CE,* 15 Jan., 4 June 1851, 4, 8, 22 Dec. 1880; 1 Jan. 1881.

27 *CDH,* 6, 11 Feb. 1886. A manufacture revival meeting called in response to pressure from the tailors' society was attended by no prominent public or business men and by none of the trades except the tailors themselves and some workers from a local match factory threatened with closure.

28 *CE,* 19 Sept. 1891, 8 Dec. 1893, 9, 23 Nov., 14 Dec. 1894, 18, 22 Mar., 25 Oct., 15 Nov. 1895; Cork Coopers' Society Minute Books, 14 Mar., 27 Aug., 24 Sept. 1895. Much of the coopers' political energies in the 1890s were, in fact, spent on unsuccessfully lobbying the local MPs for the return of the navy's salt pork contract to Cork provision merchants. This had been given exclusively to Cork merchants in the mid-1870s, but thereafter sizeable proportions were given to Danish and Dutch firms.

29 *CE,* 19 Nov. 1896.

30 For a study of the events surrounding the reform of the Cork corporation, see Maura Murphy, 'Municipal reform and the Repeal Movement in Cork 1833-44' in *JCHAS,* vol. lxxxi, no. 233, 1976, pp. 1–18.

31 *CE,* 24 Apr. 1882, 21, 23 Nov. 1883; Maura Murphy, 'Municipal reform and the Repeal Movement in Cork', pp. 9–10.

32 *CE,* 12, 24 Feb., 11 Mar. 1886.

33 *CE,* 10, 15, 23 Mar. 1886; CDH 10, 13, 15 Mar. 1886. One such contractor was Edward Fitzgerald, himself a member of the corporation and later Lord Mayor of Cork in 1902. He actually got the building contract for the municipal buildings in the 1890s and, following the demolition of the City Hall after the burning of Cork in 1920, investigations into both the granting of the contracts and the quality of work in the buildings suggested that some shady deals had, indeed, been made. Cork Corporation, *Report of the Sub-committee on the Past History of the Municipal Buildings* (Cork, 1895), *passim; County Borough of Cork, Verbatim Report of Local Government Inquiry into Administration by the Corporation* (Cork, 1925), *passim.*

34 *CE*, 23 Mar. 1886.

35 *CE*, 28 Sept. 1888, 19 Aug., 11 Nov. 1892, 2, 9, 30 Mar., 25 May, 20 July, 14 Sept. 1894, 8, 15 Mar., 26 July, 5, 13 Sept. 1895, 10 Jan., 15, 16, 22 May 1896.

36 *CE*, 14 Sept. 1894, 8 Mar., 5, 13 Sept. 1895.

37 Brendan McDonnell, 'The Dublin labour movement', p. xxviii; *CE*, 5, 6, 13 Feb., 18 Nov., 2 Dec. 1892, 16 Oct., 30 Nov. 1894, 21 Nov. 1896. The bakers' society pressed the trades council to oppose John Twomey, a master baker employing non-union men, when he stood for the North-West Ward in 1892. Twomey was elected by a small majority but nine months later the trades council was more successful in securing the defeat in the South Ward of James Fitzgibbon, another master baker employing unfair labour. Again in 1894, in answer to calls from the tailors' society, the trades council successfully opposed two municipal candidates who had clashed with the operative tailors in the strike of 1893, and when one of these men stood in a different ward in 1896 they renewed their campaign against him.

38 *CE*, 23, 24 Mar. 1886, 28 Sept. 1888, 2 Dec. 1892, 25 May 1894, 21 Aug., 10 Sept. 1896, 27 Aug., 24 Sept., 1, 15 Oct. 1897, 14 Nov. 1898. Since the mid–1860s the local Poor Law Board had given its printing contracts to houses employing society men but the town council and harbour board frequently allowed employment of unfair labour, particularly in painting and building contracts. The clothing contracts for the Lunatic Asylum and Poor Law Union were, thanks to trades pressure, finally given to fair houses in 1894–96, but when the corporation clothing contract went to the lowest tender (a non-union employer) in 1897, the trades were furious.

39 Dick Geary, *European Labour Protest*, p. 68.

40 John B. O'Brien, *The Catholic Middle Classes in Pre-Famine Cork*, O'Donnell Lecture (Dublin, 1979), p. 9.

41 Maura Murphy, 'Cork commercial society', pp. 233–44.

42 John B. O'Brien, *The Catholic Middle Classes*, p. 14; Maura Murphy, 'Cork commercial society', pp. 239–40; Ian D'Alton, 'Keeping faith', pp. 765–9.

43 Ian D'Alton, *Protestant Society*, pp. 206, 211–12.

44 Angela Fahy, 'Residence, workplace and patterns of change, Cork 1787–1863', pp. 45–50; Ian d'Alton, *Protestant Society*, p. 34.

45 For the breakdown of traditional social and economic mutualities in nineteenth-century Britain, see Asa Briggs, 'The language of "class" in early nineteenth-century England' M. W. Flinn and T. C. Smout (eds.), *Essays in Social History* (Oxford, 1974), pp. 154–77.

46 E. P. Thompson, *The Making of the English Working Class*, p. 810.

47 J. G. Kohl, *Travels in Ireland* (London, 1844), p. 95.

48 K. T. Hoppen, *Elections, Politics and Society*, p. 68; *CC*, 3 Jan. 1850; *CDH*, 15 May 1897. At the mayoral election of 1850, the butter trade background and political stance of the outgoing mayor, Sir William Lyons, was jeered from the gallery: 'You were always a humbug – firkin of butter!' In 1897

the appearance of the anti-Parnellite trades councillor, Edward Crean, was ridiculed mercilessly by hecklers. At a public meeting to organise the Ninety-Eight anniversary celebrations, a voice from the audience jeered – 'Yerra! Is it Crean you want, with the long neck and the storky face!'

49 Eugen Weber, *Peasants into Frenchmen*, pp. 243–4.

50 *CMC*, 14 July 1832.

51 In Cork during the 1830s and 1840s local newspapers cost a prohibitive sixpence when artisan's daily wages averaged three shillings, and were even further out of the reach of the unskilled workers whose daily earnings varied between eightpence and a shilling.

52 *Guy's County and City of Cork Directory 1875–76* (Cork, 1875); *Guy's Directory of Munster 1886, 1893* (Cork, 1886, 1893); *Almanac and Directory 1907* (Cork, 1907); *Census of Ireland, Province of Munster, City of Cork,* 1871–1901; *CE*, 21 Dec. 1892, 3 July 1893, 16 Feb. 1894; *Evening Echo Centenary Year Supplement*, 11 Sept. 1992. The specific category of newsagent first appeared in the local trade directory in 1875, and the numbers thus listed increased from six in that year to twenty-five by 1907. Census figures show a rise from twelve to twenty-eight 'newspaper agents, vendors and newsroom keepers' over the period 1871 to 1901.

53 J. S. Donnelly Jr., *The Land and People in Nineteenth Century Cork,* p. 249; Maura Murphy, 'The working classes of nineteenth century Cork', p. 45. By 1900 when artisans' daily wages varied between five and six shillings, and labourers' daily rates averaged half-a-crown, the local daily papers cost a mere penny while the daily evening paper, the *Evening Echo* cost a halfpenny.

54 *CC*, 3 May 1859; *CE*, 13 Oct. 1873.

55 Hoppen, *Elections, Politics and Society*, p. 309; John Foster, *Class Struggle and the Industrial Revolution*, p. 161.

56 Any attempt to pinpoint the source of artisan politicisation in the so-called middle class, however, immediately exposes one to the worst features of Marxist historical interpretation. After all, did the average small employer who enforced politicisation belong to the middle class or to the artisan class itself? Should the immediate landlord of some wretched hovel be described as bourgeois or upper working class? And what of that indefinable middle group which included not just pawnbrokers but also shopkeepers and publicans, and which had such immediate and constant contact with the city's working people? Tom Garvin, *Nationalist Revolutionaries in Ireland*, pp. 13–32.

57 Hoppen, *Elections, Politics and Society*, pp. 62–3; *Report of the Select Committee on Ministers' Money (Ireland)*, HC 1847–48, (559) xvii, 401. Maura Murphy, 'Cork commercial society', p. 238. Ministers' Money was a tax levied on certain cities and corporate towns in Ireland (Dublin, Cork, Limerick, Waterford, Drogheda, Kilkenny, Clonmel and Kinsale) for the support of Protestant clergy. Land was exempt but dwelling houses were liable at a rate of twelve pence sterling in every pound valuation. Houses valued

above sixty pounds were valued at sixty, thus rousing much public indignation as to the inequitable nature of the tax.

58 *CE*, 11 Aug. 1847.

59 K. T. Hoppen, *Elections, Politics and Society*, pp. 35–6, 127–70; *CE*, 26 Apr. 1880, 24 Apr., 10 Nov. 1882.

60 *CMC*, 24 Oct., 21 Nov. 1832; *CC*, 27 July 1848; *Griffith's Valuation*, Borough of Cork, 1852; Patrick Joyce, *Work, Society and Politics*, p. 123.

61 Tom Garvin, *Nationalist Revolutionaries in Ireland*, pp. 14, 22; John Foster, *Class Struggle and the Industrial Revolution*, p. 163, describes this group as a 'social tail to the bourgeoisie proper'.

62 A similar leading role was played by 'shopkeepers and superior artisans' in the pro-reform processions of the early 1830s in London. E. P. Thompson, *The Making of the English Working Class*, p. 894.

63 *CMC*, 6 June, 16, 23 July, 1, 8, 29 Aug., 5, 14, 21, 24, 28 Sept., 19 Nov. 1832; *CE*, 28 Aug., 11, 18, 25 Sept., 2, 23, 25, 30 Oct., 6, 13, 27 Nov., 11, 18, 30 Dec. 1850. The most prominent individuals in the manufacture revival movements of 1832 and 1850–5 are as follows (in percentages):

	1832	1850–55
Manufacturers	21·75	5·45
Master tradesmen	15·65	24·09
Journeymen	0·41	0·00
Grocers, Vintners	14·23	7·27
Merchants	14·02	9·55
Dealers, Drapers	6·30	5·91
Agents, Brokers	3·25	4·55
Lawyers, Doctors, Attorneys	2·64	7·73
Clergy	2·03	3·18
Gentlemen	1·83	5·91
Unidentified	17·89	26·36

64 *CMC*, 13 Feb. 1833; Cork Archives Institute: Day Papers, DP II, 1837, p. 57; 1839, p. 95; *SR*, 14 Dec. 1839. The precise social composition of the Cork Trades Association of 1832 is difficult to pinpoint. Of the estimated 1,200 members the names of only 77 survive, and the social background of only 58 of these can be ascertained. The anonymity of the majority of members certainly suggests humble social origins, but among those prominent in the association 24.68 per cent were manufacturers and master tradesmen, 20.78 per cent were merchants and retailers, 12.99 per cent were professionals and 7.79 per cent were described as gentlemen, while only 9.09 per cent were described definitely as journeymen and 24.68 per cent could not be identified. Artisans joining the Cork Trades Association and the People's Hall were practically press-ganged by the radical shopkeeper and pawnbroker leadership into a struggle for power against the merchant-dominated Chamber of Commerce.

65 Strong supporters of Catholic emancipation and moderate parliamentary

reform, the liberal Chamber of Commerce merchants were correctly considered lukewarm on Repeal of the Union and extension of the franchise. Therefore, the People's Hall as 'an every-day school for the People' would counteract merchant indifference by instilling 'correct notions of measures, local and national, to enable [the public] to estimate . . . the characters of public men – to respect the honest and efficient – and to defeat or discard the corrupt'. For details of this rivalry between retailer burgesses and merchant elite, see Maura Murphy, 'Municipal reform and the Repeal Movement in Cork', pp. 1–18.

66 Patrick Joyce, *Work, Society and Politics*, pp. 98, 123, 201–40.

67 *CC*, 10 Nov. 1840, 10 May 1859.

68 In general, employers tended to recruit workers of their own religious persuasion, but in firms with a large workforce of mixed or no skills, religious uniformity was impossible to achieve. It was calculated in 1877 that between three-eighths and one half of the city's employers were Catholic, while some of the larger firms – the Steam Packet Company, Cork Docks Company, Ogilvie and Company and the large tobacco spinners – were Protestant controlled, but most of their unskilled workforce was Catholic. *Proceedings of the Select Committee on the Sale of Intoxicating Liquors on Sunday (Ireland) Bill*, HC 1877, (198) xvi, Qs. 4581–2.

69 For further discussion on the size of business establishments and employer-worker relations in nineteenth-century Cork, see Maura Murphy, 'Social and economic structure of nineteenth century Cork', pp. 138–9, and Maura Cronin, 'Work and workers', pp. 722–4, 739–40.

70 *Select Committee on Fictitious Votes (Ireland)*, HC 1837–38, xxiii, I, Qs. 4267–70.

71 *CC*, 10 Nov. 1840, 6 June 1848; *CE*, 18 Nov. 1845.

72 *CE*, 23 Oct., 11 Dec. 1850. The employer in question was Fletcher of Patrick Street.

73 Patrick Joyce, *Work, Society and Politics*, pp. 220–1; R. Q. Gray, *Class Structure in Edinburgh*, p. 156; R. Price, *Labour in British Society*, p. 85.

74 Takagami, 'The Dublin Fenians', pp. 65–6, 91–2; Irish Crimes Records, Fenianism: Index of Names; Tadhg Ó Murchadha, *Sgéal Sheandúin* (Dublin, 1920), p. 34.

75 *CC*, 8 July 1830; *People's Press*, 17, 24, 31 Jan., 7, 14 Feb. 1835; Thomas Sheahan, *Articles of Irish Manufacture*, pp. 224–5; *Number of persons entitled to vote at the elections of members for cities and boroughs in Ireland: specifying the number of electors for each place*, HC 1830, (522) xxi, 321; *Number registered under the Reform Act, distinguishing qualifications*, HC 1833 (177) xxvii, 289. The size of the electorate in 1830 was uncertain. Mainly a freeman electorate, it was 'supposed to number' between 2,500 and 3,000, of which fewer than 300 were artisans. After the 1832 Reform Act it increased to 4,322. The estimated number of 500 artisan voters tallies closely with the numbers in the 1835 city pollbook (printed in the *People's Press*) in which voters in the manufacturing and building sectors accounted for 544 of the total 2,545 names, but it is not clear how many of these 544 voters

were journeymen and how many were masters and manufacturers.

76 *CMC*, 24 Aug., 24 Oct. 1832; *CE*, 9 June 1845. In 1832 the pledged trades included nailors, stonecutters, cotton weavers, broguemakers and coopers.

77 *CMC*, 29 Aug. 1832; *CE*, 28, 30 Dec. 1842; *SR*, 15 Feb., 7, 30 Mar. 1848.

78 *SR*, 30 May 1848; *CC*, 6 June, 25 July, 3 Aug. 1848; CSORP.OR, 1848: 6/866.

79 Fenian Papers, 1870: 5640–R; Takagami, 'The Dublin Fenians', pp. 81–3; Tadhg Ó Murchadha, *Sgéal Sheandúin*, pp. 33–6. It is worth noting that the coopers' society was among those who in 1873 withdrew from a public demonstration in favour of Amnesty as a protest against the introduction of Home Rule into what it was felt should have been a purely Fenian demonstration. *CE*, 9, 11 Oct. 1873.

80 Patrick Joyce, *Work, Society and Politics*, p. 289.

81 Vincent Comerford, 'Patriotism as pastime', p. 239.

82 In 1876 it was calculated by the Royal Irish Constabulary that on an average Sunday, thirty-seven per cent of Cork's population frequented public houses. Similar calculations in other centres produced the following estimates: Dublin – 50 per cent; Waterford – 35 per cent; Limerick 31 per cent; Belfast – 24 per cent; Londonderry – 16 per cent. *Minutes of Evidence taken before the Select Committee on the Sale of Liquors on Sunday (Ireland) Bill*, HC 1867–68, (280) xiv, Qs. 138, 705; Report of the Select Committee on the Sale of Intoxicating Liquors on Sunday (Ireland) Bill, HC 1877 (198) xvi, Qs. 4767; Elizabeth Malcolm, *Ireland Sober, Ireland Free: Drink and Temperance in Nineteenth-Century Ireland* (Dublin, 1986), p. 234; Patrick Joyce, *Work, Society and Politics*, p. 293.

83 K. T. Hoppen, *Elections, Politics and Society*, pp. 52–3; *Report of the Select Committee on the Sale of Liquors on Sunday (Ireland)*. HC 1867–68, (280) xiv, Qs. 2106; *Minutes of Evidence of the Royal Commission on Licensing Laws*, HC 1898 (C–8980) xxxviii, vol. vii, Qs. 61529–677.

84 Fenian Papers 1865: 233 (1 and 2); CSORP, 1870: 17146. Brian Dillon's pub in the north-side area of Dillon's Cross, the 'Cork Arms', Curtin's public house in North Main Street and 'The Ship' in Warren's Place were all Fenian meeting places, as was James Mountaine's boot trimming shop and William O'Carroll's bakery in North Main Street.

85 Patrick Joyce, *Work, Society and Politics*, pp. 286–9; Dennis Smith, 'Paternalism, craft and organizational rationality 1830–1930: an exploratory model', *Urban History*, vol. xix, pt. 2, Oct. 1992, p. 213; C. Behagg, *Politics and Production in the Early Nineteenth Century* (London, 1990), p. 126; E. P. Thompson, *The Making of the English Working Class*, p. 789.

86 Comerford, 'Patriotism as pastime', p. 247; K. T. Hoppen, *Elections, Politics and Society*, p. 53; Maura Murphy, 'The ballad singer and the role of the seditious ballad in nineteenth century Ireland – Dublin Castle's view', *Ulster Folklife*, vol. xxv, 1979, pp. 90–1; SOC, 1804: 1028/7; CSORP, 1831/1. Thomas Bartlett, *The Fall and Rise of the Irish Nation*, pp. 316–17, also notes the public house as centre of both conviviality and sedition in the 1790s.

87 E. P. Thompson, *The Making of the English Working Class,* pp. 445–6; Patrick Joyce, *Work, Society and Politics,* p. 118.

88 Comerford, 'Patriotism as pastime', pp. 246–8; Takagami, 'The Dublin Fenians', p. 132; *Proceedings of the Select Committee on the Sunday Closing Acts (Ireland),* HC 1888, (255) xix, Qs. 65851. In the last three decades of the century there were seven packs of harriers in Cork City, supported by artisans, shopkeepers and labourers. Walking was particularly popular because it allowed those who went three miles from the city to evade the Sunday licensing laws by qualifying as 'bona fide travellers'.

89 Anthony D. Buckley, 'On the club: friendly societies in Ireland', *Irish Economic and Social History,* vol. xiv, 1987, pp. 39, 42; Patrick Joyce, *Work, Society and Politics,* p. 215; Dick Geary, *European Labour Protest,* p. 45.

90 E. P. Thompson, *The Making of the English Working Class,* p. 460; R. Price, *Labour in British Society,* p. 55; *Royal Commission on Friendly and Benefit Societies, Second Report* [C–514] HC 1872, xxvi, I, Qs. 16564; *CE,* 3, 31 Dec. 1894. For a brief discussion on the role of mortality societies in nineteenth-century Cork, see Maura Murphy, 'The working classes of nineteenth century Cork', *JCHAS,* Jan.–Dec. 1980, vol. lxxxv, nos. 241–2, pp. 40–1.

91 Elizabeth Malcolm, *Ireland Sober, Ireland Free,* pp. 83, 89–90, 133; Colm Kerrigan, 'The social impact of the Irish Temperance Movement 1839–1845', *Irish Economic and Social History,* vol. xiv, 1987, pp. 20–38 and *Father Mathew and the Irish Temperance Movement 1838–1849* (Cork, 1992), pp. 107–31.

92 *CC,* 22 May 1843, 6 June 1845; *Irishman,* 29 Aug., 26 Sept. 1863; *CE,* 10 Oct. 1864, 22 Aug. 1871, 22 Nov. 1875; R. V. Comerford, 'Patriotism as pastime', p. 247; Elizabeth Malcolm, *Ireland Sober, Ireland Free,* p. 129.

93 *CE,* 5, 6 May, 23, 24, 27, 30 June, 8 July, 7, 8, 11 Oct., 10 Nov. 1879, 18 Oct., 22, 23 Nov., 13 Dec. 1880, 28 Feb., 2 Mar., 22 June 1881. The main protagonists in this inter-band quarrel in the 1870s and early 1880s were the Fair Lane and Blackpool bands, whose first open confrontation was apparently due to a disagreement about the distribution of money after playing at a wedding. By the early 1900s, they were still at one another's throats, but now the quarrel had been translated into political terms as one band backed William O'Brien and the other supported John Redmond.

94 *CE,* 26 Aug. 1872, 7 Aug., 22 Nov. 1875, 26 Feb. 1877, 9 Mar. 1888, 28 Nov. 1892, 23 Nov. 1893, 21 Nov. 1898.

95 The popular *Cork Examiner* was firmly anti-Parnellite while the local Catholic clergy passed a vote of no confidence in the fallen leader a little over a week after the scandal broke. *CE,,* 6 Dec. 1890.

96 *CE,* 10, 11 Dec. 1890, 6 Oct. 1893. Though many bands split internally as a result of the Parnell issue, those supporting Parnell can be identified as the Barrack Street Band, Butter Exchange Band, Carpenters' Brass Band, Tailors' Band, Sts Peter and Paul's Fife and Drum Band, Blackpool Band and Passage Band.

97 Hoppen, *Elections, Politics and Society,* pp. 258–9.

98 *CE*, 5 Feb., 12 Apr., 30 June 1845; *Reports of the Repeal Association*, vol. ii, pp. 332, 346, in Cork Archives Institute: Day Papers.

99 *CE*, 13 Sept., 6, 20 Oct., 6, 20, 31 Dec. 1847, 20, 25 Jan., 24 Feb. 1848; *United Irishman*, 12, 19 Feb. 1848. The newspapers and periodicals available in the reading room were: the *Daily News; Douglas Jarrold's Newspaper; Packet; Limerick Reporter; Peter Carroll's Register; Dublin University Magazine; Cork Magazine; Hewitt's Journal; Douglas Jarrold's Magazine; Sharpe's London Magazine; North American Review; Builder;* some northern newspapers; the *Cork Examiner; Cork Constitution; Southern Reporter,* and, most important of all, the *Nation.*

100 *CC*, 4, 11, 13, 18, 20 Apr. 1848; CSORP, 1848: 6/397, 405, 424, 447, 464, 489, 505, 574.

101 *CE*, 4 Feb., 7 Nov., 1859, 22 June 1860, 14 Sept. 1861, 12 Mar. 1864; *CDH*, 11 Jan. 1861. This body, which organised the McManus funeral in the city in 1861, formed a branch of James Stephens' National Brotherhood of Saint Patrick. In 1864 it severed its connection with that organisation because of an internal fissure in the nationalist camp, and became an independent Cork-based Fenian body, one of its leading lights being Michael B. O'Brien who was later to become famous as one of the Manchester Martyrs of 1867.

102 *CE*, 25 Oct. 1869, 22 Aug. 1871, 2, 18 Mar., 26 Aug. 1872, 15 Oct. 1873; *CDH*, 13 Oct. 1873.

103 CSORP, 1848: 6/866. A typical club was the Oliver Bond Club in Barrack Street, the committee of which included a timber merchant, corn buyer, clerk, gardener and journeyman shoemaker, while other identified members were a publican, sawyer, shoemaker and three carpenters.

104 *CE*, 25 Oct. 1869, 22 Aug. 1871, 26 Aug. 1872, 15 Oct. 1873. The Cork National Reading Room was led largely by clerks and shopkeepers but with a large number of artisans in the rank and file. The leadership of the Cork Working Men's Association included the inevitable clerks and drapers' assistants, but most of the rank and file were unskilled workers, quay porters, day labourers and a number of skilled artisans.

105 In the 1880s, all offices in the local branch of the National League were held by men from professional, mercantile and manufacturing backgrounds. *Guy's Directory of Munster* 1886 (Cork, 1886), p. 344.

106 For comment on the social composition of the Cork Land League leadership, see above, pp. 111–12. By the 1890s, the Home Rule side (itself internally divided) was led by merchants, retailers, professionals and minor manufacturers. See, for instance, the lists of candidates contesting the 1899 local elections, *CE*, 15 Dec. 1898, 6 Jan. 1899; *Guy's Directory of Munster* 1886–1900 (Cork, 1886–1900)

107 For brief biographies of the Young Ireland and 1848 leaders, see T. F. O'Sullivan, *The Young Irelanders* (Tralee, 1944).

108 Dick Geary, *European Labour Protest*, pp. 38, 66–7.

109 *Irishman*, 15 Sept. 1849, 16 Mar. 1850.

110 *Irishman*, 16 Nov. 1849, 2, 16 Mar., 6 Apr. 1850; *CE*, 8 Mar. 1850.

111 John Foster, *Class Struggle and the Industrial Revolution*, pp. 151–9; Tom Garvin, *Nationalist Revolutionaries in Ireland*, p. 9; John Newsinger, 'Old Chartists, Fenians and New Socialists', *Éire/Ireland* vol. xvii, no. 2, 1982, p. 20; Takagami, 'The Dublin Fenians', p. 81.

112 CSORP, 1864: 20623; 1872: 12974; Fenian Papers 1866: F–2254; Larcom Papers, National Library of Ireland, MS 7687, 31 Dec. 1865; Diarmuid O'Donovan Rossa, *Rossa's Recollections* (Irish University Press Reprint, Dublin, 1972), pp. 298, 307. *CE*, 26 Aug. 1872; *Irishman*, 9 Mar. 1850.

113 CBSR, 1890: 1229/S.

114 *CE*, 13, 15 Oct. 1873, 4 Feb. 1874, 22 Feb. 1877, 23 Aug. 1880, 10 Dec. 1890, 12 Dec. 1898; CSORP, 1867/22537.

115 Takagami, 'The Dublin Fenians', p. 81; *CE*, 25 Oct. 1869, 18 Mar. 1872, 15 Oct. 1873; Irish Crimes Records, vol. I, Fenianism: Index of Names; Fenian Papers 1870: 6224–R; The occupational structure of the Cork Fenian leadership, as indicated by numerous police and newspaper reports, was as follows:

Occupation	Number	Number as % of whole
Artisans	9	32
Publicans	8	28·5
Clerks	4	14
Shop Assistants	2	7
Shopkeepers	1	3·5
Unidentified	4	14

The four unidentified names are presumably those whose social position was too low to allow them to be included in the trade directories of the day.

116 CBSR, 1892: 904/18; 1894: 900/S; 1898: 15192/S.

117 Tom Garvin, *Nationalist Revolutionaries in Ireland*, pp. 13–14; CBSR, 1890: 94/S, 1892: 5483/S, 1894: 9057/S, 1898: 17582/S.

118 John Boyle, *The Irish Labour Movement*, p. 139.

5

CLASS AS IDENTITY

Sociologists who have stopped the time-machine and, with a good deal of conceptual huffing and puffing, have gone down to the engine-room to look, tell us that nowhere at all have they been able to locate and classify a class. They can only find a multitude of people with different occupations, incomes, status-hierarchies, and the rest. Of course they are right, since class is not this or that part of the machine, but *the way the machine works* once it is set in motion – not this and that interest, but the *friction* of interests – the movement itself, the heat, the thundering noise. Class is a social and cultural formation (often finding institutional expression) which cannot be defined abstractly, or in isolation, but only in terms of relationship with other classes; and ultimately, the definition can only be made in the medium of *time* – that is, action and reaction, change and conflict. When we speak of *a* class we are thinking of a very loosely defined body of people who share the same congeries of interests, social experiences, traditions and value-system, who have a *disposition to behave* as a class, to define themselves in their actions and in their consciousness in relation to other groups of people in class ways. But class itself is not a thing, it is a happening.[1]

Studies in the British and European contexts have suggested that, while a heightened sense of class pervaded nineteenth-century society, class consciousness among working people was, until the middle of the century, characterised less by solidarity than by internal fragmentation, white-collar workers considering themselves

to have little in common with manual workers, and skilled craftsmen looking down upon the unskilled labourer. However, by the
1870s, a wider sense of working-class consciousness emerged,
linked to the spread of union organisation among both craftsmen
and semi and unskilled workers, and to increasingly vociferous
demands by working men for political rights. This increasingly
cohesive sense of working-class consciousness emerging towards
the end of the nineteenth century has been described by modern
researchers as 'labourism' or 'workerism' – i.e. the political expression of the 'trade-union consciousness' of British workers,
characterised by the 'conviction that it is necessary to combine
in unions, fight the employers and strive to compel the government to pass necessary labour legislation'.[2]

Had such a sense of class solidarity come into existence in Cork
during the same period? At face value such was, indeed the case.
In 1899, for the first time ever, nine labour representatives were
elected to the city's corporation, a body which had been dominated throughout the century by merchants, retailers and professionals.[3] Greeting the labour victory with delight, one labourer
rejoiced in terms redolent of class solidarity

> that the time for certain tradesmen considering themselves
> superior to the labourer was now gone, and labourer and trades-
> man would in future work unitedly for the advancement of their
> interests.[4]

Such political awareness based on working-class solidarity had,
indeed, been evolving over the preceding six decades. This was
particularly obvious in the increasing use, by both public men
and by representatives of the trades and labouring classes, of what
might be termed the language of class. Just as the experience
elsewhere showed that working men could be radicalised by conflict with middle-class elements, so in Cork of the 1830s this trend
was reflected in the language directed specifically against the local
middle-class élite in the Chamber of Commerce, who were
resented for their domination of popular politics in the city. As
in contemporary Edinburgh where, in the face of the traditional
élite, the shopkeepers were 'striving to be great in their shop-
ocratic way', so too, in Cork it was the politically ambitious retailer

element which first became self-consciously assertive in local affairs.[5] In turn, the artisanate, or at least representatives of it, echoed both the language and the attitudes of their lower-middle-class leaders, presenting a political challenge to the city's traditional élite. In the parliamentary election of 1832 the Trades Association, largely manned by the retailers and trades, helped to push forward the candidature of the popular Dr Herbert Baldwin as against that of the Chamber-backed merchant politician, Daniel Callaghan. Though Callaghan did marginally better than Baldwin on polling day, Baldwin's election was portrayed as a victory for 'the people' who, in the words of the Trades Association, ' "had beaten down the Aristocracy, and the worst of all Aristocracies – the Catholic Aristocracy". (loud and prolonged cheering).'[6]

Such populist language was in keeping with the general tenor of the day. Studies of politico-social developments in different nineteenth-century British centres have noted the importance of language as both reflecting and shaping class consciousness, the insertion of the term 'the people' becoming an essential feature of public rhetoric. But who comprised 'the people'? To Cobbett in contemporary England, 'the people' essentially comprised 'artisans and labourers', though modern historians have retrospectively depicted the term in a broader way as the 'productive classes' and the 'non-élite'.[7] These latter, wider definitions appear to be particularly applicable in the context of nineteenth-century Ireland, and particularly that of Cork. O'Connell's public letters, interweaving the concepts of 'people' and 'nation', were always addressed to the 'People of Ireland', that of January 1830 trumpetting forth the slogan 'For God and the People'.[8] Such a theme was promptly taken up at local level: at all public dinners on the popular side the toast to 'the People' immediately followed that to the Queen, platform orators of high and low station laced their speeches with references to the 'rights of the people', and voters were reminded by radical spokesmen that they held their votes in trust 'for the good of the people'.[9] The city's short-lived radical newspaper of the mid–1830s was predictably called the *People's Press*, which described itself in language typical of contemporary British radicalism, as agitating for the 'welfare of the productive classes'. In 1835 the Cork Trades Association considered renaming itself the People's Society and the new radical headquarters opened in the city two years later was named the People's Hall.[10] The late 1830s saw brakes applied to this democratisation of language. As O'Connell's political alliance with the Whigs resulted in a wild canvas at local level for the co-operation of 'all the influential noblemen and gentlemen of the county', the democratic catch-phrases of earlier years were noticeable by their absence.[11] Though lip-service continued to be paid to 'the people' as a matter of form in after-dinner toasts and platform speeches, yet it was not until a decade later, with the impact of the Paris revolution of February 1848, that this populist rhetoric was once more widely used. This development was most obvious locally in the columns of the formerly moderate *Southern Reporter* newspaper which, taken over in January 1848 by two Cork Confederates, Michael Joseph Barry and Charles D. Murphy, became a violent exponent of revolution *à la française*. Similarly, local radical orators, carried along by news from France and by the force of their own rhetoric, reminded 'the respectable class' that 'the people will triumph, with or without or against you – they will triumph'.[12] After the pathetic rebellion attempts of 1848–49, such revolutionary fervour soon fizzled out. Yet both the radical ideas and the accompanying populist terminology were given a brief lease of life in the titles and programmes of two subsequent political bodies backed by the die-hards of 1848 – i.e. the Irish Democratic Association of 1850, which had a number of branches throughout the British Isles but which faded into oblivion within a few months, and the related People's Institutes which apparently had little influence outside Dublin.[13]

The increasingly widespread usage of populist terminology was not, however, confined to the political sphere. From the 1830s onwards, and particularly in the latter half of the century, there was an increasing awareness of lower-class needs and, consequently, an increased use of populist rhetoric by philanthropists and entrepreneurs alike. A People's Bakery had been opened in Cork in the late 1840s while, from the late 1850s onwards, advertisers referred to public holidays as 'people's holidays' and headed their notices with slogans like 'Fair Play' and 'Song for the Million'.[14]

This tendency did not, of course, develop in a vacuum. Rather, it reflected the fact that by mid-century, with increasing emphasis throughout the British Isles on self-betterment and opportunities for working-class leisure, the concept of popular facilities had been well established. In both Britain and Ireland, the latter half of the nineteenth century saw the expansion of popular recreational facilities geared not alone to the requirements of working people, but also to what middle-class patrons and philanthropists saw as the necessary refinement of lower-class habits.[15] Cork's experience fitted into this pattern. Throughout the 1850s, reflecting what one historian has described as the 'growth of civic Britain', successive calls were made for a public park for the use of the local working classes and for the provision of threepenny seats for working-class attenders at the Atheneum, while a company catering principally for working-class insurance was established in 1853.[16] The range of facilities widened, albeit slowly, from the 1860s onwards. A People's Baths was opened in March 1863; between 1866 and the early 1880s the Cork Refreshment Rooms Company established four rooms in the city which provided reasonably priced meals for the public; and in 1872 the Cork Improved Dwellings Society was set up to provide suitable accommodation for 'respectable' working people.[17] Against the background of such social and economic trends, the increasing emphasis on 'the people' in the language of public figures is not surprising.

From the 1870s onwards, this vague populism of public rhetoric was further sharpened by the infusion of still more radical terminology – a development already visible in other cities of the British Isles from the previous decade. In the Cork context, this trend was most apparent in labour-related court cases where legal men increasingly used what might be termed the language of class. In 1871, for example, the counsel for a journeyman shoemaker suing his employer for overdue wages described himself as 'asserting the right of his client and the class to which he belonged', while in the previous year the counsel for the defense of striking foundry workers attributed changing worker expectations to a mighty revolution [which] had recently taken place in the status of the working man – a revolution recognised by wise statesmen as a vast social advancement. The working man was now recognised as a sentient, intellectual being, not as a mere machine – as something next the brute.[18]

Though much of this 'class rhetoric' was used by legal men rather than by artisans or labourers, the available evidence, scanty though it is, suggests that by the 1870s class-based terminology was also beginning to pepper the public statements of working men, moving towards a sense of identity based on labourism. At a meeting to back the local tailors' strike in 1870, for example, trade-society spokesmen referred to the 'rights of labour', the 'dignity of labour' and the 'battle of labour against capital'.[19] Two years later, the Cork Working Men's Association, which operated in the dual capacity of Fenian front-group and protective society for unskilled workers, described itself in by now typical class terms as 'essentially a movement of the masses – the trades, the sons of labour, and the young men who are a country's best reliance'.[20] By the 1890s, as 'new unionism' spread among the semi-skilled workers, the rhetoric from trade-union platforms became even more pointedly class orientated, striking railwaymen and dockers in 1890 speaking of the workers' 'ties of brotherhood' and declaring that 'in the struggle against powerful capital', all labouring men were 'bound in common ties'.[21] By 1898, with the establishment of the first labour panel in municipal elections, local political platforms were even more severely affected by this virus of class rhetoric. This was particularly obvious in labour spokesmen's pronouncements on the local housing issue. Ignoring the fact that many slum landlords were themselves drawn from the ranks of the poor, the labour candidates used an evocative 'them-and-us' terminology to condemn the 'disgraceful condition of some of the houses of the poor . . . Hovels out of which rich people are drawing high rents'. Marginally more accurate, but still grossly oversimplifying reality in stark class terms, was labour's description of the opposing Commercial Group as part of 'an attempt to crush the working classes, from whom directly or indirectly they earn their livelihood'.[22]

If the abstract language of class was becoming more widely used in the course of the century, both by and in relation to working men, there was nothing abstract in the grievances against which it was directed. As one British labour historian concluded, 'the mode of thought of working people is . . . strongly biased to concrete and practical experience', so in Cork most apparent class confrontations were, in fact, rooted in concrete grievances.[23] This was particularly true of those occasions on which the skilled trades expressed hostility towards the local middle classes – a tendency which became increasingly common as the century passed. On such occasions the middle classes were targeted not on account of their class but because some of their representatives had in very practical ways made themselves obnoxious to the trades. Thus, when in 1843 the journeymen coopers described the local butter buyers as 'petty tyrants who look upon us as slaves that must minister to their wants', this had nothing to do with abstract class animosity. The butter buyers were hated by the journeymen because of their position as middlemen interposing between the coopers, butter merchants and farmers, and because on this particular occasion they had threatened to break the city coopers' union by buying their firkins from cooperages in the county towns.[24]

The practical issue of manufacture revival was also portrayed in over-simplified class terms, for although the trades themselves were reputedly the worst offenders against patronage of local manufacture, some of the trades' most determined anti-middle-class rhetoric was occasioned by the perceived failure of the more prosperous citizens to patronise local industry.[25] This view of middle-class perfidy hardly changed in the course of the century, the bitter anti-middle-class statements by the artisan-dominated Mallow Lane Board of Trade following the collapse of their efforts in 1842 being re-echoed almost unchanged forty years later by the local trades council when their interests were ignored in the local industrial exhibition of 1883.[26]

Whatever resentment was manifested by the organised trades towards those above them on the social scale, there was no doubt that in many ways they both needed and sought middle-class support. The phenomenon of middle-class sponsorship of respectable

working men's social activities was already clearly visible in
Britain in the shape of cultural agencies like mechanics' institutes,
savings banks and Sunday schools, 'which emphasised the virtues of work ethic, savings, education and religion within the
market economy'.[27] The successive attempts to found a Dublin
trades council at mid-century were marked by the same patron-
client relationship between prominent citizens and the trade
unions, the projected establishment of a trades hall in 1870 being accompanied by invitations to employers and prominent
citizens to contribute, and by the drawing up of an impressive
muster of trustees from among the 'right honourables', 'sirs' and
'esquires' of the city.[28] Throughout the century, the trade
societies of Cork predictably worked along the same lines. In
the election of 1832 the Cork Trades Association had sought support for the Repeal cause by sending deputations to the Catholic
clergy and the residents of the 'respectable' residential areas, while
the People's Hall of the late 1830s was largely dependent for funds
on the generosity of a small number of local middle-class individuals.[29] The repeated efforts to set up a local trades council from the 1850s onwards were marked by a similar dependence
on and courting of middle-class patronage. In 1861 the sitting
mayor, Sir John Arnott, was secured as honorary president by
the first short-lived trades council, while its successor in 1864
canvassed the support of benevolent local businessmen by stressing its conviction that depressed trade societies should emigrate
their members rather than resort to 'strikes and kindred evils'.[30]
Even the Mechanics' Hall of the early 1870s, later associated
with the militant nationalist movement, came into existence partly
as the result of benevolent middle-class attempts to 'improve the
moral and intellectual condition' of the trades.[31] For the
Catholic bishop Dr Delaney, and a number of local businessmen,
the Mechanics' Hall was less a trades council than an amalgam
of mechanics' institute and temperance society, and the trades'
own early appeals for support dutifully echoed this benevolent
paternalism:

> Though there are, as there must be, social differences and distinc-
> tions, there is . . . no difference whatever between the natural
> capacities of the children of the rich and the children of the poor

... Apprenticed at an early age to our respective trades, and employed during the entire day from morning to evening at our work, we naturally want some time for self-improvement. A well selected library, suited to the various tastes and requirements, would afford us the best of all means for this improvement, and rendering the working classes of this city more capable of holding their own in these days of unexampled progress.[32]

Similarly, the final and successful attempt to establish a permanent trades council in 1881 was marked, at least initially, by the same cultivation of middle-class sympathies, its stated objective, apart from protecting the affiliated trades, being to establish a dispute-free industrial climate. Moreover, while it genuinely saw itself as a trades council, it sought a broad social basis which would preclude over-identification with any one sector, opening its ranks to 'all persons of character, whether in the shopkeeping or labouring interest' and proposing to find 'some good business men' to accept places on the executive committee. Though this extension of the basis of membership was prompted mainly by financial considerations, it was also favoured as lending social tone and respectability to what was essentially an artisan body.[33] Thus, in spite of the articulation of some anti-middle-class sentiments, the council deliberately sought the patronage of its social superiors. It vigorously canvassed and quickly received the patronage of a number of Catholic bishops; its honorary presidency and vice-presidency were conferred on the city's two parliamentary representatives, Charles Stuart Parnell and John Daly who, in the trades' own words 'condescended to accept' the office; and when it organised an artisans' industrial exhibition in 1883 the committee thereof was largely composed, not of trade members, but of professional men and businessmen.[34] In 1884 moreover, when the radical secretary, Michael McCarthy was ousted following a split in the council, the reorganisation was entrusted to a local Catholic priest, Revd Francis Hayde, whose emphasis on temperance, self-betterment and respectability seemed set fair to consolidate the mechanics' institute image of the trades council to the detriment of its role as a champion of skilled labour.[35]

Even when Father Hayde's retirement allowed the trades council to concentrate again on its primary role of forwarding trade interests, it remained moderate in its attitude to the middle classes in general, and towards employers in particular. Its intervention in strikes seldom went further than a respectful deputation to the employer concerned to state the strikers' case and try to arrange a meeting between the protagonists. The only really aggressive stand made by the council was during the strike and lockout of operative pork butchers in 1890, when the council's president and secretary headed a picket on one local bacon factory. This display of aggression – if it can be so termed – was never repeated, and even in this case the strike was eventually settled by the usual means – a deputation and conference.[36] In most strikes, however, the trades council advocated a moderate approach to striking members. In a wage dispute among the cork-cutters in 1883, it pressed the men to accept a reduction of twenty per cent, and only when the employer tried to force a further reduction did it take up the cudgels for the journeymen's society. A similarly conciliatory position was taken regarding the boot rivetters' dispute with Dwyer and Company in 1887, the council becoming tough only when the company proved totally obdurate. Such a mild attitude was based largely on the commonsense realisation that in the context of the time, strikes were largely self-defeating, most strikers being easily replaced by blacklegs. Moreover, strikes of long duration were particularly frowned upon as interfering with the employment prospects of other trades, particularly in the building industry where the laying down of tools by one trade could hold up an entire construction scheme. Thus, a ten-week strike by operative plumbers in 1894 was ended by the trades council's insistence on settlement, and two major strikes by operative carpenters in 1892 and 1896 were similarly wound up through council pressure on the men involved.[37]

Yet, if the skilled trades and their representative bodies were the very opposite of radical, they could, in those cases where their collective interests were directly affected, prove surprisingly outspoken towards even those to whom they were usually deferential. Thus, the Catholic clergy who were seldom, if ever, criticised by the organised trades, were towards the end of the century severely censured for their failure to support the manufacture

revival movement. This trend was clearly visible in late nineteenth century Dublin labour circles where it was suggested that
trade unionists should withhold contributions from clergy who
had allowed the use of imported material for the building and
furnishing of city churches.[38] Precisely the same controversy
arose in Cork in 1881 when Canon Hegarty of Sts Peter and
Paul's Church had not only imported the materials for a new
altar but had also withdrawn the contract for carved wooden con-
fessionals and statues from a local cabinet-making firm and sent
it to a firm in Belgium. The reaction of the trades council and
affiliated trades was amazingly sharp. On the summons of the
council secretary, the masons and stonecutters withdrew from
work on the altar, placards posted throughout the city exhorted
all artisans to boycott the work, and the offending clergyman
was publicly called upon by the trades council to explain his actions. He pointed out that the greater part of the work had been
done locally and that it was the local firm's delay in executing
the work which had forced him to send it abroad. But the trades
were not in the humour for reasonable explanations. The boycott
on the work was confirmed and a committee was appointed to
investigate how many other local churches gave their contracts
to local firms. The fact that the boycott was lifted after some weeks
when the trades considered that they had made their point suggests that the wave of militancy on this occasion was an aberra-
tion, due almost certainly to the influence of the radical council
secretary, Michael McCarthy.[39] Yet, even when the latter's
replacement by more moderate spokesmen marked a return to
a more conciliatory stance, the council continued to speak out
strongly against clerical resistance to the cause of local manufacture. The clergy continued to be indifferent. In spite of the trades'
protests, altars were imported by the Augustinian community
in 1888 and a foreign-made organ installed by the Dominicans
in 1897.[40] Similarly, disappointment awaited the several trade
deputations to the Catholic bishops and clergy seeking a commitment that contractors working on church building
would use local manufacture and give preference of employment to union labour. These incidents left a particularly sour
aftertaste, for although the responsibility for providing men

and materials really lay with the contractors and architects, the trades never fully absolved the clergy from blame.[41]

What galled the trades as much as the loss of work for local artisans, however, was the clergy's frequently dismissive attitude towards the trades councils' protests. In 1891, the same clergyman whose importation activities had caused a furore in 1881, again offended the trades. By now, ironically, a member of the Irish Industrial League, he not only imported an altar for the church in the nearby rural parish of Riverstown, but also added insult to injury by telling the trades council deputation waiting on him that they were too well dressed to look like fellows in need of work.[42] Similarly, the Dominicans pointedly ignored the trades' letter of protest against the importation of the organ in 1897, causing the piqued trades council to pass a resolution against future subscriptions by its members to the Dominican church. Though the effectiveness of such a ban was doubtful in the extreme, its adoption showed that while anti-clericalism *per se* was not at all a feature of the organised trades, they were far from deferential to the clergy when their collective interests were at stake.

If the organised trades were generally cautious on economic issues, they were even more so in their political activities. While the Cork trade societies strongly supported contemporary nationalist movements, both constitutional and militant, they gave radical social movements the widest possible berth. This deep distrust of socially-orientated political movements was as characteristic of the skilled artisans of the early twentieth century as it had been of their forebears in the days of O'Connell. The social conservatism of Cork artisans in the pre-famine period was most clearly illustrated in the fate of the infant Chartist movement. In the late 1830s, when Chartism in Britain epitomised 'the ideology of the artisan outlook', it made only feeble attempts to establish itself in Ireland, and not a single report of Chartist activity came into Dublin Castle from the vigilant Cork police.[43] In fact, the only recorded exponent of the movement in the city at this stage was Joseph Hayes, a distiller and a fiercely individualistic member of the merchant-dominated Chamber of Commerce, but whatever rhetorical support for Chartism existed in such unlikely quarters, there was insufficient general interest to form the basis of a local Chartist group. Indeed, so remote was Chartism from the Cork political scene that the local press and police could confuse the Chartist movement with the directly opposed Anti-Corn Law League, describing one of the latter organisation's travelling lecturers in 1841 as 'a Chartist delegate sent over to enflame the people' – and this at a time when the Chartist *Northern Star* was the most bitter opponent of Corn Law repeal.[44] Soon afterwards when the Irish Universal Suffrage Association, a Chartist-linked body based in Dublin, canvassed support in Cork, the reception was equally unencouraging, while a decade later the radical Irish Democratic Association managed to recruit little more than one hundred members in the city, whose working class population was probably well in excess of fifty thousand.[45] Thirty years later again, the First International's attempt to establish a Cork branch failed dismally, as did similar attempts by the Fabian Society in the early 1890s and James Connolly's Irish Socialist Republican Party in the early years of the twentieth century.[46]

To what can be attributed this suspicion of radical social movements among the Cork working classes in general and particularly on the part of the skilled trades? The general failure of Chartism is surely due in part to the opposition of Daniel O'Connell, who accorded to himself the credit for having 'kept Ireland free from this pollution'.[47] O'Connell's claim had some foundation, since at all social levels veneration for him was sufficiently strong to give considerable public force to his anti-Chartist statements. On the other hand, local adulation for O'Connell was not unqualified, periodic criticism for his stance on both local and national issues coming from a number of different quarters. Even the strongly O'Connellite Chamber of Commerce and *Cork Examiner* sometimes expressed resentment at what they saw as the Liberator's political dictation, while the trade societies were disillusioned by his anti-combination stance in general, and particularly by his opposition to a strike by local tanners in 1833. Moreover, among the lower classes he was seriously rivalled in popularity by the parliamentary representative for Cork County, Fergus O'Connor, who was also

considered by more enthusiastic city Repealers to be more committed to the Repeal cause than was O'Connell himself.[48]
Thus, even if O'Connell's opposition partly accounts for the local
failure of Chartism, other factors must be sought out to give a
more satisfactory explanation.

Similarly, although the failure of later radical movements in
Ireland is frequently attributed to the influence of the Catholic
Church, this too (at least in the Cork context) is only partly correct. Certainly, local clerical denunciation of the Irish Democratic
Association of 1849–50 and of the First International in the early
1870s helped to wean away many potential supporters among
respectable workers and particularly within the ranks of the
trades, while in the case of the local branch of the Irish Socialist
Republican Party of 1899 onwards, clerical pressure was apparently responsible not only for a fall-off in the membership, but also
for the sacking of a few die-hard members from their places of
work.[49] But church influence was simply one anti-radical influence in an intensely conservative society. Lack of support from
the middle-class press was equally responsible for the silencing
of would-be radical movements. In early 1850 the popularisation of the radical Irish Democratic Association was effectively
hampered by the determined opposition of John Francis Maguire,
proprietor of the *Cork Examiner*, who stymied the movement's progress by refusing to report the proceedings of the local branch
in his paper. Relying for publicity, therefore, on the modest circulation of its own mouthpiece, the *Irishman*, the association
was denied the local publicity necessary for survival, so that six
months after its inception its existence was unknown to many
of the city's most enthusiastic nationalists and it soon perished
quietly through lack of support.[50] Twenty years later the local
branch of the First International, more difficult to ignore
because of its members' vociferous propaganda, was similarly
smothered by the partisan reporting of the local liberal press,
which not only effectively enforced clerical denunciations, but
also concealed from the public even the modicum of sympathy
which the movement received from within some of the trades.
On this particular occasion, the church–press alliance in Cork
against radicalism took on an intriguing family dimension,

the main spokesmen against the International being the *Cork Examiner*'s John Francis Maguire and his brother, Canon Augustine Maguire, a curate in the centre-city parish of Sts Peter and Paul.[51]

However, just as the single factor of O'Connell's opposition did not provide the ultimate bulwark against Chartism in the 1830s, neither can the opposition of press or pulpit on their own sufficiently explain public non-support for radical movements later in the century. The supplementary reasons for the failure of radicalism among working men in general and artisans in particular must, therefore, be sought elsewhere, particularly in the socio-economic structure of Cork's skilled workforce and in the all-consuming force of nationalism. British observers frequently noted the supremacy of nationalism over radical ideologies in the Irish context. In 1886, William Morris of the Socialist League concluded that 'the Irish . . . will not listen to anything except the hope of independence as long as they are governed by England', and twenty years later, the Fabian Edward Pease conceded that 'the application of the principles of socialism in Ireland has not yet been seriously attempted.[52] In this, as in other matters, the Cork locale proved to be the microcosm of a wider scene. Just as in contemporary south Wales, where inter-class animosity was diluted by a 'common Welshness and non-conformity', so nationalism in much of Ireland gradually assumed the role of panacea for all ills, displacing all other movements which contended with it for popular loyalty.[53] Though, in the Cork context, it could be said that nationalist rhetoric grew more sophisticated in the course of the century, the basic belief that self-government was inevitably good government was as much a feature of popular thinking in the early 1900s as it had been in the 1830s when the extravagant promises of the Chartist movement were largely ignored by a population which saw Repeal of the Union as the ultimate cure-all. In this pre-famine context, popular street ballads and the widely believed 'prophecies' of Pastorini and Colmcille forecast in relation to Repeal the same age of plenty which the English masses foresaw in the attainment of the Charter, even the more politically articulate envisaging that under Repeal 'every man who would be willing to work would be sure of procuring employment, and on satisfactory terms'.[54] It was hardly surprising, then, that a Dublin Chartist meeting, seen as undermining the Repeal cause, was broken up by an O'Connellite gang in 1839 or that the Cork populace totally ignored the new movement.[55] By the 1870s the popularisation of nationalism – and particularly of separatist nationalism – had proceeded so far that Cork organisers of the First International met the strongest possible hostility from among the city's Fenian element. Apart from the clergy, indeed, the most vehement opponents of the International were to be found in the Cork Workingmen's Association (the local Fenian cover-group) and among individual active Fenians within the trade societies. These, ignoring the fact that most of the pathetically few Cork Internationalists were also separatist nationalists, denounced the new body as being inimical to nationalism and religion. Echoing the local clergy's description of the new movement as 'hatched by English and Continental Atheists', the Fenian element pledged that 'the International shall be at once crushed in this country. The moment our religion is attacked we shall stand by it.'[56] Three decades later, when separatist nationalism was reorganising amid inevitable scenes of splits and in-fighting, the by now familiar combination of church, nationalism and artisan conservatism re-emerged to challenge the resurrected socialist movement. As usual, the issues in dispute disappeared in a morass of petty arguments and mud-slinging, the confrontation reaching its nadir with the laying of the local 'Ninety-Eight monument's foundation stone. On this occasion, the local socialist Wolfe Tone Literary Club was elbowed out of the monument committee following the latter's refusal to allow the socialist *Workers' Republic* to be placed along with other nationalist publications under the foundation stone of the monument.[57] The Wolfe Tone Club's reconstitution of itself a few months later as local branch of James Connolly's Irish Socialist Republican Party branch did little to avert its fate. Tottering between life and death, it lasted from early 1899 until 1902 under the leadership of a young clerk, Con O'Lyhane, but found itself hammered from all sides. Denounced from the altars of several Catholic churches, its members pressurised individually by priests and employers,

treated with suspicion by the trades council and cold-shouldered
by the militant nationalists, the small organisation faded into
near-oblivion.[58]

To effectively combat movements which aimed at fundamental social change, however, this commitment to nationalism had
to combine with a further ingredient – an inherent fear of
radicalism. It was obvious, for instance, that despite their increasing use of the language of class in the latter half of the century, local skilled workers regarded socialism with deep suspicion.
In the occasional throw-away remarks of their spokesmen it is
clear that they saw it less as an ideology of any intrinsic worth
than as a stick to brandish over the heads of unpopular employers
and public men. It is worth noting, for instance, that the
favourable reception given to the International by the Cork
coachmakers in 1872 was prompted less by commitment to international socialism than by the International's promise to back
the nine-hours movement which was spearheaded by the
coachmakers' society, and when clerical and public opinion swung
against the International, the coachmakers quickly inserted a
notice in the press to repudiate all connection with the Internationalists.[59] Well over a decade later, attitudes remained unchanged, a similar outlook coming across clearly in the remark
of one trades council delegate driven to extremes by the municipal
corporation's backsliding on wage promises in 1886:

> I tell you what it is, the way we are treated [by the corporation]
> will make Socialists of us soon . . . going after the Lord Mayor's
> carriage![60]

To what can be traced the roots of this suspicious attitude
towards radical change? It seems that, whatever the influence
of religion and nationalism, the real fear of radicalism among
nineteenth-century Cork artisans derived most likely from local
social and employment structures, and particularly from the
predominantly small-workshop pattern of the local economy.
Throughout the century the more overt class tensions attributed
to large-scale factories and outworking systems were, in the Cork
context, mitigated by the close relationship between master and
workers. In spite of what Joyce has aptly termed 'the exploitation

behind putative camaraderie', which caused minor employers to be hated as the most grinding taskmasters, small employers' fortunes were too closely interwoven with those of their journeymen to allow this hatred to be translated into class terms.[61] Journeymen nailors still lodged with their masters as late as the 1880s, while small master bakers, though criticised on many counts by the bakers' union, had a certain affinity with the journeymen because as working masters they themselves laboured in the bakehouses and therefore supported the successive campaigns against night-work throughout the latter half of the century.[62] The oscillating fortunes of small-scale employers, moreover, closed the gap between master and journeyman, particularly in declining trades where mutual protection was essential in the face of outside threats. Thus, both masters and journeymen joined the trade societies of the declining ropemaking and nailmaking trades, while in the hard-pressed coopering trade joint master–men committees to regulate firking making became a regular feature from the depression of the 1870s onwards – an alliance unthinkable for the powerful master coopers of forty years previously.[63] In uncertain times the small master could and did frequently fall to the rank of journeymen, while it was still possible up to the 1890s for the occasional journeyman to become a master.[64] Such mutual dependence and intermeshing of fortunes seems to have discouraged among the skilled workers any wish for radical social change, and it was no surprise, therefore, that trade-society delegates at the 1870 meeting to support the striking tailors spoke not only in the emerging militant language of class but also in traditional terms of the 'paternal care' which employers should show towards their men.[65]

Whatever social radicalism existed among the skilled artisans was confined to a small number of uncharacteristic individuals whose influence was only occasionally strong enough to infect the majority. One such individual was Michael McCarthy, delegate of the coachmakers' society and first secretary of the trades council established in 1881. A dynamic and radical individual, he was almost single-handedly responsible for securing the establishment of the Cork Boot Factory in Blackpool in the early 1880s. Wishing to exclude large capitalists from the running of the new company, McCarthy had each shareholder's quota limited to twenty shares, and invited the local trades to buy into the venture, the profits from which would help to finance the running of their individual trade societies. Though the disappointing response of the public forced McCarthy to raise the upper share limit to one hundred, thus producing a large shareholder company like any other, the original model had shown the radical bent of his thinking.[66] McCarthy was also behind the trades council's militant response to importation in the early 1880s – both the previously mentioned incident involving the importation of woodwork for Sts Peter and Paul's Church in 1881 and the simultaneous protest against the importation of stone for a hall of residence attached to the Queen's College – the latter protest becoming intertwined with the rural land agitation and a labourers' strike in the city.[67] In the following decade a similarly radical leadership was provided by the trade-council president, Eugene Crean, and by the secretary, Michael Austen. As skilled craftsmen unusually sympathetic to labourers and semi-skilled workers, Crean (a carpenter) and Austen (a printer) took a leading role in a major dispute among the operative pork butchers in 1890. The strike had begun in Shaw's bacon-curing factory in Limerick in January 1890, spreading within three days to the unionised bacon factories of Cork and Waterford.[68] Drawing the trades council into the fray, Crean and Austen made the unprecedented move of heading a picket on a local bacon factory as a protest against the drafting in of blackleg labour, while Austen visited Limerick to review the strikers' position and encourage their stand. Both men, moreover, acted for the strikers in the eventual settlement conference.[69] Later in the same year, Austen took a prominent part in unionising the seamen who worked on the cross-channel steamers operating out of the port of Cork, crossing the divide between skilled and unskilled to act for two years as secretary of the local branch of the Sailors' and Firemen's Union.[70] He was certainly responsible to some degree for the action of local branch members who in November 1890 refused to put to sea with a cargo of boycotted cattle – an issue complicated by an interwoven protest against the employment of non-union sailors by the shipping company involved.[71]

Austen was also one of the prime movers in establishing Michael Davitt's Democratic Labour Federation in the Cork region, and later worked with the Englishman, Charles Kelf, a coachmakers' delegate to the trades council, to push the latter body to take up the cause of the general labourer and to press for improved housing for agricultural workers. Kelf gave Austen unusually fulsome praise when he described him as 'the only one [in the trades council] who understands the present position of Trades Unionism . . . We get on well together and, I may say, fight together . . .'[72]

Such praise for Austen was also an indictment of his fellow-artisans. Kelf, as an apostle of Fabianism, was horrified at the social smugness of most Cork artisans whom he considered

> far from being fit subjects for a Fabian society. I found they were in favour of a few democratic demands but find they have only gobbled them up, why they know not. Scratch them and you find a conservative of the crudest type.[73]

Kelf's denunciations, sparked off by the Cork artisan's closed attitude to unskilled workers, was equally applicable to trade unionists in a wider context. Mid-nineteenth century British unions were described even by some of their supporters as 'mere organs of class tyranny', and by more detached commentators in recent times as 'sectionalist and exclusionary'.[74] In the Cork context, as elsewhere, artisans had always been suspicious of labourers and semi-skilled workers because of their capacity to undercut wages and act as blacklegs in strikes.[75] However, it was not until the last three decades of the century that the real depth of animosity towards the unskilled emerged. The open manifestation of such ill-feeling coincided with the unskilled workers' increasing capacity and will to organise themselves and thus threaten both the skilled trades' bargaining power and – equally importantly – the sense of superiority which accompanied their monopoly of unionisation. This threat to the exclusiveness of artisan unionisation emerged first in the heady days of local labour militancy in 1870 but more particularly in the late 1880s and early 1890s when the British 'new unions' established branches in the city. The artisans' reaction to the labour unrest

of the early 1870 was particularly revealing, for while they strongly
backed the local tailors' strike of 1870, they gave no support
whatever to the unskilled workers who took part in the series
of general strikes over the following two years.[76]

The trades council founded in 1881 appeared to deviate from
this élitist stance. From its inception it was open to labourers
as well as craftsmen, and admitted several newly unionised bodies
of unskilled and semi-skilled workers into its ranks in the late
1880s and early 1890s. Yet, its attitude towards unskilled workers
was, as Kelf discovered, conservative in the extreme.[77] When,
for instance, Kelf and Austen attempted to induce the trades
council to champion the housing of agricultural labourers, their
appeal was rejected on the self-interested grounds that the urban
artisans had no obligation towards rural workers and that, in
any case, building schemes of labourers' cottages would not
benefit the city trades since the contracts frequently went to non-
union employers. Moreover, though willing to support the
unionisation of semi-skilled workers like the dockers and pork
butchers, the trades council, reflecting the exclusiveness of its
largely skilled membership, opposed all attempts to unionise the
general labourer. Thus, when it was suggested in 1891 that the
council agitate for a wage rise for the unskilled labourers employed
by the municipal corporation, the motion was quashed by a large
majority of delegates because the corporation labourers were not
affiliated to the council and because the council did not wish to
be seen to stir up trouble between the corporation and its
employees.[78] The trades council's distrust of unskilled labour
was clearly shown at the same period in the grudging co-operation
given to Davitt's Democratic Labour Federation and its successor,
the Land and Labour League.[79] Although the Fermoy branch
of the Labour Federation was allowed to affiliate with the trades
council in 1891, attitudes had again hardened by the mid-1890s
so that invitations to the council to send delegates to the meetings
of the Land and Labour League were snubbed for four years
in succession. Although delegates finally attended Labour League
meetings in 1898 many members of the trades council even then
strongly opposed the move.[80] More indicative still of artisan
hostility towards unskilled workers was their outright opposition

to the South of Ireland Labour Union which emerged in 1890 as a general labour union – i.e. a union including in its ranks several categories of workers.[81] Its organisation drive in the city and, in particular, its attempted co-ordination of a local foundry workers' strike were blocked at every step by the trades-council.[82] A similarly dismissive attitude was shown towards unskilled labour in 1901, when a major strike among the gas company's workers was settled by trades-council mediation in a manner totally unacceptable to the local branch of the Gas Workers' Union.[83]

Such hostility towards workers outside the ranks of the skilled was hardly compatible with any real sense of class consciousness. This was painfully clear to the leaders of the unskilled who, reacting with understandable bitterness to what they saw as artisan snobbery and self-interest, concluded that

> it was the old, old story, that whenever a movement was started to help the working men, the greatest clog upon it were the Trades of Cork . . . [who] think more of their own ambition than of harmony and the working men's improvement.[84]

This assessment, however, did not take fully into account the complexities of artisan attitudes towards those outside their ranks. As Weber expressed it in the French context, most 'people looked down, not up', and if many Cork artisans were snobs, their snobbery was based on fear rather than self-confidence, revealing how latent socio-economic prejudices were brought into the open when the status and privileges of a plebeian élite were threatened by the attempted upward movement of those below them.[85]

The complexities of artisan snobbery were highlighted in 1890 by the totally different ways in which the Cork trades council reacted to two simultaneous local strikes by semi-skilled workers. One group, the operative pork butchers, was strongly supported while similar action by foundry workers was condemned out of hand. On the surface, the reasons for such apparent inconsistency were simple: the trades-council spokesmen claimed that the foundry men's demands were unreasonable and that, moreover, the pork butchers were supported because their society was affiliated to the trades council whereas the foundry workers were not so aligned. In reality, however, the trades council's arguments were untenable. There was little difference between the respective demands of the two groups of strikers, and the foundry men were not allied to the trades council simply because their union's application had been bluntly rejected by the trades a short time beforehand.[86] The real reasons for artisan intransigence on this occasion must be sought elsewhere – i.e. in the composition of the foundry workers' society, the South of Ireland Labour Union. Whereas the pork butchers' society was made up of clearly defined categories of workers – butchers, salters and curers – the South of Ireland Labour Union included in its ranks not just labourers but also 'handymen' – those who did the work of craftsmen without having served an apprenticeship.[87] This union was therefore seen by the craftsmen as a haven for untrained men who, operating outside trade-union control, were 'taking the bread out of [the artisan's] mouth and interfering with his business' by undercutting wages and blacklegging during trade disputes.[88] Equally significant was the fact that the artisans were unable to envisage any bona fide labour organisation which was not built on the foundations of the individual trade – hence the trades-council rule, reiterated in the controversy of 1890, against the affiliation of any body whose members followed a variety of occupations. When, on that occasion, one delegate declared that a man could sit at the council table only as a delegate of his own trade, he was simply verbalising the traditional mindset of the craft.[89] Thus, whatever lip-service the skilled artisan might pay to class solidarity, he was ultimately constrained by fear of the unskilled and by a traditional sense of identity rooted in trade rather than class.

When the matter of labour representation in local government arose in the 1890s, the same constraints of traditional thinking were visible. The trades' espousal of the cause of labour representation was based less on any real class consciousness than on a desire to further the interests of the skilled workers in the face of municipal government indifference. Indeed, the trades' periodic confrontations with the corporation over the latter half of the century were, perhaps, the clearest indication of the narrowness of skilled men's class awareness. As discussed earlier, most of the organised trades' contacts with the municipal corporation before the 1890s concerned the interests of the skilled craftsmen, centring on what the trades perceived as the corporation's lack of patronage of the local building industry and of establishments employing fair labour. Such contact, moreover, was less with the corporation as a body than with individual corporators who, predictably, were supported by the trades not on the nebulous grounds of class, but for their nationalist credentials and their record as champions of trade interests. Thus, when Daniel O'Sullivan, a pro-Fenian mayor, was pressurised to resign his office in 1869 because of his attendance at a banquet in honour of released Fenian prisoners, the trades took up his cause with gusto. At a more practical level, they also supported individual mayors and town councillors who assisted the short-lived Mechanics' Hall of the early 1870s and the more permanent trades council of the 1880s.[90]

This tug of loyalty between trade interests and nationalism left very little room among the artisans for any abstract sense of class consciousness in their dealings with the municipal corporation. Even the militant anti-corporation speeches made from time to time by trade representatives concentrated not on working-class identity but on solidarity among the trades, who

> should uphold themselves and not be so apathetic, and show what they could do. And if the trades would band themselves together for the common benefit, as they did in other cities, they could compel the mayor and corporation not to be going against them, as they [were] doing at present.[91]

With this limited outlook, it was hardly surprising that until the very end of the century the organised trades made no demand for a change in the social composition of the corporation, concentrating instead on securing the election of parties who, though favourable to trade interests, belonged to the political and social élite which had traditionally dominated the corporation. It was not, in fact, until the Local Government Act of 1898 threw open to popular election most of the public bodies hitherto elected on a restricted franchise that the Cork trades made any serious moves towards Labour representation on the town council.

Viewed in the context of the British Isles as a whole, Irish artisan interest in direct local political involvement developed
relatively late. Whereas in England there had been sporadic trade-
union forays into municipal electoral politics in 1852 and 1868,
Belfast and Dublin trade unionists did not become active in this
field until the last two decades of the century. In 1892 the Belfast
trades council had created a parliamentary and municipal election fund and in 1897 elected the first Labour group to the city's
corporation. Moreover, since 1892 the city had its own local
Labour party. This affiliated in 1893 with the newly-formed Independent Labour Party, which later formed branches in Dublin
and Waterford. In Dublin, too, the trades council formed its own
Labour electoral association in 1895, putting forward Labour
candidates for council seats in 1895 and 1896, though none were
successful.[92] Cork lagged even further behind these developments. It had no branch of the Independent Labour Party, and
not until 1901 was a short-lived branch of the Fabian Society
established in the city.[93] Moreover, as has been discussed earlier,
its labour organisations were inward-looking and lacking in enthusiasm for any broadly based Labour movement, as evident
in their dearth of interest in the Trades Union Congress and their
hostility towards unskilled labour. Above all, local trades' animosity
towards the town council was primarily a product of their resentment against that body's ineffectiveness in promoting trade interests rather than of any class consciousness in the wider sense
– an attitude which still prevailed even in the late 1890s when
the local trades council had finally come round to the idea of
fighting for Labour representation on the town council.

When the Cork Labour candidates finally entered the
municipal contest following the Local Government Act of 1898,
their canvas was based not on any abstract ideas of the rights
of labour but on the well-worn grievances which had caused friction between the trades and the corporation since the early 1880s,
particularly the questions of fair labour and the provision of public
works and – a newer issue – the switching of corporation sit-
tings from afternoon to night to facilitate the attendance of working men. The impression of a wider class commitment by the
trades was evident in the introduction of three totally new issues.

Firstly, sparring with the corporation over the latter's lack of interest in providing municipal baths and financing the city's many musical bands, the trades council presented their case in the class rhetoric of the day as an instance of the city fathers' anti-working-class bias which contrasted starkly with their recent generous grant to the middle-class patronised School of Music. Added to this were calls for higher wages for corporation labourers and for improved housing and sanitation for the working-class areas of the city.[94] However, it could be suggested that the introduction of these issues by the trades was decidedly opportunistic, and that what they had in mind was the interests of the unionised workers rather than of the working class as a whole. They had, after all, proved themselves totally indifferent to the plight of the corporation labourers earlier in the decade, and they had never before concerned themselves with the housing issue which had, in fact, been conspicuous by its absence from discussions at trades council meetings.[95] Indeed, the only recorded occasions on which the organised trades had previously mentioned the housing issue were in 1877 and 1886, in both cases the motivation being to foster employment in the building trade rather than to better the living conditions of the working classes in general.[96] Now in 1898 the trades took up the housing question with zest, accusing the municipal authorities of jobbery, implying (not incorrectly) that many corporation members were slum landlords, and refusing to give any credit whatever to the corporation for its involvement in working-class housing schemes which were dismissed as too expensive, too cramped, and too far from most places of employment.[97]

The use of the housing issue by the organised trades in their 1898 election canvas was, therefore, based on political expediency rather than social commitment. But both their previous neglect of the subject and the terms in which it was now presented also suggest that the more vocal representatives of the trades were themselves an élite, well-housed and ignorant of the squalid living conditions of the poor. This view is supported by the fact that all the Labour candidates in the 1899 election, their proposers and seconders, had relatively 'respectable' addresses, while their post-election speeches suggested that the city-centre

house-to-house canvas had been a frightening revelation of the
extent of hidden poverty in the city.[98] If, as this suggests, the
spokesmen of the organised trades were so far removed from the
most grinding aspects of contemporary local poverty, it is hardly surprising that when they came to form a labour panel in the
local elections, this panel would lack any radical commitment
to class solidarity.

The actual choice of Labour candidates, moveover, revealed
that the Labour label was in itself a misnomer, for the trades council had no direct part in candidate selection, which lay ultimately
with the individual trade societies. Under these circumstances,
the unskilled labouring sector was predictably absent from a canvas
monopolised by the skilled trades. Of the nineteen individuals put
forward by fourteen affiliated trade societies, seventeen were
members of the skilled trades while not a single labourer was included. The two non-craft candidates were members of the
Hackney Car Owners' Society, affiliated to the trades council since
1897, while also included under the Labour banner were two
master tradesmen – a cooper and a painter.[99]

The inclusion of such micro-capitalists poses problems for an
assessment of the class consciousness of the 1898 Labour panel.
On the one hand, as Foster put it in the parallel British urban
context, 'all the little master had was his skill . . .[and therefore]
shared the general working-class allegiance', so perhaps the inclusion in the Cork Labour panel of master craftsmen and car
owners – all men of relatively humble status and modest means
– revealed on the part of contemporary workingmen a broader
and more accurate understanding of the term 'Labour' than that
presented by twentieth-century Marxist interpretation. On the
other hand, the omission of any unskilled manual workers from
what purported to be a Labour panel renders somewhat suspect
the use of the political term 'Labour' in the local context of the
late 1890s. Ultimately, in the matter of 'Labour politics' in the
1899 municipal election, the trades were as hedged in by the traditional artisan sense of identity as their forebears had been in the
1830s. While they might pay lip-service to the concept of class
solidarity, their attitudes were narrow and élitist, and their
horizons stretched no further than the confines of their craft.

NOTES

1 E. P. Thompson, *The Making of the English Working Class*, p. 939 (quoting his previous article, 'Peculiarities of the English', Ralph Miliband and John Saville (eds.), *The Socialist Register* (London, 1965), p. 357.

2 E. P. Thompson, *The Making of the English Working Class*, p. 914; R. Q. Gray, 'Class formation in Edinburgh', pp. 232, 255; Richard Price, *Labour in British Society*, p. 83; Tony Bennett, 'The politics of the "popular"', Tony Bennett, Colin Mercer and Janet Woollacot (eds.), *Popular Culture and Social Relations* (Open University Press, Milton Keynes, 1986) p. 6.

3 For the social composition of the Cork Corporation, see Maura Murphy, 'Economic and social structure of nineteenth century Cork', p. 126.

4 *CE*, 16 Jan. 1899.

5 Dick Geary, *European Labour Protest*, p. 44; R. Q. Gray, 'Class formation in Edinburgh', p. 48, quoting Haiton, *The Castes of Edinburgh* (1860), pp. 4–7, 104; John Foster, *Class Struggle and the Industrial Revolution*, pp. 331–3.

6 *CMC*, 14 Nov., 26 Dec. 1832.

7 John Foster, *Class Struggle and the Industrial Revolution*, pp. 109, 122; E. P. Thompson, *The Making of the English Working Class*, pp. 819, 889; Tony Bennett, 'The politics of the "popular"', p. 20, depicts the term 'the people' as referring 'neither to everyone nor to a single group within society but to a variety of social groups which, although differing from one another in other respects (their class position or the particular struggles in which they are most immediately engaged) are distinguished from the economically, politically and culturally powerful groups within society and are hence *potentially* capable of being united – of being organised into "the people versus the power bloc" – if their separate struggles are connected'.

8 *CC*, 14 Jan. 1830. This letter called for a long list of reforms including municipal reform, universal suffrage and the ballot, and ending with the cryptic message: 'I am for the present silent on the most important of all topics – the Repeal of the Union. I will not bring that subject before Parliament until the combined wish of the Irish *people* [my italics] shall demand that Repeal in a voice too distinct to be misunderstood, and too formidable to be trifled with.'

9 *SR*, 25 May 1839; *CC*, 28 Aug. 1838, 3 Oct. 1839, 6 Oct. 1840, 20 July 1841; Sheahan, *Articles of Irish Manufacture*, pp. 224–5.

10 *People's Press*, 2 May 1835; Cork Archives Institute, Day Papers, DP II, 1837, p. 57; 1839, p. 95. Another such People's Hall was established in Limerick around the same period. *Limerick Reporter*, 6 Dec. 1844. The Cork *People's Press* was established in 1834 by some individuals who believed that the city's main radical newspaper, the *Cork Mercantile Chronicle* was 'pusillanimous and ineffective'. The new paper was strongly in favour of Repeal of the Union, its motto being 'Uniformly have the people of Ireland been plundered and oppressed'. The paper proved a flop. Its reporting was third

rate, it apparently lacked funds and a competent editor, and it folded in 1836.

11   *SR*, 22 Mar., 19 Apr., 9, 14 July 1836, 27 Apr. 1837; *People's Press*, 1 Aug. 1835.

12   *SR*, 6, 25 Jan. 1848; *CC*, 30 Mar. 1848; William Smith O'Brien Papers, National Library of Ireland, MS 442, letter 2374: Michael Joseph Barry to William Smith O'Brien, 22 Feb. 1848.

13   *Irishman*, 16 Nov. 1849, 2 Mar. 1850; *Nation*, 23 Feb., 9 Mar., 11, 18, 25 May, 1 June, 27 July, 3 Aug. 1850; CSORP.OR, 1850, 9/64; 1851: 9/125.

14   *CE*, 15, 26 Feb., 2 June 1858.

15   Peter Bailey, *Leisure and Class in Victorian England: Rational Recreation and the Contest for Control, 1830–1950* (London, 1978), *passim*; James Walvin, *Leisure and Society 1830–1950* (London, 1978), *passim*; Elizabeth Malcolm, *Ireland Sober, Ireland Free*, pp. 326–7.

16   Patrick Joyce, *Work, Society and Politics*, p. 169; *CE*, 10 July 1850, 21 Sept., 21 Dec. 1853, 7 Jan. 1857.

17   *CE*, 18 Apr. 1863, 1 Apr., 28 June 1873, 20 Jan., 13 Feb. 1874, 4 Mar. 1882; Elizabeth Malcolm, *Ireland Sober, Ireland Free*, pp. 178–9. The Cork Refreshment Rooms Company was established by the South of Ireland Temperance League.

18   *CE*, 12 Oct. 1870, 28 Apr. 1871.

19   *CE*, 6, 27 June 1870; John Boyle, *The Irish labour movement*, p. 55. The Dublin United Trades Association described itself in 1864 as seeking 'the protection of the rights of labour'.

20   *CE*, 13 Oct. 1875.

21   *CE*, 22, 23 Apr. 1890. Brendan McDonnell in his 'The Dublin labour movement', p. xvi, notes the use of similar anti-capitalist terminology among late nineteenth-century Dublin trade unionists.

22   *CE*, 20 Dec. 1898, 18 Jan. 1899; Cork Archives Institute, Cork Corporation Public Health Committee Minute Books, 1895–98. By the late 1890s quite a large number of slum landlords were obviously poor people who themselves lived in substandard accommodation.

23   R. Q. Gray, 'Class structure in Edinburgh', p. 23.

24   *CE*, 28, 30 June, 15, 18, 20, 22, 25 Sept., 9, 30 Oct. 1843; Cork Public Museum, Cork Committee of Merchants' Minute Books, 31 Aug., 17 Sept. 1840.

25   *CE*, 25 Oct. 1895, 12 Feb. 1897. The rank and file of the trades council reputedly bought their clothes, shoes and furniture from establishments dealing in cheap imported goods. The tailoring trade, in particular, in which the effects of importation and sweating had been creating problems since the 1850s, protested in the late 1890s against the level of tradesman custom given to these 'unfair' shops. To combat this tendency the tailors' society sent lists of fair employers to all the other trade societies, but without any significant result.

26   *CE*, 19 Jan., 18 Mar., 11 Apr. 1842. *CE*, 19 Jan., 15 Feb., 10, 17 Mar., 23 May 1883. In the 1840s, much of this anti-middle-class rhetoric was

directed against the reformed town council which was accused of deserting the trades in their hour of need. In the 1880s, though the trades themselves gave little real support to the exhibition, the trades council singled out some of the city's large firms whom they accused of losing interest in the manufacture revival. Besides, when the exhibition closed, it transpired that the executive committee had not fulfilled its promise to organise a sale of individual artisans' exhibits, and the disappointed parties, financially at a loss through the oversight, retained much bitterness towards the gentlemen at fault.

27 R. J. Morris, 'The labour aristocracy in the British class structure', p. 173.

28 John Boyle, *The Irish Labour Movement*, pp. 144–5.

29 *CMC*, 20, 24 Oct., 21, 28 Nov., 14 Dec. 1832; *People's Press*, 4 July 1835; *SR*, 14 Dec. 1839; Cork Archives Institute, Day Papers, DP II, 1837, p. 57; 1839, p. 95. The Hall fund received a £200 surplus from the 1837 election fund, but the remaining subscriptions came from a very limited group. Over seventy per cent of the money donated or lent to the Hall came from two individuals connected with mercantile and brewing interests – William Crawford and Francis Bernard Beamish. A further twenty-four per cent came from thirteen individuals – manufacturers, merchants, independent gentlemen and Catholic clergymen. The remaining six per cent came from four of the city's trade societies – tailors, bakers, coopers and saddlers, though others including victuallers, corkcutters, weavers and shipwrights subscribed later.

30 *CE*, 14 Sept. 1860, 3, 6, 10, 11 Dec. 1861, 2 Jan. 1862, 28 Nov. 1864; *CC*, 3 Dec. 1861; *CDH*, 2 Jan. 1862; *Morning News* (Dublin) 3, 11, 13, 17 Jan. 1862. Arnott, Scottish by birth and a conservative in politics, had become a public figure in both Limerick and Cork, and had won much public popularity by his donations towards the relief of the poor, his catch-cry of cheap bread for the poor and his campaign against Sunday work in bakeries. The involvement with Arnott may have had its disadvantages because the trades council split some time in the early 1860s as the result of squabbles between him and the *Cork Examiner* editor, John Francis Maguire.

31 *CE*, 19 Oct. 1871.

32 *CE*, 19 Oct. 1871.

33 *CE*, 21, 25 Feb., 18 May, 11, 18 July 1881, 31 Jan., 5 July, 12 Sept. 1884, 6 May 1892, 1 Jan. 1895. Non-working men or honorary members were required to pay an annual fee of one guinea, while working men members paid only one shilling a year. The association actually attracted few honorary members – a maximum of thirty per year – and periodic appeals for funds for specific purposes met with a similarly unenthusiastic response. The most generous donations came always from the same quarter – the brewing and distilling interests, traditionally generous to the trades. Yet, in spite of its limitations, this extra-trade financial support was vital to the council's existence, for though the yearly accounts were not published

in sufficient detail to show the exact dependence on such subscriptions, up to the mid-1880s from forty to eighty per cent of income came from such sources.

34 *CE*, 11 Apr., 30 May, 13 June 1881, 19 Mar. 1885. Such a quest for the patronage of prominent public men for local trades councils was also typical in Britain, as demonstrated by R. Q. Gray, 'Class structure in Edinburgh', p. 251. In the Cork context, however, it can also be argued that the courting of Parnell and Daly was prompted less by the desire for middle-class support than by the trades' anxiety to show solidarity with the forces of nationalism, while the employment of experienced businessmen on the exhibition committee was probably based on sound common sense.

35 *CE*, 31 Jan. 1884.

36 *CE*, 8 Mar. 1883, 11, 13 July 1889, 14, 27 Feb., 5 Mar. 1890, 17 Mar. 1893, 1, 8, 15 May 1896, 4, 12 Oct. 1898.

37 *CE*, 9 Dec. 1887, 10, 11, 12, 13, 14, 15 June 1892, 8, 16, 18, 19 June, 21 July, 21 Aug., 9 Oct. 1896.

38 Brendan McDonnell, 'The Dublin labour movement', pp. 10–11.

39 I have been unable to find any details on the background of Michael McCarthy. Besides being a particularly militant exponent of labour organisation, he also strikes one as having Fenian sympathies, although there is, to date, no proof whatsoever of this.

40 *CE*, 24 Aug., 2 Sept. 1888, 23 Jan., 5 Feb. 1897.

41 *CE*, 25 July 1881, 6, 7 Apr. 1886, 2 Sept. 1888.

42 *CE*, 8 Aug., 7, 8, 9, 10 Sept. 1881, 2 May 1891. Riverstown is some four miles north-east of the city.

43 Patrick Joyce, *Work, Politics and Society*, p. 62; CSORP, 1841: 1/13323, 9/9445, 11/15869, 15/399, 449, 16/14919, 14825, 18661–3, 19/17517, 22/3945–6, 29/14093; 1842: 1/979, 2219; Andrew Boyd, *The Rise of the Irish Trade Unions*, p. 45. Chartism made little headway in Ireland generally. Some moves were made to set up Chartist groups in Dublin, Waterford, Belfast, Newry and Drogheda, but with relatively little success. In the country towns of the midlands there were reports of the presence of Chartist emissaries but their efforts apparently bore no fruit, although they were sufficiently active to attract the attention of the police, who hurriedly sent reports on their movements to Dublin Castle.

44 *SR*, 12, 14 Mar. 1839, *Freeholder*, 8 Mar. 1839, *Northern Star*, 23 Mar. 1839; CSORP.OR, 1840: 6/16225; 1841: 6/8473; Charles Gavan Duffy, *Thomas Davis: The Memoirs of an Irish Patriot* (London, 1870), p. 164. The local Young Irelander, Michael Joseph Barry, writing to Thomas Davis in 1843, described Hayes as 'singularly clever, equally intemperate, thoroughly impracticable, hating everybody in general and the Murphy family in particular; cannot, I presume, do the entire work of this city himself, and will not, I am convinced, work with anyone else'.

45 *CE*, 8, 13 Sept. 1841; *Irishman*, 16 Nov. 1849, 2 Mar. 1850; *Census of Ireland 1851*. The total population of Cork in 1851 was 85,732.

46 John Boyle, *The Irish Labour Movement*, pp. 75–91, 205–215; Seán Daly, *Ireland and the First International* (Cork, 1984), pp. 72–129; *Fabian News* (London), Mar., Aug., Nov. 1892, Dec. 1893–Feb. 1897; William O'Brien Papers: Minute Books of the Irish Socialist Republican Party, 8 Feb. 1900, 2 Aug. 1901, National Library of Ireland, MS 15,700 (1). There was no Fabian group in Cork in the late nineteenth century though Belfast had a branch since February 1891 and Dublin's branch was established between August 1892 and December 1893.

47 Boyd, *The Rise of the Irish Trade Unions*, pp. 44–5.

48 *CMC*, 13, 15 June 1833, 3, 12 Mar. 1834; *CC*, 18 Nov. 1834, 16 May 1844; *Pilot*, 23 Sept. 1836; CSORP.OR, 1834: 1206/17, 34. Fergus O'Connor was parliamentary representative for County Cork from 1832 until he was unseated due to inadequate property qualifications in 1835. He later became one of the best-known Chartist leaders in Britain. For an account of his career, see Donald Read and Eric Glasgow, *Fergus O'Connor, Irishman and Chartist* (London, 1961).

49 John Boyle, *The Irish Labour Movement*, pp. 206–9; *Irishman*, 16 Nov. 1849, 2 Mar. 1850; *CE*, 13, 26 Mar. 1872; William O'Brien Papers, 13 Mar. 1900, 2, 9, 29 Oct., 4 Nov. 1901, National Library of Ireland, MS 15,700 (1).

50 *Irishman*, 16 Mar., 6 Apr. 1850; *CE*, 8 Mar. 1850.

51 John Boyle, *The Irish Labour Movement*, pp. 83–6; Seán Daly, *Ireland and the First International*, p. 94. The local coachmakers' union branch had held a meeting to receive delegates from the International, and many apparently joined the association, while the carpenters, the drapers' assistants and nine other societies were rumoured to be considering affiliation.

52 John Boyle, *The Irish Labour Movement*, pp. 174, 181.

53 Patrick Joyce, *Work, Society and Politics*, pp. 230–1.

54 Sheahan, *Articles of Irish Manufacture*, p. 187.

55 Andrew Boyd, *The Rise of the Irish Trade Unions*, pp. 49–50; John Boyle, *The Irish Labour Movement*, pp. 44–5. O'Connell praised the 'loyal demonstration' of those who disrupted the Dublin Chartist meeting.

56 Seán Daly, *Ireland and the First International*, p. 116; *CE*,, 16, 21, 27, 29, 30 Mar. 1872; Fenian Papers 1872, 8105R.

57 CBSR, 1898: 17582/S.

58 John Boyle, *The Irish Labour Movement*, pp. 203–9.

59 Seán Daly, *Ireland and the First International*, pp. 89–91, 123; John Boyle, *The Irish Labour Movement*, pp. 84–6.

60 *CE*, 21 Oct. 1886.

61 Patrick Joyce, *Work, Society and Politics*, p. 161.

62 *CE*, 25 Nov. 1881, 23, 25, 26, 28 Sept., 2, 6 Oct. 1890.

63 *CE*, 25 Nov. 1881; Cork Coopers' Society Minute Books, 16, 29 Jan. 1874, 26 July, 4 Oct. 1883, 2 Nov. 1896. In ropemaking and nailmaking, working masters were apparently the norm – hence their inclusion in the trade society. The coopers' society decided in 1896 to cut their wage rates for cask making to help the master coopers to get over a period of depression.

John Foster, *Class Struggle and the Industrial Revolution*, p. 136, similarly outlines the economically marginal position of small employers in English towns, while Dick Geary, *European Labour Protest,* p. 56, refers in the British and French contexts to the deradicalising effect of good (or, at least, close) employer–worker relations.

64 Maura Murphy, 'The economic and social structure of nineteenth century Cork', pp. 130–9; Cork Coopers' Society Minute Books, 13 June 1888, 14 June 1892; Cork Plumbers' Society Minute Books, 15 Oct. 1870; Cork Typographical Society Minute Books, 5 Apr. 1890. The local coopers' and plumbers' societies had special provisions in their rule books for the admission as society members of former masters who had fallen to the ranks of the journeymen.

65 *CE*, 27 June 1870.

66 *CE*, 31 Aug. 1881, 2 Feb., 20 May, 8 July 1882, 23 May 1884.

67 *CE*, 19, 20, 29 July, 8, 10 Aug. 1881.

68 *CE*, 27, 28 Jan. 1890. The strike was originally concerned with Shaw and Company's refusal to pay 'pig money' – i.e. an extra payment of one penny for each pig killed. This pig money was shared among the men at the end of the week and was intended to buy their clothes for the job. The strike reached the other two cities just as the employers in the three centres decided to break up the growing union by a policy of dismissing union members. In Cork the employees of three bacon factories (Shaws, Lunhams and Dennys) turned out or were locked out, and a five-week strike ensued. For a comprehensive account of the strike in Waterford, see Emmet O'Connor, *A Labour History of Waterford*, pp. 91–3.

69 *CE*, 19, 21, 27 Feb., 3, 4 Mar. 1890.

70 *Seafaring,* 22 Aug. 1891, p. 8.

71 *CE*, 31 Oct., 1, 3, 4, 5, 6, 8, 10, 12, 13, 15, 18 Nov. 1890, 5, 7 May 1892. Austen was severely censured by the union executive for his involvement in this complicated affair, and was replaced by Thomas H. Clarke who, incidentally, soon absconded with union funds.

72 *CE*, 19 Oct., 9, 12 Nov. 1894; London School of Economics, Webb Trade Union Collection, section A, vol. iii, ff. 46–7: Charles Kelf to Edward Pease, 1891.

73 Webb Trade Union Collection, section A., vol. iii, ff. 46–7: Charles Kelf to Edward Pease, 1891. The Fabian Society, founded in London in 1884, was manned largely by well-to-do supporters of socialism who were known somewhat derisively as 'gas and water socialists' because of their belief that government-sponsored reforms in vital areas affecting working people's living conditions would be more effective than violent revolution.

74 Adrian Pimley, 'The working class movement and the Irish revolution', p. 193; R. J. Morris, 'The labour aristocracy in the British class structure', p. 171; Richard Price, *Labour in British Society*, p. 83; Henry Pelling, *A History of British Trade Unionism* (London, 1971), p. 68, quoting the trade-union nominee on the Royal Commission on Trade Unionism in 1867.

Parnell – no friend, incidentally, to organised labour – described the Irish unions of his day as a 'landlordism of labour', while some early twentieth-century socialists were equally scathing, denouncing trade unions as closed, selfish and 'isolated . . . from the mass of the proletariat'.

75 E. P. Thompson, *The Making of the English Working Class*, p. 270, noted that in the early nineteenth-century context 'where a skill was involved, the artisan was as much concerned with maintaining his status as against the unskilled man as he was in bringing pressure upon the employers'.

76 *CE*, 6, 9, 20, 27 June 1870.

77 *CE*, 11 July 1881, 26 Apr., 13 Dec. 1889, 28 Feb., 11 Apr., 9 May 1890. The trades council, seven months after its inception, admitted 'all persons of character, whether in the shopkeeping or labouring interest'. Whether this decision was based on the general feeling of the council or forced through by the radical secretary, Michael McCarthy, is not now clear. Seven categories of semi-skilled worker joined the trades council in 1889–90: the pork butchers, seamen and Cork dockers in 1889, followed in 1890 by the brewery workmen, builders' labourers, railwaymen and Passage dock labourers,

78 *CE*, 4, 11, 18 Sept. 1891; Webb Trade Union Collection, sect. A, vol. iii, ff. 46–7. It must be stressed that this closed attitude was not confined to the skilled trades, for the local society of builders' labourers proved equally exclusive, refusing to open its ranks to any labourers except those employed in the building trade.

79 *CE*, 11 Jan., 22 Feb. 1890, 18 Mar. 1891, 19 Oct., 9, 12 Nov. 1894; *CDH*, 22 Jan. 1890.

80 *CE*, 19 Oct., 1, 12 Nov. 1894, 2 Aug. 1895, 6 Sept. 1897, 17 Sept. 1898. The only Cork labour society sending delegates to the Land and Labour League meetings in the late 1890s was the Builders' Labourers' Society.

81 *Irish Times*, 20 Nov. 1885; *CE*, 3, 24 Feb. 1890. The origins of the South of Ireland Labour Union are obscure. Apparently, it was originally founded by the west Waterford landed proprietor, Villiers Stuart of Dromana, not as a trade union, but as a mutual help organisation of labourers, farmers and artisans. Between 1884 and 1890 it fell into obscurity, but reappeared in 1890 as an authentic general labour union unconnected with its original founder. It also apparently had some tenuous connections with the Knights of Labour, for which see Henry Pelling, *A History of British Trade Unionism*, pp. 95–7; John Boyle, *The Irish Labour Movement*, pp. 106–7.

82 *CE*, 24 Feb. 1890.

83 William O'Brien Papers, Minute Book of the Irish Socialist Republican Party, 26 Sept. 1901; John Boyle, *The Irish Labour Movement*, p. 207.

84 *CE*, 24 Feb. 1890.

85 Eugen Weber, *Peasants into Frenchmen*, p. 246.

86 *CE*, 22 Feb. 1890.

87 Emmet O'Connor, *A Labour History of Waterford*, p. 91.

88 *CE*, 22 Feb. 1890. It was stressed by the trades delegates that if the strikers

had served their apprenticeships to the trades which they practiced, the council would have no objection in seeking standard wages for them.

89 *CE*, 22 Feb. 1890.

90 *CE*, 3 Feb. 1870, 2 Jan. 1872, 5 Jan. 1882; CSORP, 1869: 6779, 7461; Fenian Papers 1869: 4235R; Seán Daly, *Cork: A City in Crisis*, p. 73.

91 *CE*, 23 Mar., 14 Oct. 1886. The occasion of this outburst was the corporation's decision to sell municipally-owned land (which the trades felt should be used for housing) for the building of a new match factory.

92 Henry Pelling, *A History of British Trade Unionism*, pp. 61–2; Arthur Mitchell, *Labour in Irish Politics*, p. 18.

93 John Boyle, *The Irish Labour Movement*, pp. 206–7.

94 *CE*, 17 June, 23, 30 July, 8 Oct., 14 Nov., 5, 10 Dec. 1898; *Workers' Republic*, 3 Sept. 1898, p. 4; 17 Sept. 1898, p. 1; John Boyle, *The Irish Labour Movement*, p. 256.

95 *CE*, 5 Dec. 1898. Corporation workers' wages were two to three shillings per week lower than the city standard.

96 *CE*, 23 Oct. 1877, 12 Feb. 1886. In 1877 the trades called on the corporation to enforce Crosses' Act by starting a local housing scheme, and made similar calls in 1886 when the building industry was experiencing a slump.

97 *CE*, 27 Mar. 1897, 17 June, 28 Nov. 1898; *Workers' Republic*, 3 Sept. 1898.

98 *CE*, 6, 18 Jan. 1899. Only one labour candidate lived in a back lane, and this was not one of the slum lanes of the city.

99 *CE*, 22 May 1897, 18 Jan. 1899, PP 1899, xcii (493), pp. 204–5. The affiliation of the Hackney Car Owners' Society to the trades council had been agreed to only with certain reservations. The main reason for the request for affiliation was the danger of the hackney men's livelihood being eroded by the introduction of a private bus service to the city. Among the skilled trades, journeymen candidates were put forward as follows: coachmakers – three; carpenters and bakers – two each; and one each by the bootmakers, cabinet makers, plasterers, plumbers, printers, smiths, stonecutters and tailors. The masters put forward for election were Thomas Cogan, a master painter and a master cooper, the strongly pro-Fenian Cornelius P. O'Sullivan.

6

TRADE AS IDENTITY

Be careful not to say anything hurtful to the Cork United Trades
. . . [Your communication] ought to be conveyed in the most
moderate language and without any expression that could be
seized upon as hostile to the Trades.[1]

This sound advice tendered to one local politician by another
in 1897 illustrates how, by the late nineteenth century, the trade
unions of Cork had developed their own distinct collective identity, not only in economic matters but also as a relatively autonomous section of the nationalist movement.

Such an assessment of the trades would have been inconceivable seventy years previously, when neither individual artisan
nor trade society attracted the attention, much less the approval,
of either press or authorities. This former disinterest derived from
two major factors. Firstly, trade unions were outside the law until 1825, and even then, hedged in as they were by various restrictions, their legal position remained unclear. Secondly, the individual artisan, though occasionally enfranchised, was considered
to be of little political significance in his own right. Thus, it is
clear that in this period of obscurity, the primary identity of the
artisan lay not in his dubious role as citizen, but in his membership of a trade and his sharing of what Gray described as 'the
culture of the craft'.[2] While such craft solidarity — 'the strong

205

shared commitment to their own customs and interests which binds together a specialized occupational group with distinct skills' – did not necessarily involve membership of a trade society, it was most clearly articulated by the unionised artisans.[3] Such trade union-based identity was, however, difficult to articulate publicly until trade unions, criminalised under several provisions of the Irish Parliament from 1729 to 1763, were legalised following the Repeal of the Combination Acts in 1824.[4] Even after this legalisation, the very essence of the Irish trade union continued to manifest itself as solidarity rooted in defensiveness, a characteristic deriving not just from its recent admittance within the bounds of the law, but also, as discussed earlier, from a spirit of intense localism and from fear of changing economic conditions which tended to erode the traditional customs and prestige of the craft.

Such defensiveness was certainly the keynote of the first satisfactorily documented waves of trade-union militancy in nineteenth-century Cork. In 1817 major disturbances were sparked off by the unemployment of the post-war slump, while sporadic agitation over a two-year period in the late 1820s was equally defensive, deriving from wage grievances consequent upon the Irish and English currency assimilation.[5] Sharpened also by the disintegration of the traditional machinery of wage regulation from the 1820s onwards and by non-union artisans' undercutting of wages, the skilled craftsmen's sense of siege was epitomised in the titles and slogans on trade-union banners, which, reflecting their British counterparts, sought to protect craft interests and sense of community by projecting sentiments of mutuality and solidarity. The local shoemakers' banner from 1832 until 1880 typically warned – 'Beware of division! Union is Strength!', the glovers and tanners in the 1830s and 1840s declared – 'In love and unity we do subsist', while in similar vein the hatters in the 1830s and the shipwrights in the 1860s and 1870s proclaimed – 'United we stand, divided we fall'.[6] Ultimately, narrow trade-society interests triumphed over any broader sense of craft community for, whatever the expansive sentiments of fraternal goodwill traced with loving care on these banners – 'May God enable us to assist each other' (stonecutters, 1832), 'Love and friendship' (coopers, 1864), or 'Amor et Obedientia' (painters, 1890), the real nature of unionism was more aptly summed up by the clannish mottoes of the ropemakers in 1845 – 'Friendship with all *lawful* tradesmen' and 'May commerce and our plan succeed, to help each *deserving* brother in time of need' [my italics].[7] The *raison-d'être* of the trade union was, after all, to safeguard members through regulation of the labour market, beginning with a firm control over access to the union's own ranks. High membership fees for prospective members along with strict limitations on apprentice numbers acted as the first defensive rampart against an influx of unwanted outsiders. As has been indicated in chapter 1, most of these regulations proved increasingly ineffective as the century passed, yet despite this they confirmed the collective identity of the trade and the individual artisan's position within it. Moreover, the closed-shop tradition of the trade, with its emphasis on family links between journeymen, masters and apprentices, ensured that economic defensiveness was strengthened by ties of blood. Nor was this simply the blood tie between the journeyman as father and the apprentice as son, but also an implied relationship between the trade as parent and the individual journeyman or apprentice as offspring of the craft. In the Repeal processions of the 1830s and 1840s, apprentices formed an integral part of the trade representation, marching under the society banner or appearing (no doubt under duress) in the romantic tableaux arranged to portray the trade's pride in its craft and its commitment to the popular cause. In the Cork Repeal procession of March 1832, twin apprentice masons bore one of the society's banners, and two hapless tailors' apprentices were decked out in silk dresses to represent Adam and Eve standing beside the tree of knowledge, while in a similar demonstration in the city in 1845, the coopers' tableau included two apprentices who played respectively the roles of a freed African slave and, in contrast, 'young Ireland still in chains'.[8]

Confining the membership of the trade to a closed circle, while most certainly based on hard-headed economic considerations, was also designed to highlight the exclusiveness and skill of the craftsman in contrast to the unskilled worker. Here again, the system of apprenticeship was vital – not just because it was the means of transmitting skills to a younger generation, but because it was the badge of the craftsman who was, as the terminology of the 1830s put it, proud of his identity as 'a seven years' man'. In Geary's words, apprenticeship 'involved the inculcation of values concerning status and tradition, pride not just in one's craft but in one's personal worth'.[9] It was this equation between skill, trade solidarity, individual dignity and family tradition (combined, no doubt, with the fear of losing convenient cheap apprentice labour) which later in the nineteenth century accounts for the Cork trades' resistance to the attempted supplementing of apprenticeship training by classes sponsored by the educational authorities.[10]

The sense of pride in one's handiwork was certainly the most obvious characteristic of the skilled artisan. E. P. Thompson noted how small-town wheelwrights in late nineteenth-century England 'possibly (and properly) exaggerated the respect for good workmanship and material' while in the French context Eugen Weber referred to the scorn for bad work expressed by rural craftsmen.[11] This pride in production was graphically presented in contemporary trade-union banners, both British and Irish, whose work scenes, 'painted with a loving photographic exactitude, celebrate[d] a craft'.[12] Cork was no exception, for in all public demonstrations in which the trades participated in the course of the nineteenth century, both the symbolism of the banners and the tools and specimens of handiwork carried by the marching artisans bore testimony to this deeply felt pride in the craft. Most eloquently expressed in the 1830s and 1840s when basketmakers wore crosses of basketwork on their breasts, shovelmakers bore wands surmounted by tiny shovels, and the coachmakers' contingent carried a miniature model coach, this custom lasted well into the later years of the century. In a demonstration of 1864, the shipbuilders still carried a model ship and the smith's wands were topped by gilt hammers, anvils and tongs, while as late as 1890 the stonecutters bore a model of the local Father Mathew Church, on the spire of which they were currently working.[13]

In the Irish context, such craft-based pride frequently overlapped with local and national loyalties. Significantly, in the first flush of the manufacture revival movement in Cork in the early 1830s it was this pride in craft which was used to foster local pride and then to extend it to pride in a wider sense of Irishness among artisans and middle-class patrons alike:

> I was brought up in the cutlery business: but what is done in that trade in Cork? . . . Shame on the Cork people. In Dublin they at least ask for a 'Reid' or a 'Lamprey', but who in Cork asks for a Cork-made knife? . . .
> . . . Why is there such a prejudice against Irish hats? This is an Irish hat which I wear, and I am satisfied that it is as good a one as any which I could get in England . . .[14]

Such pride in craft, of course, existed independently of any political consciousness. Painters in the 1880s railed against those who, by 'getting a man with a whitewash brush to put paint on', discredited the entire trade.[15] In the early twentieth century the local stonecarvers brought their apprentices into local churches where the work of their forebears in the trade provided them with models to emulate. At the same time, reflecting typical inter-trade rivalry, they wryly mocked that same craft-based pride when it was manifested by the members of another trade:

> Sure the plasterers have cricks in their necks from looking up at the ceiling in St. Mary's. Any time I go there to look at the pulpit an' the two side altars, there's one or two of them with their apprentices standing in the main aisle and their eyes turned up, gaping at the masterpiece of the craft. They are so proud of it they had a banner of it painted for the procession the trades used to have on St. Patrick's Day long ago. It's in the sacristy of St. Mary's now. The plasterers' society used even give a contribution for the up-keep and repair of that same ceiling'.[16]

Such pride in craftsmanship as basis of the skilled artisans' sense of identity was intertwined with another perceived attribute – that most Victorian of qualities – respectability, which Geary has summed up in reference to the artisanate as 'independence, self-respect and dignity'.[17] Thus, when Cork's trade societies marched in public demonstrations, the political and skill-related objectives of participation were almost evenly balanced by the need to display publicly the respectability and sturdy masculinity of both the individual artisan and the corporate trade. Hostile local commentators, like the *Cork Constitution* in 1835, stressed the perceived raggedness and boorishness of the marching artisans:

> The edict dread had forth been sent
> Which none might dare neglect,
> And many even barefoot went
> To show the more respect . . .[18]

The popular press, on the other hand, demonstrated a positive incapacity to omit the word 'respectable' or its equivalents from its descriptions of the marching trades, lacing its accounts of trade participation with such phrases as 'very respectable appearance', 'most respectable body of operatives', 'highly creditable appearance', 'respectable and well-conducted class of men', and 'particularly fine body of men'.[19] Though at times such descriptions were possibly based more on wishful dreams than on reality, they served as much as did pride in manual expertise to bolster the artisans' sense of superiority. While his respectable appearance visibly raised him above the so-called lower classes, his skill marked him off from the mass of unskilled workers by enabling him to earn higher wages and to hold (in theory, if not in practice) more permanent employment. Most importantly it confirmed that he had, by serving a long apprenticeship, proved himself to be more industrious and deserving of public respect than the unskilled labourer or handyman who had not sacrificed his youth to the rigours of training.

From the 1840s onwards, artisan respectability took on another characteristic – i.e. the substitution of peaceful for violent methods in the sphere of trade unionism. This trend produced marked differences between the public image of pre-famine trade unionism and that of the latter half of the century. As in the case of other towns throughout the British Isles, the early manifestations of union protest in nineteenth-century Cork had been particularly violent.[20] The wave of trade-union activity in 1822 resulted in such disturbance that order was maintained in the city only through the presence of the military, while in 1828 the coopers and building trades burned and demolished the premises of employers who had refused wage increases.[21] In the early 1830s, and to a lesser extent in the early 1840s, further trade-union violence erupted, marked by rioting, damage to property, and threatening and ill-treatment of persons obnoxious to the unions.[22]

Closer examination at local level, however, suggests that although trade-union defensiveness frequently led to violent action, the trade societies were not, in essence, violent. As was the case with their British counterparts, they had a recognised method – though not a particularly successful one – of enforcing regulations with a minimum use of force. Trade-union regulation of the labour market involved a fairly sophisticated system of written admonitary notices to offending parties, followed in strict order by pressure on their employers, and only then by physical violence. Trade-union committee meetings were largely taken up with the preparation and circulation of warning notices. A slater who informed on his fellow unionists in 1829 explained to the court the purpose and procedure of these trade committee meetings:

> The object in meeting was to regulate trade and keep up prices. The payment to the society was fourpence a month . . . If they wanted to deprive a man of work they generally wrote a 'strike letter' . . . with the trade mark fixed upon it. The members were generally fined . . . for working under price, and . . . twenty shillings for not keeping the rules. The price is four-and-a-penny per day, and any man who would work under it would be liable to be fined, and if he resisted, would be struck off work.[23]

During the following two decades the slaters continued to regulate their trade in the same way: police raids on their committee rooms in 1834 and 1842 discovered the union officers drawing up warning notices to employers and journeymen who had broken society rules on wage rates, apprentice numbers and non-union labour. Similarly, a meeting of the masons' committee was surprised in session in 1838 and twenty-eight warning notices to workmen were seized, together with the society account books and brass seal.[24] In these particular cases the warning notices were worded with scrupulous politeness:

> Gentlemen, you are requested to withdraw from the employment
> of Mr. Belcher, as he holds an illegal apprentice, contrary to the
> rules of the trade.

However, in a market flooded by unorganised cheap labour on
which an employer could readily draw, rule quoting and fine im-
position was frequently a futile exercise. Polite requests soon
evolved into demands which were much more direct and menac-
ing, and had far more in common with the threatening letters
sent by the secret agrarian societies of the rural areas than with
the carefully worded notices of the city trade societies. Headed
not by the trade society crest but by a roughly sketched coffin
or skull and crossbones, they were, as the following notice prepared by the labourers in a city iron foundry in 1833 indicates,
marked by a low level of literacy and a disarming directness:

> By the Loyal Helpers of the City:
> Daniel Lyons you are where are hereby [sic] warned not to work
> in this employment on less [sic] a wrise [sic] of wages. If not,
> mind the matter.

Others were even more explicit – 'Prepare your coffin or quit
Cork'.[25]

Threatening letters, if ignored by the recipient, were usually
followed in the last resort by an attack on the house or person
of the offender. A classic example of this step-by-step union
harassment of a recalcitrant member took place in 1829 in the
case of the local slaters' society. A new committee had been elected
early in 1829 and, as was usual, the new officers examined the
society's books to check the expenditure of society funds by the
previous committee. On discovering that the funds had been spent
entirely on food and drink and that no more money remained
in the chest, the new committee heavily fined the former officers.
The stewards were required to pay two pounds each, and the
other committee men one pound each. One steward, William
Strettle, refused to pay the fine, whereupon the next stage of coercion was applied, the society successfully calling on Strettle's
employer to dismiss him. Still Strettle refused to pay, and the
third stage was tried: some men were sent by the society to attack his house and break his windows, and a notice chalked on

his door warned him that the next step would be an attack on
his person:

> If you don't come in the morning and attend on the committee,
> we will call again and serve you out . . .

Before his callers returned to implement their plan, however,
Strettle sought police protection and three of his would-be at-
tackers were arrested and committed to prison for nine months,
with six months on the treadmill.[26]

Strettle's case was certainly only one of many, and it would
hardly have reached the headlines had he not chosen to bring
it to the attention of the police. The many attacks of this sort,
as in Strettle's case, were usually made on journeymen: employers
who refused to comply with society demands were less amenable
to heavy handling, and it is significant that of the fifty-six recorded
cases of combination violence in Cork City between 1830 and
1850, only twelve were directed against the persons or property
of employers. Where personal attacks against employers did occur, however, they were no less violent than those aimed against
journeymen. During a tailors' strike in 1833, one of the proprietors of Keane and Turnbull's tailoring establishment was
waylaid by a crowd of from fifty to one hundred men, dragged
from his carriage and beaten until he agreed to 'never again oppose the Union of Trades'. In 1842, one of the proprietors of the
Cork Steam Saw Mills was blinded with vitriol for his introduction of machinery into the industry and the consequent displacement of a great number of hand sawyers.[27]

In spite of recurring violent incidents, however, the 1840s and
early 1850s saw the emergence of a self-conscious respectability
on the part of the Cork trade unions. In this, they were no different from their peers elsewhere. Pelling noted among English
artisans 'a moral earnestness akin to that of the Victorian middle class', Foster used the term 'liberalization' to describe the
general move towards moderation among the Lancashire unions
in the early nineteenth century, while Fergus D'Arcy and John
Boyle showed how, following the violence of the 1830s, the Dublin
artisans became aware in the early 1840s of the need to regain
public sympathy through peaceful agitation. The anti-night-work

campaign of the Dublin journeymen bakers and the wage strike
by the city's tanners were conducted in the early 1840s in a strictly
decorous fashion, and were presented to the public as campaigns
for social justice rather than narrow trade issues.[28] In 1842 the
parallel Cork bakers' campaign against night work was run on
exactly the same lines, launched by a petition to parliament and
supported by many prominent citizens. Though this campaign
proved unsuccessful, the abandonment of violence was permanent, so much so that in the mid-1840s the bakers were described
by the Repeal Association (no friend of combination) as 'a most
respectable body of men' while in 1846 the bakers' secretary with
a by now characteristic unctuousness expressed the hope that
'our city be [not] again disgraced by those illegal combinations
which were too prevalent heretofore' and described his fellow
members as

> humble men, doing our duty to our country, and endeavouring
> to maintain a respectable standing for our society . . . [which is]
> held together by the bonds of benevolence.[29]

The cabinet makers, too, who had been prominent in the combination outrages of the 1830s had, a decade later, been sufficiently
pacified to earn the description – 'this most deserving body of
our local trades'. Their campaign for a reduction in working
hours, moreover, mirrored their cultivation of this new-found
probity, their request to the employers pointing out that their
long hours 'deprived [them] of an . . . opportunity of participating in the scientific and general improvements of the day'.[30]

Even the coopers, traditionally a far more aggressive trade than
the bakers and cabinet makers, and who consequently received
less public sympathy, were at pains to point out (not always accurately) that they too had, since the early 1840s, avoided all
violent activity. A major strike conducted in 1843 against the
flooding of the city by country-made firkins was conducted on
clearly 'respectable' lines, with an extensive use of letters to the
press to rouse public support for their campaign against the
powerful butter-buying interest.[31] A decade later, when the
coopers' society was accused of burning obnoxious masters'
premises, it followed the now familiar pattern of publishing its

denials in indignant letters to the local press which in turn bore striking testimony to the artisans' changed image by praising their 'decent independence and feeling of self-respect'.[32] So great was this transformation from militancy to respectability among all the city trades that the police authorities assured Dublin Castle in 1851 that though trade societies were still active in Cork, there had been no 'combination' – by which they meant violent union activity – for a number of years.[33] Violent action was never, of course, totally abandoned: into late in the century strike breakers were not infrequently subjected to assault and the property of the union's opponents was still damaged, but these were regarded as the acts of maverick individuals and were either winked at or hastily repudiated by the trade societies concerned.[34] Moreover, this respectable image was further enforced by the increasing capacity of local trade societies to employ attorneys to advise them on the framing of society rules and to defend their members in court. Some of the Dublin trade societies had, as early as 1824, employed lawyers to state their case in a trade dispute, but in Cork no similar instance of union employment of a legal man was noted until 1842 when the slaters' and plasterers' society employed an attorney to draft their rules. The same attorney successfully defended a number of union members when they appeared in court on a charge of illegal combination.[35]

This increasing respectability of the unions may well have been a consequence of their progressive legalisation, but it was also closely intermeshed with the growing emphasis on temperance which was so vital a part of the middle-class and aspiring working-class image of the mid nineteenth century. Just as Thompson noted among English artisans in the 1830s 'a general moral primness' characterised by 'thrift, self-education, industry, perseverance, independence, sobriety and cleanliness', so in contemporary Ireland similar developments followed on economic change, new recreational habits, and more disciplined religious observance.[36] It was significant, for instance, that the anti-night-work campaign by the Cork bakers in 1842 was strongly supported by Fr Theobald Matthew, the 'Apostle of Temperance', and that the bakers themselves dutifully attributed their previous campaign

failures to drunkenness and placed their hopes in present
enlightenment when 'temperance and good will preside at our
council . . . [and] bid us rely on the justice, wisdom and humanity
of parliament.'[37] Similar interweaving of the themes of
temperance and economic betterment was also obvious in contemporary manufacture revival attempts, both middle-class and
artisan revivalists seeing the commitment to revive home industry
as dovetailing with the temperance pledge. Those who launched
the local manufacture revival movement in 1832 were at pains
to persuade working men that their situation would be improved
by the twin policy of supporting home industry and leading 'a
sober and well-conducted life', while the Irish manufacture pledge
drawn up in 1842 was consciously referred to as 'the second
pledge', those who took it being reminded that

> the great moral foundation is laid in the temperance movement.
> Found your pledge on it, and . . . let them go hand in hand
> together, as they are the cardinal virtues of Irish freedom and
> happiness.[38]

In the course of the century successive artisans' umbrella
organisations similarly emphasised the temperance theme. The
founders of the local People's Hall in 1835 canvassed public support by stressing the 'cheerful sobriety and easy order' which
the new facility would establish among the city's working classes.
Over thirty years later the seventeen trades who met to establish
a Mechanics' Hall in the city did so in conjunction with the
recently revived Temperance Movement which aimed to provide
new accommodation for the trade committee meetings in order
to 'bring them away from the temptations they had to encounter'
in their usual public house venues.[39]

Closely tied to this temperance image was the dual ethic of
hard work and self-improvement. This, as suggested earlier, was
an essential, though latent, part of craft-based pride, but it was
also openly articulated by both the organised trades themselves
and by sympathetic middle-class observers. The bakers involved
in the anti-night-work campaign in 1842 had been described by
the local press as 'deserving and industrious' while in the same
year the journeymen cabinet makers assured their employers who
had conceded shorter hours that

this act of benevolence [would] be repaid tenfold in diligence and good feeling . . . [and that] the hour gained from severe toil [would] not be spend in idleness or dissipation.[40]

By the 1860s, at least among sympathetic observers, the organised trades had been fully identified with the temperance idea. When the Father Mathew monument was unveiled in the city's principal street in October 1864, the *Cork Examiner* waxed lyrical on the trades' perceived links with the temperance movement:

> In such a ceremonial the trades of Cork had a right to occupy a prominent position. The labours of the man they had assembled to honour were directed altogether to their social elevation. To the trades of the country he principally looked for support, and the trades nobly rallied round him. In all the great temperance processions they bore a prominent part. From their ranks the temperance societies were reinforced. And by their contributions and their adherence, the battle of temperance was gained . . .[41]

A cynical observer might well point out that, in order to preserve their temperate image on the very day of the unveiling, the trade societies found it necessary to threaten a fine on any member found drunk or disorderly. But the temperance image stuck, and as late as the 1880s, therefore, when a new local trades' council was established, its programme of objectives stressed not alone the protection of trade interests but also the ambition to foster in its members the virtues of 'self-denial, perseverance, industry and thrift'.[42] Adding in the further ingredient of self-education, the new body organised instructive lectures by well-disposed gentlemen and established the inevitable library for the use of members.[43]

This triple emphasis on respectability, temperance and self-betterment was, of course, an integral feature of the middle classes and aristocracy of labour in Victorian society. The experience in Cork was no exception, the trade unions being inevitably affected by a self-improvement ideal reflected not only in successive temperance movements but also in the development of improved housing schemes, savings banks, friendly societies and institutions like the Young Men's Christian Association and the Catholic Young Men's society.[44] Nonetheless, the march of temperance and self-betterment did not sweep all before it. In 1853 complaints were made that the Cork working classes were 'singularly and shamefully improvident' while in the 1870s it was claimed that the demand for liquor was so great in the city that the whiskey in the stills was sold before it had sufficiently matured.[45] Neither, in spite of the undoubted commitment of individual artisans to the ideals of temperance and industry, was the anti-drink and self-improvement image of the organised trades much more than skin-deep. A local Mechanics' Institute established in 1851 to give working men 'the means of rational recreation and the opportunity of intellectual improvement' attracted no support from the trades. While its library of newspapers, maps and scientific periodicals remained empty, the unemployed artisans frequented the public houses or lounged against the wall in Daunt's Square, the traditional spot for gatherings of the unemployed.[46] Two decades later, the organisers of the Mechanics' Hall failed to break the trade societies' tradition of meeting in licensed premises, while later in the decade it was stated that young artisans in the city spent all their Saturday half-day in the public houses.[47] Moreover, the continuing connection between the artisan's recreational habits and the consumption of alcohol was obvious in the organised trades' adamant opposition to any proposed changes in public house opening laws. These changes, supported in the last three decades of the century by local temperance advocates, aimed to close public houses on Sunday and to strictly curtail opening hours on Saturday.[48] It was indicative of the trades' strong feelings on the subject – and of the shallowness of the temperance image to which they had periodically subscribed since the 1840s – that at the meeting held to discuss the issue only thirty out of six hundred trade representatives present voted in favour of Sunday closing, and while the question was in the air trades council meetings paid little attention to any other issue.[49]

This powerful sense of collective identity among the trades had been developing in the course of the century in the successive attempts to establish a local trades' council as an umbrella organisation in which the various trade societies could come together for the advancement of their mutual interests. In general,

Irish trade unions up to mid-century lacked any permanent umbrella organisation, their collective views finding expression only through irregular meetings and *ad hoc* organisations which
crumbled when the immediate need had passed.[50] Unlike the
trades of Limerick who were associated early in the century in
the Congregated Trades, the Cork trades apparently had no
permanent cover-all organisation in the 1830s and 1840s.[51]
Contemporaries, however, assumed the existence of a widespread
trades conspiracy, and blamed labour violence on the influence
of a supposed 'union of trades', which reputedly controlled all
the trades of the city. The existence of a similar union of trades
in Dublin has long been a matter of debate, and in the case of
the Cork union of trades, the same uncertainty prevails, for
although contemporaries never doubted its existence, their accounts of its precise composition varied considerably.[52] In 1821
it was claimed that the trades, with the exception of the cotton
and linen weavers, 'formed a kind of federal union', while in 1822
a Cork correspondent to Dublin Castle complained that

> the great source of mischief here, as in Limerick and in most
> large towns, is what is called a Union of Trades: it is carried on
> by meetings and clubs which assist the promotions of the con-
> spiracies as the present, at once the means of receiving and of
> circulating their plans.

In 1828, a further variation on the theme was suggested when
reference was made to the 'general body of combinators' to which
the coopers alone did not belong. Two years later when attempts
were made to reduce wages in the building trades to three shillings a day, measures to prevent the reduction were reputedly
discussed at a meeting of the 'general body of the trades' and
in 1833 it was claimed that the committee of the union of trades
had set a minimum wage for all artisans.[53] It is much more
likely that in the latter two cases the umbrella bodies referred
to were simply committees of the building trades, such as existed many decades later in the 1890s, and that the much feared
'union of trades' may have existed only in the prolific imagina-
tions of nervous contemporaries who regarded any inter-trade
co-operation as evidence of a dangerous conspiracy.[54] Much

of this co-operation had probably evolved in an *ad hoc* fashion
from the personal interaction between individuals of different
trades, many of whom lived in close proximity to each other in
the crowded lanes and alleys of the city. Joyce points out the 'cen-
trality of neighbourhood to community feeling' in nineteenth-
century English industrial society.[55] In the Cork context, too,
there are hints that such day-to-day contact between neighbours
could also help to strengthen trade unionism at local level, for
it seems that at least some trade-union recruitment was done
not by the officers of the unions but by tradesmen who saw to
it that their neighbours in other trades joined the relevant trade
society. Thus, a sawyer charged in 1834 with illegal combination described how he had first been brought to his society rooms
for enrolment by a neighbour who was a member of the
ropemakers' union.[56] On the other hand, however, co-operation
between the different trade bodies of the city was on occasions
sufficiently well co-ordinated to suggest that even in this early
period there was indeed some general directing body. In 1833,
when a number of journeymen bakers were sentenced to
transportation for a combination outrage, a well-organised
deputation of tradesmen, one from each trade society in the city, waited on the two city MPs in an unsuccessful attempt to pro-
cure their intervention on behalf of the convicted men. Moreover,
the combination outrages in Cork in these years were, like those
in Dublin, perpetrated through inter-union connivance. In 1824
the Select Committee on Combination was told how the Dublin
trade societies used the unemployed men of other trades to carry
out attacks on those breaking society rules, the tailors figuring
prominently in assault cases since they were 'a numerous body,
and more unemployed, and therefore more ready to be had'.
Likewise in Cork, the tailors, together with the numerous and
distressed bakers, sawyers and cabinet makers, all took leading
parts in attacks on masters and strike breakers in trades other
than their own.[57]

If any formal inter-trade body did exist in the 1830s, it was
almost certainly defunct by the late 1840s when the local Irish
Confederates seeking artisan support had to approach each trade
society in turn.[58] Not until 1857 was a short-lived trades council

founded by nine of the city trades, followed in 1864 by another transient body modelled on a similar organisation recently established in Dublin.[59] While the Dublin United Trades Association survived into the 1870s, neither of Cork's early trades councils had much chance of survival for they lacked self-confidence, funds and public support. Yet, even their brief existence was in itself indicative of some sense of collective purpose, geared as it was to their mutual protection and what was rather grandiosely termed, in imitation of their Dublin model's programme, 'the protection of labour'.[60] This idea of mutual protection was even more obvious in 1870 in the third attempt to establish a trades council. This latter body, the Mechanics' Hall, was originally envisaged by its benevolent middle-class sponsors as an association geared to the moral improvement of local artisans. Significantly, however, it failed to make any real headway among the organised artisans until its management was taken over by the trade societies themselves who swiftly changed its mechanics' institute image and attempted to shape it into an organisation geared to further the trades' economic interests and provide them with a unified voice in public affairs.[61] As in the case of the earlier experiments, the Mechanics' Hall proved only partly effective as a trade federation: fewer than half the trades of the city were affiliated while the association was rocked by obscure personal and political quarrels.[62] Moreover, the Hall's failure to act as a cohesive force among the local trades was evident in its absence from the nine-hours movement of the early 1870s which was, in fact, launched by unaffiliated local trade societies. Thus, while most trades reaped the benefits of the nine-hours campaign, the Mechanics' Hall lost its opportunity to cement its identity under the banner of one of the most important labour issues of the day.[63] Finally, the Fenian movement's increasing domination of the Hall's affairs meant that within a few years the association was more identified with militant nationalism than with trade solidarity, and it was not until the early 1880s that permanently successful attempts were made to form a general trades association whose principal *raison-d'être* was the protection of trade interests.[64]

In February 1881, eleven city trades met to form the United

Trades Association and Irish Industrial League which, like its transient predecessors, aimed to combat trade depression through the promotion of home industry and to protect the interests of the affiliated trades. The association grew steadily so that by mid-1881 sixteen trades had joined, this number rising to twenty-seven a year later.[65] In 1883 a major internal dispute caused the near collapse of the association so that by early 1884 only nine societies remained affiliated, but it was indicative of the increased resilience and cohesion of the trades that, unlike previous bodies, the association did not disintegrate at this first major set-back. Internal dissensions were ironed out by organisational changes, and affiliations resumed so that by late 1885 the association included fifteen affiliated societies, this figure rising to nineteen in 1888, twenty-one in 1894 and by the end of the century to twenty-five – apparently the total complement of unions in the city at that time.[66]

From the 1830s, when the first comprehensive documentation on trade society activity appeared, to the end of the century when a permanent trades council had been established, the skilled trades saw themselves collectively as separate from other local interest groups. Such collective identity, of course, derived to a great extent from economic realities, since the common experience of unemployment, undercutting of wages and erosion of traditional trade customs ensured a considerable degree of solidarity between the unionised members of different crafts. While in earlier decades this had manifested itself in clandestine recruitment and violent enforcement of regulations on an inter-trade basis, in the closing decades of the century it took the form of highly publicised moral and financial support for strikers in trades other than one's own. The first expression of this latter form of inter-trade solidarity was in the form of a general meeting of the trades in June 1870 to support the local tailors' strike. Even contemporaries were aware of the occasion's significance: the authorities reacted nervously, banning a planned procession of the trade societies, while the trades themselves saw the occasion as 'a new and happy sign' of solidarity. Trades enthusiasm, moreover, expressed itself practically as well as rhetorically. The coopers' society placed all its funds at the tailors' disposal and members agreed to buy their clothes only from tailoring establishments which conceded the tailors' demands. The local branch of the Amalgamated society of Engineers made similar commitments while other trades promised financial support.[67] Two decades later, during the anti-night-work strike by journeymen bakers, the same sense of inter-trade co-operation was evident. As in 1870, pledges of financial aid and boycotting of night-working bakeries were made by several local trade societies, while other disputes in the 1890s among seamen, tailors, coopers and builders' labourers received similar aid from uninvolved trade societies.[68]

Solidarity both within and between trades, however, was just about as durable as economic conditions and sectional rivalries would permit. Trade society pledges to buy only clothes made by unionised tailors and bread baked by day-working bakers were sincerely intended, but their fulfilment frequently proved beyond the financial capacity of the artisan – and, more importantly, of his wife, mother or sister. In spite of the rhetoric of solidarity and promises to patronise fair-labour shops, it was widely recognised among the trades themselves in Cork, as in Dublin, that working men both skilled and unskilled were the greatest patrons of the cheap-clothing establishments dealing in both imported and sweat-shop produced garments, and that artisans' wives were reputedly the worst offenders in 1890 in buying from strike-bound bakeries.[69]

Moreover, deep rivalries existed between different trade societies. Some inter-trade enmities were quite obscure. The quarrel which divided the infant trades council into two hostile camps in 1884 probably derived from personal animosities and fear of the monopolisation of office by the representatives of particular trades.[70] More common were those clashes which resulted from demarcation disputes between different crafts. The shipbuilding industry in Cork, as elsewhere, was particularly prone to such disputes, especially between the shipwrights and joiners, one such dispute in the Passage Docks dragging on almost without interruption between early 1894 and late 1895, while another perennial inter-trade quarrel was that between the large and aggressive local carpenters' union on the one hand and the tiny cabinet makers' society on the other.[71] Moreover, the tenuous nature of

internal union solidarity was particularly evident in the facility
with which former union members who entered the rank of
master cast aside their union principles. These 'men of small
or equivocal capital', who barely managed to hold their position
as employers through penny-pinching on wages and getting the
last ounce of work out of their largely non-union workforce, were
regarded with hostility by their former co-unionists who, however,
were no less adept at jettisoning union principles should the occasion of becoming a master present itself.[72]

The necessity to safeguard the identity of the individual trade
society was further underlined by the way in which the trade
jealously guarded the right of its members to determine when
a strike was necessary and when to reach settlement with employers. While, from the 1880s onwards, the local trades council
committee claimed the right to decide whether a projected strike
in any of its constituent societies should proceed, many affiliated
societies regarded such a claim as an unacceptable intervention
in internal trade matters.[73] Though it seems that in late 1894
the trades council, after consultation with the affiliated trades,
established its own board of arbitration, its record was not impressive, intervening successfully in only eighteen per cent of
recorded strikes in the 1890s. The reasons for this lack of success were multiple. In some situations, it was almost impossible
to appoint arbitrators acceptable to both sides, particularly if dealing with obdurate employers willing to replace strikers by non-
union labour. Such a typically insurmountable difficulty was evident when the bakers' strike of 1883 ended in triumph for the
masters who settled directly with their men without any reference
to either the bakers' society or the trades council. Similarly, strong
trades council support for printers locked out by the determined proprietor of the *Cork Constitution* in 1888 had no effect, the
lockout still operating ten years later.[74] This situation had not
changed in the 1890s. Trades-council attempts at intervention
in single-establishment strikes by engineers, pork butchers, mill-
sawyers, bakers and boot rivetters between 1892 and 1897 all failed
because of a tough line taken by the employers concerned, while
arbitration attempts proved even more futile in the case of the
multi-establishment strikes by operative bakers in 1890 and tailors

in 1893 because of the easy availability of blackleg labour.[75] The choice of arbitrators, too, proved problematic, for while churchmen were generally regarded as the most impartial and conscientious, it was significant that their offices were availed of only in disputes concerning unskilled and semi-skilled workers organised in the 'new unions'.[76] The craft unions, while agreeing with the principle of arbitration, actually shied away from it as a practice encouraging outside interference in internal trade matters. They preferred to bring masters and men in the one trade to a general conference at which all questions could be fully discussed by both sides before any solution was imposed from outside craft boundaries.[77] Secondly, the arbitration process was further sabotaged by the complex rivalries between trade societies, particularly in the building trade, where the interests of several categories of skilled and unskilled workers were frequently incompatible. In 1890, for example, the builders' labourers' strike against the Master Builders' Association, in spite of being backed by the trades council, was wrecked by the masons' and plasterers' societies. The members of the latter unions, who had been kept in enforced idleness during the strike, eventually agreed to work with blackleg labourers. Finally, the most difficult of all arbitration was that which involved those previously mentioned inter-trade demarcation disputes. Such disputes, though generally referred to the trades council by the employers and trades involved, proved almost impossible to solve when one or both of the trades concerned refused to compromise, a typically protracted demarcation dispute between carpenters and cabinet makers in 1896 and 1897 causing much difficulty to the trades council when the strong and aggressive carpenters' union tried to over-ride the trades council's decision in favour of the weak society of cabinet makers.[78]

If disputes between societies threatened the cohesion of the trades, disputes within societies were even more disruptive. Union records reveal that within most trade societies, the enforcement of internal unity was at least as great a problem as were disputes with employers and other unions. The weekly meetings of local union branches were periodically enlivened by fist fights over real or supposed maladministration of funds or because members

refused to pay their union dues. As surviving records show, these
non-paying members were the bane of every union secretary's
existence, the plumbers' secretary typically recording in 1890
after a 'pay up or get out' ultimatum to defaulters that

> such latitude will never again be given to members of the Cork
> lodge. It is better to have six good men than forty like [those]
> we have to grapple with from time to time . . . The good and
> clear members are paying up the levy, but it is hard on men pay-
> ing for men we will never get a penny from . . .[79]

If the plumbers on this occasion managed to maintain unity by
a tough line with recalcitrant members, internal squabbles in
other societies proved dangerously divisive, both the plasterers'
and coopers' societies splitting in the 1890s because of disputes
regarding benefit payment. The coopers' dispute was particularly
dramatic with the rebels repeatedly breaking into the society
rooms, wrecking the furniture and – in the ultimate gesture of
rebellion – threatening to tear up the union's books and banner. In the plasterers' case, inter-faction recriminations became
so bitter that the quarrel was re-enacted at the weekly trades'
council meeting, to the delight of the press reporters present,
and to the horror of the council committee, which only with difficulty persuaded the plasterers present to resolve their differences
within the sanctum of their own committee rooms.[80]

Within every craft, moreover, the fragile unity of the trade
society was further weakened by the presence in its ranks of
employees of several different business concerns. Indeed, one
might well suggest that the ultimate sense of identity of the skilled
artisan was rooted in his place of work rather than in his trade
union. Studies of nineteenth-century British industrial society
suggest that, while this identification with workplace was strongest
in the case of factory workers in large establishments, the artisan's identity was equally moulded by his place of employment,
making him part of a fraternal culture dominated by the 'gang'
or the 'shop'.[81] In the Irish context, the dearth of artisan
autobiographies and working-class reminiscences makes it very
difficult to penetrate what one British historian has termed 'the
opacity of workplace culture'.[82] Yet, it does seem that the Cork

artisan's identity was, no less than that of his British counterpart, strongly influenced by the 'all-pervasive face-to-face occupational community'.[83] Union structures were generally tailored to reconcile this internal diversity of the trade with the need for centralised authority. Committee members were therefore drawn from the different workplaces of a given trade, the coopers' society committee being composed of representatives from the local breweries, distilleries, provision stores and principal coopers' shops. Similarly, the Cork printers' society committee, like its counterparts throughout the British Isles, was drawn from the membership of the various 'chapels', each of which consisted of all the workmen in a particular office or shift. Traditionally monitoring work quality and maintaining order in the individual workplace, the chapel became progressively integrated into the structure of trade unionism in the course of the nineteenth century. But it was never fully swallowed up by union structures, and actually kept considerable autonomy in the hands of the individual printing offices, all matters of importance being voted on in the chapels before they were decided upon by the local union branch.[84] Thus, in some crafts, considerable influence still lay in the collective membership of the individual workplace, and this workplace loyalty frequently proved stronger than loyalty to the union, leading to considerable friction between union committee and workshop team. In the Cork context, there was, in fact, little apparent conflict between the printers' committee and the constituent chapels, but the coopers' society waged a constant struggle to enforce society rules in its constituent workshops. It contended for five years with the members in Murphy's brewery over the non-payment of union dues, while similar confrontations took place with the men in Arnott's and Beamish and Crawford's breweries and those in certain master coopers' shops.[85]

Nonetheless, despite this undoubtedly stronger personal allegiance to his own workshop, the artisan of the late 1890s, no less than his forebears of the 1830s, regarded himself and was regarded by others primarily as a member of the craft, and then as part of that collectivity known as 'the trades', whose distinctive sense of identity spanned both political and economic issues.

As already suggested, although the artisans might be drawn into public affairs by elements outside trade ranks, their subsequent tendency was to form, parallel to the parent movement,
a separate organisation based on the membership of the several
trade societies. In the course of the century this trend was most
obvious in the successive manufacture revival campaigns which
were so vitally relevant to all skilled craftsmen, and particularly
to those in declining trades. Thus, while most of these campaigns
were middle-class initiated with only a subsidiary role envisaged
for the trades, the latter almost always branched out with their
own particular revival movement which then ran parallel to the
original. In 1832 the Cork Trades Association for the Encouragement of Irish Manufacture was formed specifically as a trades'
counterpart to the local middle-class Irish Manufacture Association, while a decade later the employer-dominated Cork Board
of Trade (no friend to the trade unions) was faced with another
parallel artisan movement in the form of the Mallow Lane Board
of Trade.[86] Forty years later again, following a run of industrial
exhibitions patronised by middle-class business people, gentry
and prominent public figures, the Cork trades attempted their
own revival campaign by staging an Artisans' Exhibition confined to the work of individual craftsmen and small firms rather
than to the products of large concerns which had dominated the
previous exhibitions.[87]

The most obvious arena for collective trades participation was,
as discussed in chapter 5, that of municipal politics where, particularly from the 1880s onwards, it was clear that the interests
of the skilled craftsmen provided the main motive force towards
so-called 'labour' representation. It was in this arena, too that
the trades displayed that other characteristic which gave them
such a sense of cohesion – i.e. their tremendous and, indeed,
inflated sense of their own dignity. This was particularly obvious
in their reaction to local public bodies whose real or perceived
snubs to the trades were seized upon with fury. The greatest indignation was reserved for those occasions when municipal officials were seen to treat trade delegations with condescension:
in 1896 the mayor, John Scott, hitherto favourably regarded by
the trades, deeply affronted them when he gave a carpenters'

deputation a curt reception, while in 1897 the corporation's sign-
ing of a controversial tender before trades' council delegates
arrived was seen by the trades as a gross offence to their
dignity.[88]

This suspicion that other public bodies might sell out trade
interests or challenge trade dignity was equally obvious in the
field of nationalist politics. Even in the earlier decades of the century, the trades' separate sense of identity was translated into
political terms, as a tendency to form Repeal pressure groups
with a specifically artisan membership. Thus, the Cork Trades
Association of 1832, while not confined to the trades, was, besides
being a manufacture revival pressure group, the artisans' retort
to upper-middle-class domination of the local Repeal movement.
Again, in 1842, the city trade societies renewed their effort to
preserve their political distinctiveness by establishing a Repeal
meeting room exclusively 'for the use of the working classes' and
by founding their own Operative Repeal Association.[89] Above
all, when public demonstrations of support for nationalism
became a regular event in the city from the 1860s onwards, the
distinctive presence of unionised artisans marching both under
the banners of their individual trade societies and as members
of the trades council, reiterated the essentially autonomous nature
of 'the trades' in the arena of popular politics. Despite many
tiffs between trades and nationalist pressure groups in the city,
the support of the former was courted by the latter right through
the century. No Fenian demonstration was complete without at
least some trade presence in the ranks, trade backing and
subscriptions were essential for the success of any popular project, and constitutional politicians were very much aware that,
collectively, 'the trades' were a force to be reckoned with. The
local politician who, in the late 1890s, warned his colleague 'not
to say anything hurtful' to the Cork trades was simply stating
the obvious. The artisan who, in the 1830s, could be safely ignored or derided by press, pulpit and public, had been integrated
into the local social and political structures. His traditional sense
of superiority based on skill, which survived in spite of the forces
of change, was now supplemented not only by Victorian social
respectability but by close identification with the mainstream of

popular nationalism. Whatever his multiple economic problems
might be, politically and socially the artisan of the late 1890s had
arrived.

NOTES

1   William O'Brien Papers, National Library of Ireland, MS 13427: William
    O'Brien to J. F. X. O'Brien, 7 Aug. 1897.
2   R. Q. Gray, 'Class structure and the class formation of skilled workers
    in Edinburgh 1850–1900' (Ph. D. thesis, University of Edinburgh, 1972),
    p. 116.
3   Dennis Smith, 'Paternalism, craft and organizational rationality 1830–
    1930: an exploratory model', *Urban History*, vol. xix, Part 2, Oct. 1992,
    p. 227; C. Behagg, *Politics and Production in the Early Nineteenth Century* (Lon-
    don, 1990), p. 152.
4   Andrew Boyd, *The Rise of the Irish Trade Unions,* pp. 11–18; Emmet O'Con-
    nor, *A Labour History of Ireland 1824–1960,* p. 6.
5   SOC, 1817: 1835/15; British Museum Additional MS 38270, f. 450; Cork
    Archives Institute, Cork Petition to Parliament *re* Unemployment, 1822.
    CMC, 13, 15 Feb., 31 Mar. 1818; *SR,* 10, 12, 15, 19, 24 Jan. 1826;
    CSORP.OR 1828:C/10.2. In 1826 the shoemakers struck unsuccessfully
    to maintain the wage rate paid since 1810, while the tailors demanded
    and won the same concession. The various workers in the breweries and
    distilleries made similar demands, which these establishments, long con-
    sidered the most generous employers, readily conceded. These limited con-
    cessions and – more importantly – the refusal of the other employers to
    concede – led to a delayed protest in 1828 when the greatest dissatisfaction
    was expressed by the coopers and the building trades who engaged in a
    campaign of burning and demolition against non-compliant employers.
6   *CMC*, 21 Mar. 1832; *CE,* 9 June 1845, 10 Oct. 1864, 13 Oct. 1873.
7   John Gorman, *Banner Bright* (London, 1973), p. 4; John Boyle, *The Irish
    Labour Movement,* p. 16; *CMC*, 21 Mar. 1832; *CE,* 9 June 1845, 10 Oct. 1864,
    11 Oct. 1890.
8   *CMC*, 19 Mar. 1832; *CE,* 9 June 1845.
9   Dick Geary, *European Labour Protest,* p. 73.
10 John Lee, 'Aspects of the development and decline in the building in-
    dustry in Cork City 1850–1899, p. 61; Kieran R. Byrne, 'The origin and
    growth of technical education in Ireland 1731–1922', (unpublished Ph. D.
    dissertation, National University of Ireland, 1982), pp. 338–9. In the 1890s
    the master builders' attempts to have apprentices in the industry attend
    classes at the local School of Art collapsed within a few months due to
    low attendance, while the proposal to hold carpentry classes in the same
    institution were strongly resisted by the local carpenters.
11 E. P. Thompson, *The Making of the English Working Class,* p. 261, citing

G. Sturt, *The Wheelwright's Shop* (1923), chs. 10, 37; Eugen Weber, *Peasants into Frenchmen*, p. 20. For a modern study of the artisan's rightful pride in his craft, see Kevin Corrigan Kearns, *Dublin's Vanishing Craftsmen: In Search of the Old Masters* (Belfast, 1986), *passim*.

12 John Gorman, *Banner Bright*, p. 10; Belinda Loftus, *Marching Workers: An Exhibition of Trade Union Banners and Regalia* (Belfast, 1978), pp. 22, 29.

13 *CMC*, 21 Mar. 1832; *CE*, 22 May 1843, 9 June 1845, 10 Oct. 1864; *CDH*, 11 Oct. 1890.

14 *CMC*, 11 June 1832. Reid and Lamprey were Dublin cutlers.

15 *CE*, 23 Mar. 1886.

16 Loftus, *Marching Workers*, p. 78.

17 Dick Geary, *European Labour Protest*, p. 52.

18 *CC*, 6 Aug. 1833.

19 *CMC*, 19 Mar. 1832; *CE*, 9 June 1845, 10 Oct. 1864, 22 Aug. 1871, 7 Oct. 1880.

20 Emmet O'Connor, *A Labour History of Ireland 1824–1960*, pp. 9, 11–12; J. D. Clarkson, *Labour and Nationalism in Ireland*, p. 119; F. A. D'Arcy, 'The murder of Thomas Hanlon: an episode in nineteenth century Dublin labour history', *Dublin Historical Record*, vol. xxiv, no. 4, September 1971, pp. 89–100; John Foster, *Class Struggle and Industrial Revolution*, pp. 48–75.

21 *CMI*, 16, 18 Jan., 8 Feb., 13 Mar., 12, 26 May, 19 June 1821; *Freeholder*, 12, 21, 29 June 1822; SOC 1822: 2344/5, 2345/81; CSORP.OR, 1828: C/10.2. Trade-union organisation in the early 1820s spread even to the tradesmen of the suburbs so that vigorous agitation occurred among the coopers, nailors, bakers, sawyers, wheelwrights, tailors and building trades.

22 *CC*, 27 Apr., 29 May, 1, 6 June 1830, 7 Feb., 5, 10, 12, 19, 22, 31 Mar. 1835; *CE*, 2, 4, 9, 11, 14, 28 Mar., 11, 15, 18, 22, 27 Apr., 13, 27 May, 6, 15, 20 June, 5, 19 Aug. 1842. CSORP, 1833: 5859; CSORP.OR, 1835: 6/6, 7. In 1835 during a wage dispute among the journeymen bakers, a master baker's brother was seriously burned with vitriol. Matters were then brought to a head when two men were capitally convicted, for although the sentence was commuted to transportation, the discovery and conviction of the perpetrators put an almost total end to vitriol-throwing until in 1842 an isolated case occurred when a local sawmill owner was burned and a number of journeymen sawyers who had planned and carried out the attack were transported for life.

23 *SR*, 10 Sept. 1840; SOC, 1822:2435/81; John Foster, *Class Struggle and the Industrial Revolution*, p. 51, refers to the unions' use of 'small-scale violence and threats'.

24 *CC*, 7 Feb. 1829, 9 Mar. 1834, 24 Nov. 1838; *CE*, 9 Sept 1842; CSORP.OR, 1838: 6/227.

25 *CC*, 10 Dec. 1833, 2 May 1844. These threatening notices were sent by both unskilled labourers and skilled artisans.

26 *CC*, 7 Feb. 1829, 21 Nov. 1833; *Poor Enquiry*, HC 1836, (35) xxx, App. C to 1st Report, 27–30.

27   *CC*, 28 Dec. 1833; *CE*, 2, 4, 9, 11, 14, 28 Mar., 11, 15, 18, 22, 27 Apr., 13, 27 May, 6, 15, 20 June, 5, 19 Aug. 1842.

28   Henry Pelling, *A History of British Trade Unionism*, p. 57; John Foster, *Class Struggle and the Industrial Revolution*, pp. 203–50; Fergus D'Arcy, 'Dublin artisan activity', pp. 64, 93–119; John Boyle, *The Irish Labour Movement*, p. 47.

29   *CE*, 23 Aug. 1843, 6 May 1846.

30   *SR*, 2 Feb. 1826; *CE*, 31 Oct., 10, 12 Nov. 1845. Since the early 1820s the journeymen cabinet makers' working day had been one hour longer than that worked by other trades, so their request for a reduction in 1845 was simply to put them on a par with other crafts.

31   *CE*, 18, 25 Sept., 6 Oct. 1843, 4 Feb. 1846.

32   *CE*, 12 Jan. 1853, 22 Jan., 7 May, 22 Aug., 16 Oct. 1855.

33   CSORP.OR, 1851: 6/611.

34   *CE*, 7 May, 22 Aug., 16 Oct. 1855, 25 May, 7 Nov. 1870, 8, 10, 22, 29 June, 27 July 1893.

35   D'Arcy, 'Dublin artisan activity', pp. 17–18; *CE*, 9 Sept. 1842. By the early 1870s artisans were apparently using legal men on a regular basis to state their case in court. Striking foundry labourers were thus defended in 1870 (*CE*, 12 Oct. 1870) while in 1871 a journeyman shoemaker suing his employer for overdue wages used legal counsel in court. (*CE*, 28 Apr. 1871).

36   E. P. Thompson, *The Making of the English Working Class*, pp. 814–16; Elizabeth Malcolm, *Ireland Sober, Ireland Free*, pp. 326–7.

37   *CE*, 13, 25 July, 26 Aug., 2, 5, 21 Sept., 18, 25 Nov. 1842. This move towards moderation in the bakers' case actually predates the 1840s. In 1836 the society, whose members had frequently been involved in combination outrages in the early 1830s so as to save the life of a member convicted of outrage, entered into a pledge against all violent action in the future.

38   *CMC*, 27 June 1832; *CE*, 11 Apr. 1842. It is also significant that the exhortation of the revivalists in 1842 also included the phrase 'call Repeal to your assistance', thus interweaving a third theme – the regeneration of the country through political change.

39   *People's Press*, 2 May 1835; *CE*, 3 Feb. 1870; Seán Daly, *Cork: A City in Crisis*, pp. 7–9. The temperance role of the Mechanics' Hall was originally envisaged by the Catholic bishop, Dr Delaney in 1869. For an analysis of the Temperance Movement in the late 1860s, see Elizabeth Malcolm, *Ireland Sober, Ireland Free*, pp. 181–91.

40   *CE*, 13 July 1842, 10, 12 Nov. 1845.

41   *CE*, 10 Oct. 1864.

42   *CE*, 7 Oct. 1864, 3, 7 Feb., 18 Mar., 13 Oct. 1884. For a brief period in 1884, the reorganisation of the trades' council under a Father Hayde ushered in a period of de-radicalisation. It is from this period that the stress on self-denial comes.

43   *CE*, 3, 7 Feb., 18 Mar., 30 Oct. 1884; 12 Feb. 1885, 20, 27 Feb. 1886. Lectures were given on the following subjects: 'Trade Organisation',

'Workmen', 'Workmen and the Employer' and Thomas Davis.

44 *CE*, 5 Nov. 1852, 7 Jan. 1857, 13 Feb. 1860, 3 Oct. 1862, 26 Mar. 1864, 8 Oct. 1874. For a brief reference to the temperance note in the housing campaign in late nineteenth-century Cork, see Maura Murphy, 'The working classes of nineteenth century Cork', pp. 30–1.

45 *CE*, 21 Dec. 1853; *Proceedings of the Select Committee on the Sale of Intoxicating Liquor on Sunday (Ireland) Bill*, HC 1877 (198) xvi, Qs. 4767–75.

46 *CE*, 8 Jan. 1, 19 Feb. 1851.

47 *Proceedings of the Select Committee on the Sale of Intoxicating Liquor on Sunday (Ireland) Bill*, HC 1877 (198) xvi, Qs. 4767–75.

48 For a detailed analysis of the attempts to legally restrict Saturday and Sunday public house opening hours, see Elizabeth Malcolm, *Ireland Sober, Ireland Free*, pp. 192–275.

49 *Report of the Select Committee on the Sale of Liquors on Sunday (Ireland) Bill*, HC 1867–68, (280), xiv; *Report of the Select Committee on the Sale of Intoxicating Liquors on Sunday (Ireland) Bill*, HC 1877, (198) xvi; *Proceedings of the Select Committee on Sunday Closing Acts (Ireland)*, HC 1888, (255), xix; *Minutes of Evidence taken before the Royal Commission on Liquor Licensing Laws*, [C – 8980] HC 1898, xxxviii, vol. VII; *CE*, 14, 24 Apr. 1888, 30 Apr., 17 June 1898.

50 John Boyle, *The Irish Labour Movement*, p. 54.

51 *Limerick Evening Post and Clare Sentinel*, 21, 24 Oct. 1828.

52 Andrew Boyd, *The Rise of the Irish Trade Unions*, pp. 28–9; John Boyle, *The Irish Labour Movement*, p. 16; J. D. Clarkson, *Labour and Nationalism in Ireland*, p. 112; *Report from the Select Committee appointed to inquire into the State of the Law in the United Kingdom, and its consequences, respecting artisans leaving the Kingdom, and residing abroad; respecting the exportation of tools and machinery; and so far as relates to the Combination of Workmen and others to regulate their wages and hours of working*, HC 1824, (51), v, 1–589. *Report from the Select Committee appointed to inquire into the effects of the Act 5, Geo. iv, C. 95, in respect to the conduct of workmen and others, in different parts of the United Kingdom, and how far it may be necessary to repeal or amend the said act*, HC 1825, (437) iv, 499, 565. Contemporaries gave conflicting accounts of the existence of such a body, and historians still disagree on the subject.

53 *CMI*, 16 Jan. 1821; *CMC*, 15 Feb. 1828; SOC, 1822: 2344/5; *Limerick Evening Post and Clare Sentinel*, 26 Feb. 1830; *CC*, 16 Nov. 1833.

54 *Royal Commission on Labour*, [C-6795–vi] HC 1892, xxxvi, Qs.16882–5, 17011. The Cork United Building Trades was founded between 1890 and 1892, and included carpenters, masons, stonecutters and plasterers, all of whom had their own individual societies, but co-ordinated their efforts through the umbrella body.

55 Patrick Joyce, *Work, Society and Politics*, p. 117.

56 *CC*, 22 Apr. 1834.

57 J. D. Clarkson, *Labour and Nationalism in Ireland*, p. 119; *CMI*, 18 Jan., 18 Feb. 1821; *CMC*, 13, 18 Dec. 1833; *CC*, 13, 19, 28 Dec. 1833, 11 Jan., 3 Apr., 2 Aug. 1834, 19 Sept. 1835.

58 *SR*, 14 Mar. 1848.

59 *CE*, 29 July 1857, 19 Mar., 29 Oct. 1858, 19 Mar. 1859, 14 Sept., 28 Nov. 1864; *Irish People*, 19 Nov. 1864; Arthur Mitchell, *Labour in Irish Politics*, p. 14. The trades council of 1857 only came to the public notice in 1859 after which it again fell into obscurity.

60 *CE*, 19 Mar., 29 Oct. 1858, 28 Nov. 1864; John Boyle, *The Irish Labour Movement*, pp. 55–8.

61 Middle-class sponsors of the Mechanics' Hall were apparently pushed gently aside and the committee formed from among the ranks of seventeen city trades (plasterers, coopers, dyers, bakers, house painters, cabinet makers, paperhangers, carpenters, millwrights, curriers, tailors, ironworkers, masons, block-and-pump makers, corkcutters, tinplate workers and bootclosers). *CE*, 3 Feb. 1870; Seán Daly, *Cork: A City in Crisis*, p. 9.

62 In the 1890s the Webbs were told that the organised trades of Cork had split sometime in the 1870s following internal political disagreements. It is not clear whether this break-up occurred because of squabbles regarding local recruiting attempts by the First International or because of a different disagreement regarding the parliamentary election of 1872. On this latter occasion different factions of the trades supported rival nationalist candidates, one group supporting the pro-Fenian Joseph Ronayne while the other backed the more moderate nationalist John Daly, Mayor of Cork and benefactor of the Hall. Webb Trade Union Collection, sect. A, vol. iii, f. 45; *CE*, 2 Jan., 11, 21 Nov. 1872.

63 *CE*, 1 Jan., 27 Feb., 12, 13, 19, 21, 22, 23, 25, 28 Mar. 1872; *United Kingdom Society of Coachmakers, Monthly Report*, June 1872, p. 1; Henry Pelling, *A History of British Trade Unionism*, pp. 83–4. The Nine-Hours League was founded among the engineering and ironworkers in the north-east of England in 1859 following the successful campaign to reduce working hours among the mining trades of the region. Both unionised and non-society men joined the league, winning considerable concessions from the employers. Cork was, in fact, the first Irish centre to become involved in the Nine-Hours movement, which was initiated by the coachmakers, engineers and ironfounders. Significantly, the local Nine-Hours League met not in the Mechanics' Hall but – following the pattern in Britain – in the club rooms of the Amalgamated Society of Engineers in Devonshire Street.

64 *CE*, 2 Jan., 11, 21 Nov. 1872.

65 *CE*, 21, 25 Feb., 11, 25, 28 July, 23 Sept. 1881, 27 Jan., 24 Apr., 4 Aug. 1882. The trades involved in establishing the United Trades Association were the coopers, bootmakers, tailors, cabinet makers, ladies' shoemakers, coachmakers, farriers, shipwrights, stonecutters, bakers and carpenters. The building trades – masons, plasterers, plumbers and painters – joined after some hesitation, and were followed by a number of small declining trades like the nailors, millers, french polishers, ropemakers, corkcutters, upholsterers and sawyers and by the printing trades.

66 *CE*, 24 Sept. 1885; *Select Committee on Sunday Closing Acts (Ireland)*, HC 1888,

(255) xix, Qs. *8,490;* Reports on Trade Unions, [C–8232] HC 1896, xciii, 277, 420; [C–8644] HC 1897, xcix, 275, 250; [C–9013] HC 1898, ciii, 127, 208–9; [C–9443] HC 1899, xcii, 493, 204–5.

67   *CE*, 6, 27 June 1870; CSORP, 1870: 13023; Cork Coopers' Society Minute Books, 30 Oct. 1870.

68   *CE*, 15, 16, 22 Sept. 1890; Cork Typographical Society Minute Books, 13 Sept., 20 Dec. 1890, 15 July 1893, 13 June 1896; Cork Coopers' Society Minute Books, 20 June 1888; *CE*, 20 May 1890. On this occasion the printers, tailors and trades council each contributed ten pounds, the pork butchers, pig buyers and cattle buyers five pounds each, and the boot and shoemakers three pounds, all agreeing to give their custom only to bakeries run on day-work.

69   *CE*, 10, 28, 29 Sept., 2, 3, 9 Oct. 1890; Brendan McDonnell, 'The Dublin labour movement', p. 18.

70   *CE*, 18 Apr. 1881, 18 Dec. 1882, 15 Feb., 8, 15, 23 Nov. 1883, 13 Feb., 20 Mar., 23 May, 9 Aug., 12 Sept. 1884. From its foundation in 1881 until 1884 the committee of the United Trades Association had been representative of the coachmakers, tailors, printers, stonecutters, cabinet makers and plasterers. While most affiliated trades seemed content with this, the printers (themselves represented on the committee), carpenters and masons felt a clique was developing and called for a new election mechanism. The carpenters were generally believed to have brought up the matter through malice, having failed to secure the election of officers of their own choice, but the masons and printers who had no grievance of this kind, were equally vehement in calling for changes.

71   *Financial Report of the Associated Shipwrights' Society*, 1894, p. 2; *CE*, 16 Feb., 22 Nov. 1895; 28 Nov. 1896. One such dispute concerned the making of sideboards for use on the ships overhauled in the Passage Dock Yard. When the foreman promised the work to the cabinet makers, the carpenters claimed that they had done such work for fifty years, and only reluctantly allowed the trades council to mediate in the dispute.

72   *CE*, 19 Jan 1855. For a discussion on the role and oscillating fortunes of the small master in nineteenth-century Cork, see Maura Murphy 'The economic and social structure of nineteenth century Cork', pp. 132–9.

73   *CE*, 10, 12, 13 Mar. 1883, 10 Mar. 1893, 6 July, 2 Nov. 1894. The bakers' strike of 1883 was called without trade-council sanction. As a result, the council was sharply divided in its attitude to the dispute, some delegates openly siding with the master bakers against the strikers.

74   *CE*, 8, 10, 13, 14, 19 Mar. 1883, 4, 23 June, 4 July, 10 Sept. 1888, 5, 12, 22 Jan. 1889, 23 Mar. 1891, 5 June, 9 Aug. 1895, 12 Nov. 1898.

75   *CE*, 1, 8 Sept., 2 Oct. 1890, 22 Feb., 29 July 1892, 14, 22, 30 June, 11 July, 25 Aug. 1893, 8 May, 5 June 1896, 1, 12 Feb., 23 Mar. 1897; *Royal Commission on Labour*, Group C [C–6894–ix] HC 1893–94, xxxiv, 28,952–3, 29,037–9; [C–7063–vc] HC 1893–94, xxxviii, Qs. 17,123; *Monthly Report of the National Union of Boot and Shoe Rivetters and Finishers*, Mar. 1897, p. 4.

76 *CE*, 7 Mar., 21 May, 25 June, 4 Sept. 1890.

77 *Royal Commission on Labour*, [C–6795–v] HC 1892–93, xxxvi, pt ii, vol. ii, Qs. 14,714, 16,353, 16,917, 16,938–53; *CE*, 31 May, 1 June 1893; 27, 28 Mar., 12, 14, 25 May 1894. Brendan McDonnell, 'The Dublin labour movement', p. xxxiv, notes the same hesitancy among the Dublin unions regarding arbitration.

78 *CE*, 9, 13, 14, 20, 21 May, 5, 21, 25 June 1890, 2, 9, 13 Feb., 6, 13 Apr. 1894.

79 Cork Plumbers' Society Minute Books, 17 Mar. 1890.

80 Cork Coopers' Society Minute Books, 29 Nov. 1892; *CE*, 28 Aug., 26 Sept. 1893, 16 Oct., 19 Nov. 1894; Belinda Loftus, *Marching Workers*, p. 1.

81 Dennis Smith, 'Paternalism and craft', p. 213; Clive Behagg, *Politics and Production in the Early Nineteenth Century*, pp. 146–8.

82 C. Behagg, *Politics and Production*, p. 124.

83 R. Q. Gray, 'Class structure in Edinburgh', p. 158.

84 Cork Typographical Society Minute Books, 21 Apr. 1888, 17 Dec. 1891, 23 Apr. 1892, 25 Feb. 1893, 1, 8 June 1895; Cork Coopers' Minute Books, 19, 25 Jan. 1883, 1 Feb., 13 Apr., 30 Sept. 1886, 8 Aug. 1888. For a detailed account of the working of the chapel system in nineteenth-century Edinburgh, see R. Q. Gray, 'Class structure in Edinburgh', pp. 236–7.

85 Cork Coopers' Society Minute Books, 19, 25 Jan. 1883, 1 Feb., 13 Apr., 30 Sept. 1886, 8 Aug. 1888, 30 May 1889, 19 June 1895, 17 Feb., 6, 15 July 1896, 18 Jan. 1898, 26 Jan. 1899.

86 *CMC*, 27 June 1832; *SR*, 15 May, 27 Mar. 1841; *CE*, 8 Dec. 1841. The unionised artisans in 1841 were particularly alienated by the Board of Trade's pressure in favour of the employment of female labour as a cost-cutting exercise in local manufacture.

87 *CE*, 21, 31 Aug., 2, 21 Sept., 5, 24 Oct. 1881, 1, 8 Feb., 15 Mar., 22 Dec. 1882, 19 Jan., 29 Mar., 4 July 1883, 19 Mar., 11, 20, 27 Apr., 21, 25 May 1885. The first major exhibition was held in Dublin in August 1882 while another was held in Cork in July 1883.

88 John Scott, when accused in 1896 of sanctioning the importation of carpentry work for the corporation, retorted that he, at least, wore Irish clothes, something which most of the trades did not do. The controversy in 1897 concerned the giving of a corporation clothing tender to the lowest bidder, who was not an employer of unionised labour. *CE*, 15 Mar. 1895, 10 Jan., 15, 16, 22 May 1896, 17 Aug., 24 Sept., 1, 15 Oct. 1897.

89 *CE*, 19, 28, 30 Dec. 1842, 17 May 1843.

Conclusion

The term politicisation has been defined by one scholar as 'the process whereby a social group becomes capable of both making demands and exerting pressures on governments' and by another as the change which occurs 'when individuals and groups shift from indifference to participation because they perceive that they are involved in the nation'.[1] This study of the artisans of nineteenth-century Cork certainly confirms these definitions, but it also brings to the fore other dimensions of the process. These are, firstly, the development of an increasingly sophisticated and multilayered sense of identity on the part of both the individuals and the social group in question and, secondly, the degree to which group members remained constrained by that collective identity or emancipated themselves from it to become politically conscious individuals in their own right.

The limitations of this study are obvious insofar as the politicisation it examines is that of the artisans on the nationalist side of Cork society, while those on the Protestant and unionist side of the local divide have been largely passed by. This bias of the study is to a large extent determined by the nature of both the sources and, as far as can be deciphered, the realities of nineteenth-century Cork society. The minority status of unionist artisans ensured that, whatever vital community of economic interests existed between them and their nationalist counterparts,

their political opinions were always submerged beneath the all-
engulfing tide of nationalist opinion. Thus, however individually
politicised they were by the end of the nineteenth century, this
politicisation never became enmeshed in their craft and trade-
union identity. Some local trade societies did, it is true, attempt
to prevent their unionist members from being suffocated by
majority nationalist feeling through the simple (or not so simple) means of eschewing collective participation in nationalist
activities, but ultimately it proved impossible to avoid the identification of trade unionism with nationalism.[2]

This politicisation was a long time in the making. Garvin,
writing in a somewhat different though related context, concluded
that 'revolutions . . . have long gestations and do not run their
courses even in the timespan of a generation. Many European
revolutions have taken two generations to run their course from
beginning to end'.[3] Though the term revolution may be considered too grandiose for the politicisation of craftsmen in a provincial centre, the time-scale indicated by Garvin does seem
applicable here. The multiple processes which constitute craftsman politicisation certainly came into the open for the first time
in the 1830s, and artisans were both collectively and individually immersed in politics as the old century gave way to the new.
Whereas in the first two decades of the nineteenth century political participation by a trade union was either inconceivable,
unreported, or both, by 1898 the unions of Cork City had become
noted for both their political self-confidence and their flamboyant
participation in both labour and nationalist demonstrations alike.
Similarly, in the matter of the parliamentary franchise, the artisan's position improved considerably in the course of the century. It was not, of course, that the craftsman was unrepresented
in the electorate of the earlier decades, for the city poll book of
1835 revealed an identifiable artisan voting force of 544 individuals – some twenty-two per cent of the total vote. The dearth
of poll books in the decades after 1835 and the passing of the
Ballot Act of 1872 render impossible any similar social analysis
of subsequent elections, and make one pine, however undemo-
cratically, for the good old days of open voting when the individual's political stance was subject to the scrutiny of both his

contemporaries and of historians. However, the lack of recorded complaints by the organised artisans between 1832 and 1895 regarding the franchise may suggest (which seems unlikely) that they were not interested in gaining the vote, or (more probably) that, as a group, they were well served by the successive franchise reforms of the nineteenth century. It seems reasonable to suggest that the widening household franchise enforced by the Reform Acts of 1868 and 1884 brought a substantial number of artisans into the electorate. The 1884 Act, in particular, increased the city electorate from less than five thousand to over fourteen thousand, and this new electorate certainly included many working men, for the trades council considered it a satisfactory arrangement.[4] In the matter of the municipal franchise, the gates were thrown open to the artisans in an even more dramatic fashion at the end of the century when, under the provisions of the Local Government Act of 1898, the extremely limited local franchise and the considerably broader parliamentary franchise were assimilated and – even more significantly – property qualifications were abolished for candidates to municipal office.[5]

The increasing politicisation of the artisan is also evident in the way in which, by the end of the nineteenth century, local politicians became aware of the need to court the working-class vote. Up to the 1890s, if the craftsmen wished to influence politicians either between or during elections, the onus lay on the trades themselves to exert pressure on public men through the customary 'respectful deputation' which, while it might prove quite forceful in its language, could never do more than attempt to exert pressure from outside the ramparts of political decision-making. By the 1890s, however, with the above-mentioned extension of the franchise to working men, and with the frantic political competition precipitated in rival nationalist circles by the Parnellite split, the pattern was beginning to change. The phenomenon of trade deputations to election candidates survived, but it was now accompanied by the new feature of deputations in the opposite direction, as political hopefuls and their backers went on canvassing expeditions to the various workplaces of the city. In 1895, reviewing the general developments in the island, the Irish Trades Congress noted this new 'tendency of candidates of various constituencies to appeal to the labour element, with regard at all events to securing their vote'.[6] As far as Cork was concerned, this phenomenon can be dated accurately to the election of 1891 when, for the first time since 1832, candidates appealed directly to the working-class vote by doing the rounds of the quayside coal yards, breweries, bacon factories, gas works and railway termini.[7] Well might the local politician quoted in chapter 5 above warn his colleague 'not to say anything hurtful' to the local trades council, while the sympathetic local press, reflecting the general feeling among skilled and semi-skilled workers, concluded that at both political and social level, 'working men were beginning to feel a good deal more independent . . . [and developing] a feeling of confidence in themselves [which] they otherwise would not have'.[8]

The mesmerising effect of politics – and particularly of nationalist politics – on the artisan and labourer is hardly surprising in the context of nineteenth-century urban Ireland. In Cork, the competing politics of nationalism and unionism permeated the town council, the poor law boards, and the Chamber of Commerce, while the internecine squabbles between the various factions within nationalism were played out vigorously not only in these same public boards but also on a wider scale in the political and recreational organisations patronised by the lower middle and working classes.[9] Indeed, the average Cork working man of the nineteenth century was more likely to be involved (however peripherally) in politics than in trade unionism. In 1865, for instance, there were reputedly four thousand sworn Fenians in the city, and even allowing for the exaggeration tendencies of informers, this is almost twice the estimated local trade-union membership at the same period. It was not, in fact, until the last decade of the century that the number of trade unionists in the city was as large as Fenian membership had been in the 1860s.[10]

On closer analysis, however, the depth of this apparently all-pervasive politicisation is open to question, for there is a sense in which the perceived power and independence of the artisan and, more particularly, of the non-craft working man was illusory. At the most practical level of all, i.e. that of unionisation within the workforce, success was far from complete. The erratic nature of documentation, and fluctuations from occupation to occupation and from decade to decade, render it impossible to calculate the percentage rate of unionisation in the Cork workforce until the 1890s. Varying from an estimated fourteen to ninety-one per cent in the 1830s and 1840s to between twenty-five and almost one hundred per cent in the 1880s and 1890s, unionisation levels appear by 1900 to have averaged seventy per cent among the craftsmen but as little as thirty per cent among the unskilled workers.[11] Independence of social thinking among artisans proved equally slow to grow. By the later decades of the century, it is true, the organised trades had begun to shake off the paternal control of employers and clergymen. Thus the attempt in 1870 to harness the newly founded Mechanics' Hall to the resurrected temperance movement was rejected, while ten years later the trades council cut its links with any employers who, hitherto benevolent, had taken an anti-union stand in trade disputes.[12] On the other hand, however, the general ethos of the trades reflected what, at the risk of over-simplification, can be termed middle-class values – i.e. a determined pursuit of respectability, snobbish attitudes towards unskilled labour, and the socio-economic aspirations, as Garvin expressed it, of 'tiny capitalists'. They possessed a skill, prospects of even limited advancement from journeyman to master, and occasionally even operated as landlords in working class tenement-land, all of which indicated that in mentality if not in fact, they were an upwardly mobile group with a mind-set shaped as much by their 'social betters' as by any independent opinions based on class consciousness.[13]

Politically, too the supposed independence of the artisans is open to question. Even when, from the mid-1880s onwards, the local trades council attempted and claimed to have influenced the course of municipal elections, its power was certainly curtailed by the outsider status of most artisans in relation to the municipal franchise, and the limited degree of its influence was amply illustrated in 1894 by its euphoric reaction at turning the grand total of *three* voters against one particular candidate.[14] One can calculate that, even as late as 1900, roughly one in three adult males (at the lower end of the socio-economic scale) still had no vote at either municipal or parliamentary level.[15] Moreover, even those who were enfranchised were still constrained by the political mould in which they had been gradually shaped in the course of the previous half-century: no matter how much the organised artisans might, for example, quiz the election candidates in 1891, they never pressed them to make specific commitments of either a social or a political nature. Indeed, looked at more closely, these apparent inquisitions revealed not so much independent artisan pressure on nervous candidates (though they certainly were nervous) as rival groups of artisans who, in the bitterness of the Parnellite split, were intent on demonstrating their loyalty to their respective political heroes.[16] It is true that as the concept of independent labour representation took shape by the late 1890s, platform rhetoric suggested that organised artisans were shaking off the political controls of the past, and were moving towards a more autonomous position in politics. As one labour orator put it in 1898,

> The time had come when they should look at the social and not the political. What had they got by politics? They had so-called Nationalists coming forward, denying them the benefits of an act of parliament given them by a Conservative government, and saying that the masses should vote on the political ticket as in the past.[17]

The fact was, however, that while the concept of independent Labour did achieve its triumph at the local election of 1899, capturing nine of the fifty-six corporation places, it was equally significant that the 'traditional' nationalist parties (Nationalist and Parnellite) between them won four times as many seats as Labour, a victory achieved not only in the more middle-class wards, but also in wards with a sizeable working-class population.[18]

Despite the increasingly frequent use of the language of class, the admission of bodies of semi-skilled workers to the trades council and, ultimately, the triumph of the labour panel in the local election of 1899, class consciousness was a minor part of the artisan's world view. His awareness of a common identity with the wider working class was considerably dimmed by his fears of the growing threats to his position as part of a plebeian élite. This sense of beleaguerment by the forces of socialism, modernisation, mechanisation and the undercutting capacity of women, immigrants and unskilled labour ensured that his loyalties were based less on class than on the narrower ambit of the craft.

Thus, one aspect of politicisation probably negated the other: the more nationalistically politicised were the artisans and working classes generally, the less orientated they were towards a sense of political independence based on class. When all came to all, it seemed, Michael Austen's claim in 1890 that nationality was the 'essential characteristic of every Irishman' summed up the position.[19] On the other hand, one might well ask whether, in the Cork experience, artisan nationalist politicisation was ever more than skin-deep. Emmet O'Connor, in his *A Labour History of Ireland* (1992) makes the point that among Irish working men generally, nationalism's real function was to provide 'a rallying point for trade unions and a platform for grievances'.[20]

There is a similar sense in which all the nationalist posturing and rhetoric of Cork artisans, if not totally superficial, was certainly dragged out on occasions of crisis to help underline and articulate grievances of an economic nature. From the early 1830s, when the trades of Cork equated Repeal of the Act of Union with economic prosperity, to 1898, when some local labour spokesmen fused the concepts of labour representation with the commemoration of 'Ninety-Eight, one gathers that, however sincere the commitment to the abstract concept of nationalism, hard-headed economic considerations came first. And who would blame them? Just as the development of civic ritual and the growing cult of monarchy in late nineteenth-century Britain helped integrate working people into mainstream party politics, so in the Irish context nationalist rhetoric and participation in political demonstrations could also give to the artisan a cosy sense of belonging to a wider community from whose upper reaches he was economically and socially excluded.[21] On the other hand, nationalism cost money, demanding financial contributions by the individual craftsman or his trade society to the expenses of political processions, collections for political prisoners, election funds, and (with increasing frequency as the century passed) the inevitable memorials to dead patriots. Practically speaking, there was little return from any of these outlays, and while most artisans and trade societies were proud to participate in such nationalistic activities, there was a point at which practicality took over. This was amply illustrated in a series of controversies breaking out in the trades council in 1887. On this occasion, the local tailors' and farriers' societies strongly condemned the National League's hunting ban, which was detrimentally affecting their employment prospects in the normally busy hunting season. At the same time, objecting to a trades-council backed corporation boycott of the pro-landlord *Cork Constitution*, the typographical society claimed that, in view of possible layoffs at the office in question, the material interests of its members came above all else, and that it was particularly unfair that the *Constitution* printers, many of whom were unionist in politics, should suffer for a nationalist cause. Though on each occasion the protesting societies were treated with tight-lipped patriotic disapproval by the other trades, it was obvious that considerations of nationalism outweighed economics only when a trade's immediate interests were not at stake.[22] Perhaps this triumph of the trade over the nation was best summed up in 1904 when one irate cooper, confronted with the prospect of yet another costly political demonstration, objected that it 'would be throwing ten pounds away for the purpose of putting a green sash around his neck, and it was too Irish . . .'[23]

The wider sense of awareness based on class and nationalism also came out as a poor second when it competed with local loyalties. In chapter 2 above, we have seen just how rooted in the immediate urban context was the average Cork artisan's sense of loyalty and identity. As far as the skilled craftsman was concerned, the world of 'deserving brothers' stopped short at the city bounds. Even unionised artisans from without that magic frontier were regarded as interlopers in the city labour market; goods coming in from Limerick, Waterford and Dublin were considered to be 'imports', just as much as those from across the Channel; and British amalgamated unions, despite all their advantages, were still viewed as alien organisations.

The artisan's sense of oneness with his locality and his craft was, perhaps, ultimately fused in his association with that collectivity which, in the course of the nineteenth century, became progressively known as 'the trades of Cork', whose sense of distinctive identity spanned both political and economic issues. Under that umbrella, the artisan and the trade union to which he belonged, became more and more active in public affairs. From the Repeal campaign of the 1830s, through the successive manufacture revival movements of the ensuing decades to the Fenian and Home Rule campaigns of the latter half of the century, both the trade societies and the collectivity of 'the trades' played a distinctive part. Yet, although the trade was certainly the main political mouthpiece of the artisans up to the 1850s, it was not their sole channel of political activity. In the early 1840s most politically active artisans joined the mainstream Loyal National Repeal Association rather than transfer their allegiance to the separate Operative Repeal Association. Hence, while the latter struggled along as an independent body until mid-1843, its activities were never publicised and it apparently collapsed or lost its separate identity within the expanding Repeal movement in the city. Viewed with the benefit of hindsight, this was not surprising, because in other ways, too, the Cork trade societies appear to have had a less autonomous role within the structure of the local Repeal movement than had their Dublin counterparts. In the capital city, some trade societies had their own Repeal wardens who directed the political activities of the trade and collected the Repeal Rent from within its ranks; in Cork, on the other hand, Repeal wardens were not apparently appointed from among the rank and file of the trade societies but were mainly manufacturers, merchants, retailers and master craftsmen who had no particular connection with the organised trades.[24]

The partial supplanting of the trade society as the artisans' main political mouthpiece in the O'Connellite years was indicative of future trends. From the late 1840s onwards the growth of broadly based nationalist bodies, both constitutional and militant, further accelerated the demise of the trade as the primary organ of artisan political organisation and participation. Though, as already noted, some Confederate Clubs in 1848 were occupation-based, most were of a mixed occupational composition with locality rather than trade as the basis of organisation.[25] Moreover, while it was, indeed, through the trade societies that the Fenians first publicly recruited working class support in 1861, and while certain trades continued to identify closely with Fenianism, the trade had by the later nineteenth century disappeared as the primary unit of artisan political organisation and expression.[26] Though in the sphere of manufacture revival the local unionised artisans continued to assert their separate collective identity, they did not again form specifically artisan political bodies, but participated as individuals in the mainstream organisations which crossed class and occupational boundaries.

This declining political importance of the artisan's occupational community was to some extent evidence of the skilled working man's political coming of age.[27] No longer was his role in public affairs shaped solely by his craft membership, for by the eve of the twentieth century the progressive extension of the franchise, the proliferation of alternative political pressure groups and – most significantly – the general public recognition of the working man as an intelligent political being, allowed him an individual political role inconceivable seventy years previously. Yet, in this same political emancipation of the individual artisan from the shackles of the trade, there lay another problem: i.e. was the trade (or the collectivity of the trades) to be elbowed aside by other political groupings whose membership partially overlapped with that of the craft? Certainly, towards the end of the century, the trades' suspicions of the municipal corporation were replicated in relation to the organisations involved in both the agrarian agitation and the underground separatist movement.

In its dealings with the Land League, the trades' council was particularly given to outbursts of pique. Though, as already discussed in chapter 3, this was largely due to practical issues, artisan resentment against the League was more often expressed in terms of trade dignity. When the Land League accorded the trades a subsidiary role in the local pro-Parnellite demonstration of 1880, this slight was not forgotten, and when similar attempts were made two years later to tighten the League's monopoly of public demonstrations in the city, the most vociferous protestors were the trades who refused to support an event in whose planning they had no part. Without the colour and pageantry lent by trade-union participation, the demonstration was sure to be a fiasco, and it was reluctantly called off – a development which caused much satisfaction among the trades whose sense of righteous indignation reached new heights:

> It was well once and for all to make it known that the trades of the city would not be dragged at the tail of any man . . . It seemed as if the trades of Cork were at the beck and call of anybody who thought to get up a demonstration in Cork . . . The trades of Cork knew how to respect themselves; they were independent of anybody, and it was rather impertinent of anybody to dictate to the trades of Cork. (hear, hear) . . . They saw the semblance of a dictatorship at present, and the sooner that such a thing was put a stop to the better. (applause).[28]

The prickliness of the trades was obviously due to their awareness that, as a political force, they were lagging far behind the League. This was amply illustrated by the case of Eugene Crean who, as an active trade-unionist and equally active Leaguer, represented the tug of loyalties experienced by the average nationalist artisan in the later years of the century. A carpenters' delegate to the trades council and, since 1886, a member of the municipal corporation, Crean acted in the latter body as a trades' spokesman and watchdog, slating the city fathers for their inaction on trade-related issues, and complaining in status-conscious terms that 'the members of the [town council] cared no more for his opinion than they did for that of a common donkey boy'.[29] Moreover, even when his anti-Parnellite stand in 1890 resulted in his removal from the presidency of the trades council, he loyally maintained his pro-trades stance within the corporation.[30] Yet, Crean's identification with the trades was evenly matched by the intensity of his party-political loyalties; his election to the corporation in 1886 and his maintenance of his seat thereafter was more dependent on the influence of the National League than on that of the trades, and even if he was primarily a trades' representative thereafter, he did not allow his trade loyalties to dilute his anti-Parnellism. Not so much a trades representative as a

pro-trades nationalist councillor, Crean epitomised both the dual
identity of the nationalist artisan and the tension between the
two powerful local pressure groups – trades council and Home
Rulers.

Between the city's organised trades and the militant nationalists, too, considerable and ill-concealed hostility had developed
by the 1890s. This was so because, while many individual artisans continued to be actively involved in the underground movement, the latter was now in competition with the trades council
for the loyalty of the artisan. As a result, although the trades
prided themselves on their identification with the nationalist
cause, they found themselves increasingly cold-shouldered by the
republican underground on the occasion of public nationalist
events. The first major confrontation was in 1893 on the occasion of an abortive attempt to erect a memorial to the Manchester
Martyrs in the city. Approached by a deputation from a group
calling itself the Manchester Memorial Committee (in reality
an IRB front), the trades council agreed to subscribe two hundred pounds towards the monument.[31] It seems that by this
stage, whatever individual artisans or trade societies had IRB
links, the trades council as a body was not in the confidence of
the city's extreme nationalists. Later that year, in fact, the Manchester Memorial Committee was deliberately reconstituted to
weaken the trades' role and ensure a majority of IRB men. The
inevitable split appeared in the ranks of the committee, with the
trades on one side and the extreme nationalists on the other. Six
months of desultory discussions followed, the trades refusing to
sit on the reconstituted committee and – more importantly –
holding back their two hundred pound subscription until the matter had been settled to their satisfaction. By mid-1894 the Manchester Memorial Committee had collapsed.[32]

In 1898 a similar confrontation occurred between the trades
and the city's IRB element regarding the pending celebrations
of the centenary of the 1798 rebellion. Following the pattern
throughout the country, a local Centenary Committee was set
up, comprising a mixed group of Parnellites, anti-Parnellites,
trade representatives and a few socialists, but dominated by
the IRB.[33] Aptly described by the vigilant Castle authorities

as 'not a happy lot', the committee was plagued by interminable squabbling between the trades and the IRB element, firstly about the demotion of one of the trade representatives to a subordinate place in committee ranks, and later about attempts to link the committee with that of Dublin – a body equally dominated by the IRB. Even on the day when the foundation stone of the local 'Ninety-Eight monument was laid, yet another quarrel broke out between the IRB committee members and the trades council president – this time regarding the latter's claim that he had been given insufficient notice to deliver his speech at the ceremony.[34] Small wonder that in September 1898 one bewildered Dublin Castle official confided in another apropos of the Cork Centenary Committee: 'It is difficult to follow these squabbles between extremists in Cork . . .', to which the second wrote back: 'I am unable to treat all this seriously – I regret it, but I can't'.[35]

This *cri de coeur* of the hapless Castle correspondent investigating Cork nationalist circles in 1898 might well serve as the closing note of this study, prefiguring as it does the confusion of the historian who today attempts to untangle the many strands of Cork artisan identity at the end of the nineteenth century. The neglected unionist artisans apart, where did the identity of the artisan *qua* artisan ultimately lie? In the nation? In the city? In the working class? In the collectivity of the trades? In the craft? In the workshop? No doubt, it lay in all these areas, the relative importance of each varying with individual, time and circumstance. In his public rhetoric, the nationalist artisan portrayed himself primarily as that amalgam of devotion to motherland and class – the patriotic working man. In his day-to-day round of work, his loyalty was to the narrower circle of the workshop. In his confrontations with town council, land agitators and Fenians, he ranged himself with the collective strength of the trades council. Ultimately, however, he gave his fealty to the craft and the city. Though it means moving outside the strict time limits of this study, it does seem appropriate to give the last word to Seamus Murphy who, in his book *Stone Mad*, has opened up to us outsiders the rich and complex sense of identity of the traditional Cork craftsman. One of his most vibrant characters, Tomit, who served his time in the nineteenth century, summed up as follows his dual and overlapping pride in craft and city:

> Twas only years afterwards I realized how fortunate I was. With the coaching I got I was able to take off me coat with the best men in the country, an' they used to say to me: "You are wan of the best men to come outa Cork as long as we can remember". An' a strange thing about it, I used to feel that I was working for the honour of the oul' city, an' when I would be bankered with Galway men an' Kilkenny men an' men from all over Ireland, I used to say to meself: "Tomit, you're a Corkman, show them what the old city be the Lee can do".[36]

NOTES

1   Sam Clark, 'The social composition of the Land League'; Eugen Weber, *Peasants into Frenchmen*, p. 242

2   *CC*, 2 Dec. 1887; *CE*, 1 Dec. 1887. The printers' society which, while not formally amalgamated with the British-based Typographical Association, worked in close harmony with it, particularly in the mutual relief of tramps, and included in its ranks a large number of English and unionist members. It consequently openly recognised the diversity of political opinion within its ranks by avoiding any part in political demonstrations from 1843 until 1880.

3   Tom Garvin, *Nationalist Revolutionaries in Ireland*, p. 33.

4   The parliamentary electorate in Cork city in the course of the century fluctuated as follows (electorate as percentage of total male population given in parentheses): 1830 – 2,500 (13·78); 1833 – 4,322 (23·82); 1841 – 4,364 (21·59); 1851 – 3,039 (17·49); 1859 – 3,073 (16·68); 1872 – 4,307 (21·41); 1880 – 4,626 (22·42); 1890 – 14,569 (75·1); 1900 – 13,362 (66·73). The municipal franchise rose from 1,236 (6·8 per cent) in 1830 to 3,865 (19·12 per cent) in 1841, to 10,000 men (49·94 per cent) and 3,000 women in 1899. *People's Press*, 17, 24, 31 Jan., 7, 14 Feb. 1835; *Number of persons entitled to vote at the elections of members for cities and boroughs in Ireland: specifying the number of electors for each place*, HC 1830 (522), xxxi, 321; *Number registered under the Reform Act, distinguishing qualifications*, HC 1833 (177), xxvii, 289; *Abstract of the return of parliamentary electors, Ireland*, HC 1841 (240-1), xx, 615; *Abstract of the number of registered electors in each county in Ireland, under the Act 13 and 14 Vict., c.69, distinguishing each class of electors; and similar return for each county of a city, county of a town, and borough in Ireland*, HC 1851 (393), i, 879; *Return of the qualification required for the municipal and parliamentary franchise in each borough in Ireland having a town council; and number of municipal and of parliamentary*

electors at the last revision, specifying the number of electors of each distinct king of parliamentary franchise, HC 1868-69 (233), i 203; *Return showing for each of the parliamentary cities and boroughs of Ireland, number of electors on the register, distinguishing occupiers, lodgers, freemen, etc., also total income assessed to the income tax in each city and borough,* HC 1872 (17), xlvii, 409; *Return showing the population in each county, city and borough in Ireland returning members to parliament; the acreage and value of rateable property in each; number of registered housed in each county, city and borough, according to rating,* HC 1884 (164) lxii, 221; *Return as to each municipal borough and municipal town or township in Ireland, showing the rateable value, according to the ratebook of the property therein rated to the relief of the poor; the population within the municipal boundaries according to the census of 1881; the number of dwelling houses, the number of burgesses on the roll or number of persons entitled to vote at municipal elections; and the number of aldermen and councillors or commissioners,* HC 1886 (84 – Sess. I), lvii, 53; *Return showing, as regards each parliamentary county and borough, or division thereof, in Ireland, the population and the number of inhabited houses in 1891, and the number of the several classes of electors on the parliamentary register on 1st Jan. 1893,* HC 1894 (126), lxiii, 315; *Dod's Parliamentary Companion,* 1880, 1890, 1898. The *People's Press* published the poll for the 1835 city election – a total of 2,545 voters, of whom 2,181 were identifiable by occupation. Included among the identified voters were 147 labourers. The estimate of 544 artisan voters may, indeed, understate reality, for a further 184 unidentified voters may well have belonged to the labourer and artisan classes.

5   John Boyle, *The Irish Labour Movement,* p. 303.

6   *Report of the Second Irish Trades Congress,* 1895, p. 16.

7   *CE,* 18 Mar., 27, 30 Oct., 4 Nov. 1891.

8   *CE,* 4 Nov. 1891.

9   *Minutes of Evidence taken before the Select Committee on Local Government and the Taxation of Towns (Ireland),* HC 1877, (357), xii, Qs. 2,503; see above pp. 148–54.

10 It is impossible to give accurate figures of trade-union membership in the 1860s, but basing our estimates on the number of trade members marching under union banners in the 1860s and 1870s, there appear to have been just over two thousand trade unionists in the city. By 1892 the local trades council calculated that its membership (which covered most of the trades in the city) amounted to some three thousand men. Lest one exaggerate the degree of nationalist politicisation, however, it must be borne in mind that a man's position as a sworn Fenian, as a member of a constitutional nationalist organisation, or simply as a participant in a political demonstration or election riot, does not necessarily imply a deep political commitment. *CE* 10 Oct. 1864, 13 Oct. 1873; *Royal Commission on Labour,* [C-7063-vc] HC 1893–94, xxxviii, Qs. 17019; K.B. Nowlan, 'The Fenian Rising of 1867', T. W. Moody (ed.), *The Fenian Movement,* p. 31.

11 For detailed figures on unionisation, see Maura Murphy, 'The working classes of nineteenth century Cork', p. 42. By the late 1890s the local trades council, which included in its ranks all the unionists of the city, claimed

a membership of four thousand men, of whom some two thousand were skilled artisans. This would suggest unionisation of approximately seven in every ten skilled craftsmen, three in ten unskilled men, and one in every three men in the working class as a whole. *Minutes of Evidence taken before the Royal Commission on Liquor Licensing Laws*, [C–8980] HC 1898, xxxviii, vol. vii, Qs. 65,882–4; *Census of Ireland*, 1901.

12 *CE*, 3 Feb. 1870, 5 Jan. 1882, 7, 8, 9 Mar. 1883, 4 Apr. 1885, 4, 33 June 1888, 5 June, 9 Aug. 1895. Daniel Galvin, Mayor of Cork in 1882, had earned the trades' gratitude by helping to finance their hall when times were hard, but when he led the opposition to a general strike by the operative bakers in 1883, he fell quickly from favour. Similarly, Henry L. Tivy, proprietor of the local conservative newspaper, the *Cork Constitution*, had been popular with the trades council in the early 1880s, but a major dispute with his printing staff led (along with certain political quarrels) to a complete breakdown in relations between him and the trades in the late 1880s.

13 The cabinet makers' delegate to the trades council in 1888, in the context of a debate regarding immigrant Jewish labour, referred to his own tenants, though no further detail was given. *CE*, 16 Mar. 1888.

14 *CE*, 30 Nov. 1894.

15 *Return showing, as regards each parliamentary county and borough, or division thereof, in Ireland, the population and the number of unheated houses in 1891, and the number of the several classes of electors on the parliamentary register on 1st Jan. 1893*, HC 1894, (126), lxviii, 315; *Dod's Parliamentary Companion*, 1898; *Census of Ireland*, 1901.

16 *CE*, 30 Oct., 4 Nov. 1891.

17 *Workers' Republic*, 17 Sept. 1898, p. 1.

18 *CC*, 18 Jan. 1899. For a similar view that in the British context, 'organised labour . . . offered little by way of an alternative to the collectivities of work and religion upon which politics was based', see Patrick Joyce, *Work, Society and Politics*, p. 311.

19 See above p. 159.

20 Emmet O'Connor, *A Labour History of Ireland*, p. 201.

21 Patrick Joyce, *Work, Society and Politics*, pp. 278–80.

22 *CC*, 18, 19 Nov., 2, 3 Dec. 1887; *CE* 18, 25 Nov., 3 Dec. 1887.

23 Belinda Loftus, *Marching Workers*, p. 30, quoting Cork Coopers' Society Minute Books, 2 March 1904.

24 *Pilot*, 7 Apr. 1840; Fergus D'Arcy, 'Dublin artisan activity', p. 68; Jacqueline Hill, 'The role of Dublin in the Irish National Movement 1840–48 (Ph.D. thesis, Leeds University, 1973).

25 *SR*, 30 May 1848; *CC*, 6 June, 25 July, 3 Aug. 1848; CSORP, 1848: 6/866. The Glanmire club, on the other hand, may have been locality rather than occupation-based, and included a large number of shipwright members simply because it was based in a riverside locality where a large number of shipwrights lived.

26 *CE* 14 Sept., 9, 31 Oct., 4 Nov. 1861; CSORP, 1861: 8418 (filed with 1877: 3591).

27 For discussion of a similar trend in nineteenth-century Edinburgh, see R. Q Gray, 'Class structure in Edinburgh', pp. 155–60.

28 *CE*, 11, 13 Dec. 1882

29 *CE*, 17 Feb. 1887.

30 *CE*, 22 Oct. 1886, 17 Feb. 1887, 9 May, 10 Dec. 1890, 16 Jan. 1891, 28 Jan., 2 Dec. 1892, 24 Sept. 1897, 1, 15 Oct. 1897. Crean took a prominent part in pressing for the establishment of public building works, campaigning for a fair labour clause in corporation contracts, and seeking the assimilation of the parliamentary and municipal franchises, in 1897 leading the narrow majority of councillors who pledged support for these measures.

31 *CE* 10, 24 Feb., 13 May, 15 Sept. 1893. The recorded trades' subscriptions were: tailors – £30; masons – £25; builders' labourers – £25; plasterers – £20; boot makers – £5; bootrivetters – £2; balance unaccounted for – £93.

32 *CE*, 2 Feb., 15, 22 Sept., 13 Oct. 1893, 20 Apr. 1894; CBS, 1898: 17582/S. The trade societies had originally been allotted two representatives each on the committee, but under the new arrangements the several reading rooms and musical bands of the city – reputedly Parnellite and IRB strongholds – were each allowed four representatives.

33 CBSR, 1890: 631/S; 1897: 14851/S; 1898: 15192/S, 17345/S, 17582/S; *CDH* 15 May 1897. Of the six original officers of the committee, four were IRB men, members of the local Brian Dillon Branch of the National Foresters. When the committee membership was increased to twelve, at least eight members, and probably nine, were IRB members: P. H. Meade (mayor), John O'Keeffe, John Slattery, G. S. Crowley, A. O'Driscoll, D. O'Leary, Michael Power, David Walsh and Patrick Corcoran. Corcoran was not listed as an IRB man by the Castle, but he may well have been a member since he was present among a number of committed Fenians at the unveiling of a monument to a local Fenian in 1890. The non-IRB members of the committee were J.C. Flynn, MP; Eugene Crean, MP, member and president of the trades council, and Joseph O'Brien, secretary of the trades council.

34 CBSR, 1898: 14851/S; 15567/S; 17345/S; *CE*, 11 Dec. 1897, 3 Mar., 2 Apr., 8 Oct. 1898; *CDH*, 22 Nov. 1897.

35 CBS, 1898: 17582/S.

36 Seamus Murphy, *Stone Mad*, p. 147.

BIBLIOGRAPHY

Primary Sources

MANUSCRIPT MATERIAL

Archives Institute, South Main Street, Cork

Cork Bankruptcy Court Records 1890–1916.
Cork Coopers' Society Minute Books 1870–1900.
Cork Petition to Parliament *re* Unemployment in Cork City 1822.
Cork Plumbers' Society Minute Books 1868–95.
Cork Trades' Association Letter to P. J. Madden, Mayor, *re* Artisans' Exhibition 1885.
Cork Typographical Society, Idle Members' List 1868–1900.
Cork Typographical Society Minute Books 1887–1900.
Cork Union Workhouse Registers 1850–90.
Day Papers (including papers of Richard Dowden 1830–45).
Griffith's Valuation, Borough of Cork, 1852.
Letter Book of a Cork Merchant, Richard Hare 1770s (MS. U. 259).
Minute Books of the Cork Master Tailors' Association 1897–1957.

Cork Public Museum, Fitzgerald's Park, Cork

Records of the Cork Butter Market:
A (v) 24, Coopers' Petition *re* Standard of Casks 1840.
G (130) Committee of Merchants' Minute Books 1837–57.

National Library of Ireland, Dublin
Broadside Ballad Collection.

Diaries of Otto Travers (1830s).
James F. X. O'Brien Papers 1847–1905.
John Mitchel Papers (Hickey Collection).
Larcom Papers (1860s).
Loyal National Repeal Association Papers 1840–47.
William O'Brien Papers 1852–1928.
William O'Brien Papers 1881–1968 (Minute Books and Letter Books of the Irish Socialist Republican Party 1898–1903).
William Smith O'Brien Papers 1803–64.

Royal Irish Academy, Dublin

Charles Gavan Duffy Papers.
Irish Confederation Papers.

National Archives, Bishop Street, Dublin

Chief Secretary's Office Registered Papers, Outrage Reports 1832–49.
Chief Secretary's Office Registered Papers 1850–1900.
Crimes Branch Special Reports 1887–1900.
Fenian Papers 1860–80.
Irish Crimes Records 1865–70, vol. I, Fenianism: Index of Names.
State of the Country Papers 1800–32.
Unregistered Papers (i.e. classified papers, miscellaneous) 1821–78.

Cambridge University Library, Cambridge

Bradshaw Irish Collection, vol. v.

Public Record Office, Kew, London

Police Reports, South–Western Division 1893–94, CO. 904.63.
Secret Societies: Register of Home Associations 1890–93, CO. 904.16.
Secret Societies: Register of Suspects 1890–98, CO. 904.18.

London School of Economics

Webb Trade Union Collection, sect. A., vol. iii.

Vehicle Building and Automotive Museum, Holyhead Road, Coventry

Cork Coachmakers' Minute Books 1812–25.
Cork Coachmakers' Society Rules and Regulations 1823, Panel 2A, Museum.

Modern Records Centre, University of Warwick, Coventry

Amalgamated Society of Lithographic Printers of Great Britain and Ireland, Minute Books 1880–88.

Dublin Branch Minute Books, Amalgamated Society of Carpenters and Joiners 1884–90.

NEWSPAPERS

Cork Papers

Cork Constitution 1820–1900.
Cork Examiner 1841–99.
Cork Daily Herald 1850–99.
Cork Mercantile Chronicle 1802; 1832–35.
Cork Morning Intelligencer 1821.
Freeholder 1822.
People's Press 1835.
Southern Industry 1881–85.
Southern Reporter 1820–50.

Dublin Papers

Irish Builder 1864–68.
Irish People 1864–65.
Irish Times 1885.
Irish Trades Advocate 1851.
Irishman 1849–50.
Morning News 1862.
Pilot 1840–46.
United Ireland 1883.
United Irishman 1848.
Workers' Republic 1898-99.

Other Irish Papers

Kerry Journal 1830.
Limerick Chronicle 1890.
Limerick Evening Post and Clare Sentinel 1828–35.
Limerick Reporter 1848.
Limerick Reporter and Tipperary Vindicator 1889–90.
Waterford Chronicle 1832.

British Papers

The Anti-Sweater (London) 1886–87.
Bakers' Record and General Advertiser (London) 1889–90.
Fabian News (London) 1891–97.
Journeymen Bakers' Magazine (London) 1900.
Labour Gazette (Board of Trade) 1894–99.
Northern Star 1839.
Seafaring: The Organ of the Seafaring Class 1889–92.

Trade Union Reports

Annual Reports of the United Society of Boiler Makers and Iron Shipbuilders 1877–1900 (Bishopsgate Institute, London, hereafter cited as BIL).

Monthly Report of the National Union of Boot and Shoe Rivetters and Finishers ____ 1875–89 (National Union of Footwear, Leather and Allied Trades, The Grange, Earls Barton, Northampton).

____ 1889–1900 (London School of Economics, hereafter cited as LSE).

Annual Report and Balance Sheet of the Alliance Cabinet Makers' Association.

____ 1878–84 (BIL).

____ 1884–1900 (LSE).

Annual Report of the Societies in the House Furnishing Department 1834–38 (Modern Records Centre, Warwick University, Coventry, cited hereafter as MRC).

Yearly Account of the Income and Expenditure of the Journeymen Cabinet Makers', Carvers' and Woodturners' Friendly Society 1844–88 (MRC).

Friendly Society of Operative Cabinet Makers: Trade Report and Financial Statement 1875–77, 1890–1900 (LSE).

Annual Report of the Amalgamated Society of Carpenters and Joiners 1866–1900 (BIL).

Annual Report of the General Union of Friendly Operative Carpenters and Joiners 1893–1900 (MRC).

Monthly Report of the General Union of Friendly Operative Carpenters and Joiners 1893–1900 (MRC).

Minutes and Resolutions of the General Delegate Meetings of the Friendly Operative Carpenters and Joiners of Great Britain and Ireland 1837, 1841 (LSE).

Annual Report of the Associated Carpenters and Joiners of Scotland 1874–94 (MRC).

Quarterly Report of the United Kingdom Society of Coachmakers 1851–1900 (Vehicle Building and Automotive Museum, Holyhead Road, Coventry).

Amounts of Various Benefits Paid by the United Kingdom Society of Coachmakers 1868–1918 (Panel 5, Vehicle Building and Automotive Museum, Holyhead Road, Coventry).

Mutual Association of Coopers of Great Britain and Ireland, Monthly Report 1900 (LSE).

National Union of Dock Labourers of Great Britain and Ireland: Report of Executive 1891–95 (LSE).

Annual Reports of the Amalgamated Society of Engineers 1851–1900 (Amalgamated Union of Engineering Workers, 110 Peckham Road, London).

Half-yearly Report of the Ironfounders' Friendly Society of England, Wales and Ireland 1875–1900 (BIL).

Half-yearly Report of the Ironmoulders' Friendly Society of England, Ireland and Wales 1839–53 (BIL).

Annual Report of the National Amalgamated Society of Operative House Painters and Decorators 1893, 1901 (MRC).

Quarterly Report of the General Alliance of Operative House Painters 1873–82 (MRC).

Monthly Report of the National Association of Operative Plasterers 1894–99 (MRC).

National Association of Operative Plasterers, Auditors' Reports 1891–1900 (MRC).

United Operative Plumbers' Association of Great Britain and Ireland, Annual Reports 1876–91 (MRC).

United Operative Plumbers' Association of Great Britain and Ireland Quarterly Returns 1876–94 (MRC).

United Operative Plumbers' Association of Great Britain and Ireland, Minutes of the Delegate Meetings 1881, 1883, 1888, 1891 (MRC).

Amalgamated Society of Railway Servants of England, Ireland, Scotland and Wales, General Secretary's Report 1889–90 (MRC).

Amalgamated Society of Railway Servants of England, Ireland, Scotland and Wales, Report and Financial Statement 1889–99 (BIL).

Amalgamated Society of Railway Servants: Conference of Delegates of the Irish Branches April-July 1890 (MRC).

Amalgamated Society of Railway Servants, Quarterly Report 1898 (MRC).

National Amalgamated Sailors' and Firemen's Union of Great Britain and Ireland, Annual Report 1889–91 (LSE).

Financial Report of the Associated Shipwrights' Society 1893–1900 (BIL).

Quarterly Report of the Associated Shipwrights' Society 1893– 1900 (BIL).

United Operative Stonemasons' Fortnightly Report 1835–41 (MRC).

Journal of the Amalgamated Society of Tailors May 1898 (National Union of Tailors and Garment Workers, Radlett House, West Hill, Aspley Guise, Milton Keynes).

Quarterly Report of the Amalgamated Society of Tailors 1874–75, 1885, 1887 (BIL).

Yearly and Financial Report of the Amalgamated Society of Tailors 1867–1900 (National Union of Tailors and Garment Workers, Milton Keynes).

Minutes of the Midland Board of the National Typographical Association 1845–48 (MRC).

Provincial Typographical Association, Half-yearly Reports
_____ 1851–61 (MRC).
_____ 1875–99 (BIL).

Typographical Society Monthly Circular 1852–60 (MRC).

Half-yearly Report of the National Typographical Association 1845, 1846, 1860, 1870, 1871 (Webb Trade Union Collection, sect. B, vol. lxxxvii, 4, LSE).

Proceedings of a Meeting of Delegates from the Typographical Societies of the United Kingdom, at Manchester 1861 (Webb Trade Union Collection, sect. B, vol. lxxvii, 4, LSE).

Typographical Protection Circular 1849, 1850, 1853 (MRC).
Irish Trades Union Congress, Annual Reports 1894–99 (National Library of
Ireland, microfilm).

TRADE DIRECTORIES (listed chronologically)

Pigott's National Commercial Directory of Ireland 1824 (Dublin, 1824).
Connor's Cork Directory for 1828 (Cork, 1828).
Jackson, F., *The County and City of Cork Post Office General Directory 1842–
43* (Cork, 1843).
Aldwell, Alexander, *The County and City of Cork Post Office General Directory
1844–45* (Cork, 1844).
Purcell and Company's Commercial Cork Almanac for the Year of Our Lord 1852
(Cork, 1852).
Henry Riding's Cork Directory 1852 (Cork, 1852)
Slater's Royal National Commercial Directory of Ireland 1856 (Manchester, 1856).
Thom's Irish Almanac and Official Directory 1860–1900 (Dublin, 1860-1900).
Laing, Robert H., *Cork Mercantile Directory for 1863* (Cork, 1863).
Henry and Coughlan, *General Directory of Cork for 1867* (Cork, 1867).
Fulton and Company, *The City of Cork Directory 1871* (Liverpool, 1871).
Wilkie's Cork City Directory 1872 (Cork, 1872).
Guy and Company, *Guy's County and City of Cork Directory 1875– 76* (Cork,
1875).
Guy, Francis, *Almanac and Directory 1883* (Cork, 1883).
Francis Guy's City and County Cork Almanac and Directory for 1884 (Cork, 1884).
Guy's Directory of Munster 1886–1900 (Cork, 1886–1900).
Guy's Cork Almanac and Directory 1907 (Cork, 1907).

PARLIAMENTARY DEBATES AND GUIDES (listed chronologically)
Hansard's Parliamentary Debates, Third Series (London, 1830–1850).
Dod's Parliamentary Companion (London, 1880–1900).

PARLIAMENTARY PAPERS (listed chronologically)

(i) *Accounts and Papers*

PARLIAMENTARY AND MUNICIPAL ELECTORATES:

*Number of electors who polled at the contested elections in Ireland since 1805, with
the names of the candidates for whom they voted, distinguishing freeholders from
freemen,* HC 1829, (208) xxii, I.
*Number of persons entitled to vote at the elections of members for cities and boroughs
in Ireland: specifying the number of electors for each place* HC 1830, (522) xxxi,
321.
Number registered under the Reform Act, distinguishing qualifications, HC 1833,
(177) xxvii, 289.

Return of Registration Places in County Cork, HC 1834, xlii, 575.

Number registered; also number who voted at the last general election in counties, cities, etc. in Ireland, HC 1836, (227) xliii, 469.

Number of electors appearing by the lists or books of Clerks of the Peace, registered for each county, city, town and borough in Ireland 1835–41 HC 1841, (240–1) xx, 587.

Abstract of the Return of Parliamentary Electors, Ireland, HC 1841, (240–1) xx, 615.

Abstract of the number of registered electors in each county in Ireland, under the Act 13 and 14 Vict. c. 69, distinguishing each class of electors; and similar return for each county of a city, county of a town, and borough in Ireland, HC 1851, (393), 1, 879.

Number of electors on the register, 1852–53, in each county, city, and borough in Ireland, distinguishing their qualifications, HC 1852–53 (957) lxxxiii, 413.

Number of electors in every county, city and borough in Ireland on the register of 1858 and 1862–63, HC 1859, (140–I, sess. I) xxiii, 145; 1864, (350) xlvii, 235.

Number of tenements in each parliamentary borough in Ireland rated at and over £8, being householders, on the register of 1865–66; number of inhabited houses; and number of persons who would be entitled to vote by household suffrage, assuming the proportion of electors to householders to be the same above and below £8, HC 1867, (277) lvi, 527.

Returns as to rating, population, number of electors, area, etc. of counties, parliamentary boroughs, cities and towns in Ireland, HC 1867–68, (236) lvi, 509.

Return of the qualification required for the Municipal and Parliamentary Franchise in each borough in Ireland having a town council; and number of municipal and of parliamentary electors at the last revision, specifying the number of electors of each distinct kind of parliamentary franchise, HC 1868–69, (233) l, 203.

Return showing for each of the parliamentary cities and boroughs of Ireland, number of electors on the register, distinguishing occupiers, lodgers, freemen, etc., also total income assessed to the income tax in each city and borough, HC 1872, (17) xlvii, 409.

Return showing the population in each county, city and borough in Ireland returning members to Parliament; the acreage and valuation of rateable property in each; number of registered voters; number of lands, tenements or hereditaments and inhabited houses in each county, city and borough, according to rating, HC 1884, (164) lxii, 221.

Return as to each municipal borough and municipal town or township in Ireland, showing the rateable value, according to the rate book of the property therein rated to the relief of the poor; the population within the municipal boundaries according to the census of 1881; the number of dwelling houses, the number of burgesses on the roll or number of persons entitled to vote at municipal elections; and the number of aldermen and councillors or commissioners, HC 1886, (84–sess. I) lvii, 53.

Return showing, as regards each parliamentary county and borough, or division thereof, in Ireland, the population and the number of inhabited houses in 1891, and the number of the several classes of electors on the parliamentary register on 1st Jan. 1893, HC 1894, (126) lxciii, 315.

POPULATION

Abstract of Answers and Returns, pursuant to Act 55, Geo. III, for taking an Account of the Population of Ireland in 1821, HC 1824, (577) xxii, 411.

Population of Counties in Ireland 1831, HC 1833, (254) xxix, 3.

Census of Ireland for the Year 1841, HC 1843, (504) xxiv, 274-5.

Census of Ireland, 1851.

Pt. I, showing the area, population and number of houses, by townlands and electoral divisions; Vol. II, Province of Munster, HC 1852–53, xci, 383–723.

Pt. IV, General Report, with appendix, county tables, miscellaneous tables, and index to names of places, HC 1856, (2134) xxxi, 1.

Census of Ireland for 1861: Pt. I, showing the area, population and number of houses by townlands and electoral divisions; Vol. II, Province of Munster, HC 1863, (3204) liv, pt. I, 387.

Census of Ireland 1871: Pt. I, Area, houses and population; also the ages, civil condition, occupations, birthplaces and religion and education of the people; Vol. II, Province of Munster, [C–873–i–iv] HC 1873, lxxii, pt. I.

Census of Ireland 1881: Area, houses and population; also the ages, civil or conjugal condition, occupations, birthplaces, religion and education of the people; Vol. II, Province of Munster, [C–3148] HC 1882, lxxvii, 1.

Census of Ireland 1891: Pt. I, Area, houses and population; also the ages, civil or conjugal condition, occupation, birthplaces, religion and education of the people for each county; with summary, tables and indexes; Vol. II, Province of Munster, [C–6567] HC 1892, xci, pt. I.

Census Returns of Ireland for 1901, giving details for the area, houses and population, also ages, civil or conjugal condition, occupations, birthplaces, religion and education of the people, in each county, and summary tables for each province; Vol. II, Province of Munster, [Cd–1058] HC 1902, xcciv, cxxv, 1.

WAGES, HOURS AND TRADE UNIONISM

First Report on changes in the rate of wages and hours of labour in the United Kingdom for 1893; with statistical tables, [C–7567] HC 1894, lxxxi, pt. II, 1.

Second Report, [C–8075] HC 1896, lxxx, pt. I, 1.

Third Report, [C–8374] HC 1897, lxxxiii, pt. I.

Fourth Report, [C–8444] HC 1897, lxxxiii, 287.

Fifth Report, [C–8975] HC 1898, lxxxviii, pt. I.

Sixth Report, [C–9434] HC 1899, xci, 419.

Seventh Report, [Cd–309] HC 1902, lxxxi, 409.

Statistical Tables and Reports on Trade Unions, First Report, [C–5104] HC 1887, lxxxix, 715.

Second Report, [C–5505] HC 1888, xvii, 135.
Third Report [C–5808] HC 1889, lxxxiv, 147.
Fourth Report, [C–6475] HC 1890-91, xcii, 73.
Fifth Report, [C–6990] HC 1893-94, cii, 85.
Sixth Report, [C–7436] HC 1895, xciv, 55.
Seventh Report [C–7808] HC 1895 cvii, 71.
Eighth Report, [C–8232] HC 1896 xciii, 277.
Ninth Report, [C–8644] HC 1897, xcix, 275.
Tenth Report, [C–9013] HC 1898, ciii, 127.
Eleventh Report, [C–9443] HC 1899, xcii, 493.

(ii) *Reports of Select Committees and Royal Commissions*

Report from the Select Committee appointed to inquire into the State of the Law in the United Kingdom, and its consequences, respecting artisans leaving the Kingdom, and residing abroad; respecting the exportation of tools and machinery; and so far as relates to the Combination of Workmen and others to regulate their wages and hours of working, HC 1824, (51) v, 1–589.

Report from the Select Committee appointed to inquire into the effects of the Act 5, Geo. IV, c. 95, in respect to the conduct of workmen and others, in different parts of the United Kingdom, and how far it may be necessary to repeal or amend the said act, HC 1825, (437) iv, 499, 565.

Minutes of Evidence taken before the Select Committee on the Disturbances in Ireland, HC 1825, (20) vii, pt. I.

Minutes of Evidence taken before a Select Committee of the House of Lords appointed to enquire into the State of Ireland, HL 1825, (181, 521), ix, pt. I, 249 (27).

Minutes of Evidence before the Select Committee on Irish and Scottish Vagrants, HC 1828, iv, 14.

Report of the Select Committee on the State of the Poor in Ireland, HC 1830, vii (667).

Report from the Commissioners appointed to enquire into the state of the municipal corporations in Ireland, HC 1835, (23) xxvii, pt. I, 1.

Royal Commission on the State of the Poorer Classes in Ireland, First Report, App. C, HC 1836, (35) xxx.

First and Second Reports of the Select Committee on Fictitious Votes, HC 1837–38, xxiii, pt. I.

Report of the Royal Commission on the Hand Loom Weavers, HC 1840 (43–11), xxiii, pt. III.

Minutes of Evidence before the Select Committee on the Laws relating to the Relief of the Destitute Poor in Ireland, HC 1846, xi, pt. I.

Report of the Select Committee on Ministers' Money (Ireland), HC 1847–48, (550) xvii, 401.

Minutes of Evidence before the Select Committee on the Cork Election 1852, HC 1852–53, (521) xi, (528) xi.

Report of the Select Committee on the Sale of Liquors on Sunday (Ireland) Bill, HC
1867–68, (280) xiv.

*Royal Commission on Friendly and Benefit Building Societies, Report of the Assis-
tant Commissioners (Ireland)* [C–995] HC 1874, xxiii, pt. II.

*Report of the Select Committee on the Sale of Intoxicating Liquors on Sunday (Ireland)
Bill*, HC 1877, (198) xvi.

*Minutes of Evidence taken before the Select Committee on Local Government and Tax-
ation of Towns (Ireland)*, HC 1877, (357) xii.

*Municipal Boundaries Commission (Ireland), pt. IV; Report and Evidence with
appendices and maps, relating to the towns of Cork and Belfast*, HC 1881, l, 65.

*Report of the Royal Commission Appointed to Enquire into the Boundaries and
Municipal Areas of Certain Cities and Towns in Ireland*, [C–3089] HC 1881,
1, 65.

*Third Report of Her Majesty's Commissioners for Inquiring into the Housing of the
Working Classes in Ireland*, [C–4547] HC 1884–85, xxxi.

Proceedings of the Select Committee on Sunday Closing Acts (Ireland), HC 1888,
(255) xix.

Minutes of Evidence taken before the Royal Commission on Labour
_____ [C–6795–iv] HC 1892–93, xxxvi, pt. i, vol. ii.
_____ [C–6795–v] HC 1892–93, xxxvi, pt. ii, vol. ii.
_____ [C–6795–vi] HC 1892–93, xxxvi, vol. ii.
_____ [C–6894–vii] HC 1893–94, xxxii.
_____ [C–6894–viii] HC 1893–94, xxxiii.
_____ [C–6894–ix] HC 1893–94, xxxiv.
_____ [C–7063–v–c] HC 1893–94, xxxviii.

Minutes of Evidence taken before the Royal Commission on Liquor Licensing Laws,
[C–8980] HC 1898, xxxviii, vol. vii.

Secondary Sources

CONTEMPORARY WORKS

Anon., *A Full and Accurate Report of the Prodeedings at the Election for the City
of Cork, 1820* (Cork, 1820).

Anon., *The Entire Prodeedings of the Election for the City of Cork, which commenced on Saturday 13th and terminated on Monday 19th March 1830* (Cork,
1830).

Binns, Johnathon, *The Miseries and Beauties of Ireland* (London, 1837).

Carr, John, *The Stranger in Ireland, or a Tour in the Southern and Western Parts
of that Country in the Year 1805* (London, 1805).

Caulfield, Richard, *The Council Book of the Corporation of the City of Cork
1609–1800* (London, 1878).

Cork Special Commission: Report of the Proceedings 1865 (Dublin, 1865).

Denieffe, Joseph, *Personal Recollections of the Irish Revolutionary Brotherhood 1855–1867* (New York, 1906).

Gavan Duffy, Charles, *Report on the Organisation and Instructions for the Formation and Government of Confederate Clubs – Publication 3 of the Irish Confederation* (Dublin, 1847).

____ *Thomas Davis: The Memoirs of an Irish Patriot 1840–46* (London, 1870).

Gibson, Rev. C., *History of the County and City of Cork* (London, 1861).

Johnson, James, *A Tour in Ireland with Meditations and Reflections* (London, 1844).

Kohl, J. G., *Travels in Ireland* (London, 1844).

Maddyn, Daniel Owen, *Ireland and Its Rulers* (London, 1844).

____ *Revelations of Ireland in the Past Generation*, 2 vols. (Dublin, 1848).

Maguire, John F., *The Irish Industrial Movement* (Cork, 1853).

O'Donovan Rossa, Diarmuid, *Rossa's Recollections* (Irish University Press Reprint, Dublin, 1972).

Report of the Cork Franchise Association (Cork, 1836).

Sheahan, Thomas, *Articles of Irish Manufacture: Or Portions of Cork History* (Cork, 1833).

Thackeray, William Makepeace, *Irish Sketch Book* (London, 1843).

MODERN WORKS

Bailey, Peter, *Leisure and Class in Victorian England; Rational Recreation and the Contest for Control 1830–1850* (London, 1978).

Bartlett, Thomas, *The Fall and Rise of the Irish Nation: The Catholic Question 1690–1830* (Dublin, 1992).

Behagg, Clive, *Politics and Production in the Early Nineteenth Century* (London, 1990).

Bennett, Tony, Mercer, Colin and Woollacott, Janet (eds.) *Popular Culture and Social Relations* (Milton Keynes, 1986).

Bennett, Tony, 'The politics of "the popular" and popular culture', Tony Bennett, Colin Mercer and Janet Woollacott (eds.), *Popular Culture and Social Relations* (Milton Keynes, 1986).

Bielenberg, Andy, *Cork's Industrial Revolution 1780–1880: Development or Decline?* (Cork, 1991).

____ 'The growth and decline of a textile town: Bandon 1770–1840', *Journal of the Cork Historical and Archaeological Society* (cited hereafter as *JCHAS*), vol. lxxxxvii, 1992, pp. 111–19.

Bowley, Arthur L., *Wages in the United Kingdom in the Nineteenth Century* (Cambridge, 1900).

Boyce, D. G., ' "The marginal Britons": the Irish', Robert Colls and Philip Dodd (eds.), *Englishness: Politics and Culture 1880–1920* (London, 1984), pp. 230–53.

____ *Nineteenth-century Ireland: The Search for Stability* (Dublin, 1990).

____ (ed.), *The Revolution in Ireland 1879–1923* (London, 1988).

Boyd, Andrew, *The Rise of the Irish Trade Unions 1729–1970* (Tralee, 1972).

Boyle, John W. *The Irish Labour Movement in the Nineteenth Century* (Washington, 1988).

Briggs, Asa, *Chartist Studies* (London, 1959).

____ *Victorian Cities* (Harmondsworth, 1968).

____ 'The language of "class" in early nineteenth-century England', M. W. Flinn and T. C. Smout (eds.), *Essays in Social History* (Oxford, 1974).

Browne, Harry, *The Rise of British Trade Unions 1825–1914* (London, 1979).

Buckley, Anthony D., 'On the club: friendly societies in Ireland', *Irish Economic and Social History* (cited hereafter as *IESH*), vol. xiv, 1987, pp. 39–48.

Buckley, Kenneth D., *Trade Unionism in Aberdeen 1878–1900* (Edinburgh and London, 1955).

Casey, Albert E., *O'Kief, Coshe Mang, Slieve Lougher and Upper Blackwater in Ireland* (Birmingham, Ala., 1966–68).

Checkland, S. G. and E. O. Checkland, *The Poor Law Report of 1834* (Harmondsworth, 1974).

Clark, Sam, 'The social composition of the Land League', *Irish Historical Studies* (cited hereafter as *IHS*), vol. xvii, no. 68, Sept. 1971.

Clark, Samuel and James S. Donnelly, Jr., *Irish Peasants. Violence and Political Unrest 1870–1914* (Dublin, 1983).

Clarkson, J. D., *Labour and Nationalism in Ireland* (New York, 1925).

Clegg, H. A., Alan Fox and A. F. Thompson, *A History of British Trade Unions since 1889* (Oxford, 1964).

Colls, Robert and Philip Dodd, *Englishness: Politics and Culture 1880–1920* (London, 1984).

Comerford, R. V., 'Patriotism as pastime: the appeal of Fenianism in the mid-1860s' *IHS,* vol. xxii, no. 85, 1981, pp. 239-50.

____ *The Fenians in Context: Irish Politics and Society 1848–82* (Dublin, 1985).

Conlon, M. V., 'The census of the Parish of St. Mary Shandon, Cork, *c.* 1830', *JCHAS*, vol. xlix, 1944, pp. 10–18.

Corrigan Kearns, Kevin, *Dublin's Vanishing Craftsmen: In Search of the Old Masters* (Belfast, 1986).

Cronin, Maura, 'Work and workers in Cork City and County 1800–1900', O'Flanagan and Buttimer (eds.), *Cork: History and Society* (Dublin, 1993), pp. 721–54

Cullen, L. M., *An Economic History of Ireland since 1660* (London, 1992).

Cullen, L. M. and P. Butel (eds.), *Cities and Merchants: French and Irish Perspectives on Urban Development 1500–1900* (Dublin, 1986).

Cummings, D. C., *A Historical Survey of the Boiler Makers and Iron*

Shipbuilders' Society from 1834 to 1904 (Newcastle-on-Tyne, 1904).

Cummins, N. U., *Chapters of Cork Medical History* (Cork, 1957).

Curtis, L. P., 'Stopping the hunt: an aspect of the Irish Land War', C. H. E. Philpin (ed.), *Nationalism and Popular Protest in Ireland* (London, 1987), pp. 349–402.

D'Alton, Ian, *Protestant Society and Politics in Cork 1812–1844* (Cork, 1980).

____ 'Keeping faith: an evocation of the Cork Protestant character, 1820–1920', O'Flanagan and Buttimer (eds.), *Cork: History and Society,* (1993), pp. 755–92.

Daly, Mary E., *Dublin, the Deposed Capital: A Social and Economic History 1860–1914* (Cork, 1985).

____ 'Woman in the Irish Workforce from pre-industrial to modern times', *Saothar: Journal of the Irish Labour History Society,* no. 7, 1981, pp. 150–63.

Daly, Seán, *Cork: A City in Crisis* (Cork, 1978).

____ *Ireland and the First International* (Cork, 1984).

D'Arcy, Fergus, 'The artisans of Dublin and Daniel O'Connell 1830–1847', *IHS,* vol. xvii, no. 66, 1970, pp. 221–43.

____ 'The murder of Thomas Hanlon: an episode in nineteenth century Dublin labour history', *Dublin Historical Record,* vol. xxiv, no. 4, 1971.

____ 'The National Trades' Political Union and Daniel O'Connell 1830–48', *Éire/Ireland,* vol. xvii, no. 3, 1982, pp. 7–16.

____ 'Wages of labourers in the Dublin building industry, 1667– 1918, *Saothar: Journal of the Irish Labour History Society,* no. 14, 1989, pp. 17–35.

____ 'Wages of skilled workers in the Dublin building industry', 1667– 1918', *Saothar: Journal of the Irish Labour History Society,* no. 15, 1990, pp. 21–38.

D'Arcy, Fergus and Ken Hannigan, *Workers in Union: Documents and Commentaries on the History of Irish Labour* (Dublin, 1988).

Dare, Edward, 'Thoughts of a journeyman baker', *History Workshop,* Issue 3, Spring 1977, pp. 138–42.

Davies, A. C., 'The First Irish Industrial Exhibition', *IESH* vol. ii, 1975.

Digby, Anne and Charles Feinstein, *New Directions in Economic and Social History* (London, 1989).

Donnelly, James S. Jr., *The Land and the People of Nineteenth Century Cork* (London, 1975).

Dougan, David, *The History of the Ship Constructors and Shipwrights' Association 1882–1963* (Newcastle-on-Tyne, 1975).

Eliott, Marianne, 'Origins and transfer of early Irish Republicanism', *International Review of Social History,* vol. xxiii, 1978.

Fahy, Angela, 'Residence, workplace and patterns of change, 1778–1863', Cullen and Butel (eds.), *Cities and Merchants* (Dublin, 1986)

_____ 'Place and class in Cork', O'Flanagan and Buttimer (eds.) *Cork: History and Society* (Dublin, 1993), pp. 793–812.

Flinn, N. W. and T. C. Smout, (eds.), *Essays in Social History* (Oxford, 1974).

Foster, John, *Class Struggle and the Industrial Revolution: Early Industrial Capitalism in Three English Towns* (London, 1974).

Foster, R. F., *Modern Ireland 1600–1972* (London, 1989).

Fox, Alan, *A History of the National Union of Boot and Shoe Operatives 1874 to 1958* (Oxford, 1958).

Fraser, William Hamish, *Trade Unions and Society* (London, 1974).

Garvin, Tom, *Nationalist Revolutionaries in Ireland 1858–1928* (Oxford, 1987).

Gash, Norman, *Reaction and Reconstruction in English Politics* (Oxford, 1965).

Gauldie, Enid, *Cruel Habitations: A History of Working Class Housing 1780–1918* (London, 1974).

Geary, Dick, *European Labour Protest 1848–1939* (London, 1981).

Gorman, John, *Banner Bright: An Illustrated History of the Banners of the British Trade Union Movement* (London, 1973).

Gwynn, Denis, *Young Ireland and 1848* (Cork, 1949).

Harkness, David and Mary O'Dowd (eds.), *The Town in Ireland* (Belfast, 1981).

Harrison, Royden, 'From labour history to social history', *History*, vol. 60, 1975, pp. 236–9.

Hobsbawm, Eric J., *Labouring Men. Studies in the History of Labour* (Sixth impression, London, 1979).

Hoppen, K. Theodore, *Elections, Politics and Society in Ireland 1832–1885* (Oxford, 1984).

Horn, Pamela L. R., 'The National Agricultural Labourers' Union in Ireland 1878–79', *IHS* vol. xvii, no. 67, March 1971.

Jones, Garret S., *Outcast London: A Study in the Relationship between Classes in Victorian Society* (Oxford, 1971).

Jones, Mary, *These Obstreperous Lassies: A History of the Irish Women Workers' Union* (Dublin, 1988).

Joyce, Patrick, *Work, Society and Politics. The Culture of the Factory in Later Victorian England* (London, 1980).

Keogh, Dermot, *The Rise of the Irish Working Class: The Dublin Trade Union Movement and the Labour Leadership, 1890–1914* (Belfast, 1982).

Kerrigan, Colm, 'The social impact of the Irish Temperance Movement 1839–1845', *IESH*, vol. xiv, 1987, pp. 20–38.

_____ *Father Mathew and the Irish Temperance Movement 1838–1849* (Cork, 1992).

Kiddier, William, *The Old Trade Unions: From Unprinted Records of the Brushmakers* (London, 1930).

Loftus, Belinda, *Marching Workers: An Exhibition of Trade Union Banners and Regalia* (Belfast, 1978).

Lynch, Patrick and John Vaizey, *Guinness's Brewery in the Irish Economy* (Cambridge, 1960).

Lyons, F. S. L., *Ireland since the Famine* (Glasgow, 1971).

McCarthy, Charles, *Trade Unions in Ireland 1894–1960* (Dublin, 1977).

McCartney, Donal, *The Dawning of Democracy: Ireland 1800–1870* (Dublin, 1987).

McGrath, Walter, 'The Fenian Rising in Cork', *The Irish Sword*, Winter 1968.

_____ *A Cork Felon: The Life and Death of Brian Dillon* (Cork, 1969).

McIntyre, Angus, *The Liberator* (London, 1965).

Malcolm, Elizabeth, *'Ireland Sober, Ireland Free': Drink and Temperance in Nineteenth-Century Ireland* (Dublin, 1986).

Mitchell, Arthur, *Labour in Irish Politics 1890–1930* (Dublin, 1974).

Moody, T. W. (ed.), 'Michael Davitt and the British Labour Movement', *Transactions of the Royal Historical Society*, 5th series, vol. iii, 1953, pp. 53–76.

_____ *The Fenian Movement* (Cork, 1968).

Morris, R. J., 'The labour aristocracy in the British class structure', Anne Digby and Charles Feinstein (eds.), *New Directions in Economic and Social History* (London, 1989).

Maura Murphy, 'Municipal reform and the Repeal Movement in Cork 1833–44', *JCHAS* vol. lxxxi, no. 233, 1976, pp. 1–18.

_____ 'Repeal, popular politics, and the Catholic clergy of Cork 1840–1850', *JCHAS* vol. lxxxii, no. 235, 1977, pp. 39–48.

_____ 'The ballad singer and the role of the seditious ballad in nineteenth century Ireland – Dublin Castle's view', *Ulster Folklife*, vol. xxv, 1979, pp. 79–102.

_____ 'Fenianism, Parnellism, and the Cork trades 1860–1900', *Saothar: Journal of the Irish Labour History Society*, no. 5, 1979, pp. 27–38.

_____ 'The working classes of nineteenth century Cork', *JCHAS*, vol. lxxxv, nos. 241–2, 1980, pp. 26–51.

_____ 'The economic and social structure of nineteenth century Cork', David Harkness and M. O'Dowd (eds.) *The Town in Ireland* (Belfast, 1981), pp. 125–54.

_____ 'Cork commercial society 1850-99: politics and problems', Cullen and Butel (eds.), *Cities and Merchants: French and Irish Perspectives on Urban Development 1500–1900* (Dublin, 1986), pp. 233–44.

Murphy, Seamus, *Stone Mad* (London, 1966).

Newsinger, John, 'Old Chartists, Fenians and New Socialists', *Éire/Ireland*, vol. xvii, no. 2, 1982, pp. 19–45.

Ní Coindealbháin, Ide, 'Fenians of Kilclooney Wood', *JCHAS* vol. xlix, no. 170, 1944, pp. 128-36.

Norman, E. R., *The Catholic Church and Ireland in the Age of Rebellion 1859–1873* (London, 1965).

Nowlan, Kevin B., *The Politics of Repeal* (London, 1965).

O'Brien, Conor Cruise, *Parnell and His Party* (London, 1960).

O'Brien, John B., 'Agricultural prices and living costs in pre-famine Cork', *JCHAS* vol. lxxxii, no. 235, 1977, pp. 1–10.

_____ *The Catholic Middle Classes in Pre-Famine Cork: The O'Donnell Lecture Delivered at University College, Cork, 29th March 1979* (Dublin, 1979).

_____ 'The Hacketts: glimpses of entrepreneurial life in Cork 1800–1870', *JCHAS*, vol. xc, no. 249, 1985, pp. 150–7.

_____ 'Population, politics and society in Cork', 1780–1900', O'Flanagan and Buttimer (eds.) *Cork: History and Society*, pp. 699–720.

Ó Broin, Leon, *Fenian Fever: An Anglo-American Dilemma* (London, 1971).

_____ *Revolutionary Underground* (Dublin, 1976).

Ó Coindealbháin, Seán, 'John Swiney, the Cork United Irishman', *JCHAS* vol. lx, 1955, pp. 22–7.

_____ 'The United Irishmen in Cork County', *JCHAS* vol. liii, 1948, pp. 115–129; vol. liv, 1949, pp. 68–83; vol. lv, 1950, pp. 50–61, 73–90; vol. lvi, 1951, pp. 18–28, 95–103; vol. lvii, 1952, pp. 87–98; vol. lviii, 1953, 91–96.

O'Connell, Maurice R., *O'Connell Correspondence*, vols. iv, v (Dublin, 1980).

O'Connor, Emmet, *A Labour History of Ireland 1824–1960* (Dublin, 1992).

_____ *A Labour History of Waterford* (Waterford, 1989).

O'Ferrall, Fergus, *Catholic Emancipation: Daniel O'Connell and the Irish Democracy 1820–30* (Dublin, 1985).

O'Flanagan, Patrick, and Cornelius G. Buttimer, *Cork: History and Society. Interdisciplinary Essays on the History of an Irish County* (Dublin, 1993).

O'Higgins, Rachel, 'Irish trade unions and politics 1830–50', *Historical Journal*, no. 4, 1961, pp. 208–17.

O'Keeffe, Timothy J., 'The 1898 efforts to celebrate the United Irishmen: the '98 centennial', *Éire/Ireland*, Summer 1988, pp. 51–73.

O Mahony, Colman, *The Maritime Gateway to Cork: A History of the Outports of Passage West and Monkstown from 1754 to 1942* (Cork, 1986).

_____ 'Shipbuilding and repairing in nineteenth-century Cork', *JCHAS*, vol. xciv, no. 253, 1989, pp. 74–87.

Ó Murchadha, Tadhg, *Sgéal Sheandúin* (Dublin, 1920).

O'Sullivan, T. F., *The Young Irelanders* (Tralee, 1944).

O'Sullivan, William, *An Economic History of Cork from the Earliest Times to the Act of Union* (Cork, 1937).

Patterson, Henry, *Class Conflict and Sectarianism: The Protestant Working Class and the Belfast Labour Movement 1868–1920* (Belfast, 1980).

Pelling, Henry, *A History of British Trade Unionism* (London, 1971).

Pimley, Adrian, 'The working-class movement and the Irish Revolution 1896–1923', D. G. Boyce (ed.) *The Revolution in Ireland* (London, 1988).

Pochin Mould, Daphne D. C., *Discovering Cork* (Dingle, 1991).

Postgate, R. W., *The Builders' History* (London, 1923).

Price, Richard, *Labour in British Society: An Interpretative History* (London, 1986).

Read, Donald and Eric Glasgow, *Fergus O'Connor, Irishman and Chartist* (London, 1961)

Roberts, B. C., *The Trades Union Congress 1868–1921* (London, 1958).

Rostow, W. W., *British Economy of the Nineteenth Century: Essays* (Oxford, 1948).

Smith, Dennis, *Conflict and Compromise: Class Formation in English Society 1830–1914. A Comparative Study of Birmingham and Sheffield* (London, 1982).

_____ 'Paternalism, craft and organisational rationality 1830–1930: an exploratory model', *Urban History*, vol. xix, pt. 2, Oct. 1992, pp. 211–28.

Smyth, Jim, *The Men of No Property. Irish Radicals and Popular Politics in the Late Eighteenth Century* (Dublin, 1992)

Stewart, Margaret and Leslie Hunter, *The Needle is Threaded* (Southampton, 1964).

Swift, John, *History of the Dublin Bakers and Others* (Dublin, 1948).

Thompson, E. P., *The Making of the English Working Class* (Harmondsworth, 1963).

Thornley, David, *Isaac Butt and the Home Rule Party* (London, 1964).

Treble, J. H., 'O'Connor, O'Connell and the attitudes of the Irish immigrants in the north of England 1838–48', *The Victorians and Social Protest: A Symposium* (Newtownabbott, Devon, 1973).

Walvin, James, *Leisure and Society 1830–1950* (London, 1978)

Webb, Sidney and Beatrice Webb, *History of Trade Unionism* (London, 1894).

Weber, Eugen, *Peasants into Frenchmen: The Modernisation of Rural France 1870–1914* (London, 1977).

Winchester, F. S., *A Short History of the National Union of Vehicle Builders 1834–1959* (Manchester, 1959).

UNPUBLISHED DISSERTATIONS

Byrne, Kieran R., 'The origin and growth of technical education in Ireland 1731–1922' (Ph.D. thesis, NUI, 1982).

D'Alton, Ian, 'Southern Irish Unionism: a study of Cork City and County Unionists 1885–1914' (MA thesis, NUI, 1972).

D'Arcy, Fergus, 'Dublin artisan activity, opinion and organisation 1820–50' (MA thesis, NUI 1968).

Gough, M. J., 'History of the physical development of Cork City' (MA thesis, NUI, 1973).

Gray, R. Q., 'Class structure and the class formation of skilled workers in Edinburgh 1850–1900' (Ph.D. thesis, University of Edinburgh, 1972).

Hill, Jacqueline R., 'The role of Dublin in the Irish National Movement 1840–1848' (Ph.D. thesis, Leeds University, 1973).

Holohan, Patrick, 'Daniel O'Connell and trade unions' (MA thesis, NUI, 1968).

Lee, John, 'Aspects of the development and decline in the building industry in Cork City 1850–1899' (MA thesis, NUI, 1988).

Leo, Mary, 'The influence of the Fenians and their press on public opinion in Ireland 1863–70' (M. Litt. thesis, Trinity College, Dublin 1976).

McDonnell, Brendan, 'The Dublin labour movement 1894–1907. (Ph.D. thesis, NUI, 1979).

Murphy, Maura, 'Repeal and Young Ireland in Cork politics 1830–50' (MA thesis, NUI, 1975).

_____ 'The role of organised labour in the political and economic life of Cork city 1820–1899' (unpublished Ph.D. thesis, University of Leicester, 1980)

Takagami, Shin-ichi, 'The Dublin Fenians 1858–1879' (Ph.D. thesis, Trinity College, Dublin, 1990).

INDEX

273